The Beach Babes

Judith Keim

BOOKS BY JUDITH KEIM

THE HARTWELL WOMEN SERIES:

The Talking Tree – 1
Sweet Talk – 2
Straight Talk – 3
Baby Talk – 4
The Hartwell Women – Boxed Set

THE BEACH HOUSE HOTEL SERIES:

Breakfast at The Beach House Hotel – 1
Lunch at The Beach House Hotel – 2
Dinner at The Beach House Hotel – 3
Christmas at The Beach House Hotel – 4
Margaritas at The Beach House Hotel – 5
Dessert at The Beach House Hotel – 6
Coffee at The Beach House Hotel – 7
High Tea at The Beach House Hotel – 8 (2024)

THE FAT FRIDAYS GROUP:

Fat Fridays – 1
Sassy Saturdays – 2
Secret Sundays – 3

THE SALTY KEY INN SERIES:

Finding Me – 1
Finding My Way – 2
Finding Love – 3
Finding Family – 4
The Salty Key Inn Series – Boxed Set

THE CHANDLER HILL INN SERIES:

Going Home – 1
Coming Home – 2
Home at Last – 3
The Chandler Hill Inn Series – Boxed Set

SEASHELL COTTAGE BOOKS:

A Christmas Star
Change of Heart
A Summer of Surprises
A Road Trip to Remember
The Beach Babes

THE DESERT SAGE INN SERIES:

The Desert Flowers – Rose – 1
The Desert Flowers – Lily – 2
The Desert Flowers – Willow – 3
The Desert Flowers – Mistletoe & Holly – 4

SOUL SISTERS AT CEDAR MOUNTAIN LODGE:

Christmas Sisters – Anthology
Christmas Kisses
Christmas Castles
Christmas Stories – Soul Sisters Anthology
Christmas Joy – (2022)

THE SANDERLING COVE INN SERIES:

Waves of Hope – 1
Sandy Wishes – 2
Salty Kisses – 3

THE LILAC LAKE INN SERIES

Love by Design – 1
Love Between the Lines – (2024)
Love Under the Stars – (2024)

OTHER BOOKS:

The ABC's of Living With a Dachshund
Once Upon a Friendship – Anthology
Winning BIG – a little love story for all ages
Holiday Hopes
The Winning Tickets – (2023)

PRAISE FOR JUDITH KEIM'S NOVELS

THE BEACH HOUSE HOTEL SERIES – Books 1 – 6

"Love the characters in this series. This series was my first introduction to Judith Keim. She is now one of my favorites. Looking forward to reading more of her books."

BREAKFAST AT THE BEACH HOUSE HOTEL is an easy, delightful read that offers romance, family relationships, and strong women learning to be stronger. Real life situations filter through the pages. Enjoy!"

LUNCH AT THE BEACH HOUSE HOTEL – "This series is such a joy to read. You feel you are actually living with them. Can't wait to read the latest one."

DINNER AT THE BEACH HOUSE HOTEL – "A Terrific Read! As usual, Judith Keim did it again. Enjoyed immensely. Continue writing such pleasantly reading books for all of us readers."

CHRISTMAS AT THE BEACH HOUSE HOTEL – "Not Just Another Christmas Novel. This is book number four in the series and my introduction to Judith Keim's writing. I wasn't disappointed. The characters are dimensional and engaging. The plot is well crafted and advances at a pleasing pace. The Florida location is interesting and warming. It was a delight to read a romance novel with mature female protagonists. Ann and Rhoda have life experiences that enrich the story. It's a clever book about friends and extended family. Buy copies for your book group pals and enjoy this seasonal read."

MARGARITAS AT THE BEACH HOUSE HOTEL – "What a wonderful series. I absolutely loved this book and can't wait for the next book to come out. There was even suspense in it. Thanks Judith for the great stories."

"Overall, Margaritas at the Beach House Hotel is another

wonderful addition to the series. Judith Keim takes the reader on a journey told through the voices of these amazing characters we have all come to love through the years! I truly cannot stress enough how good this book is, and I hope you enjoy it as much as I have!"

THE HARTWELL WOMEN SERIES – Books 1 – 4

"This was an EXCELLENT series. When I discovered Judith Keim, I read all of her books back to back. I thoroughly enjoyed the women Keim has written about. They are believable and you want to just jump into their lives and be their friends! I can't wait for any upcoming books!"

"I fell into Judith Keim's Hartwell Women series and have read & enjoyed all of her books in every series. Each centers around a strong & interesting woman character and their family interaction. Good reads that leave you wanting more."

THE FAT FRIDAYS GROUP – Books 1 – 3

"Excellent story line for each character, and an insightful representation of situations which deal with some of the contemporary issues women are faced with today."

"I love this author's books. Her characters and their lives are realistic. The power of women's friendships is a common and beautiful theme that is threaded throughout this story."

THE SALTY KEY INN SERIES – Books 1 – 4

FINDING ME – *"I thoroughly enjoyed the first book in this series and cannot wait for the others! The characters are endearing with the same struggles we all encounter. The setting makes me feel like I am a guest at The Salty Key Inn...relaxed, happy & light-hearted! The men are yummy and the women strong. You can't get better than that!!"*

FINDING MY WAY- *"Loved the family dynamics as well as uncertain emotions of dating and falling in love. Appreciated the morals and strength of parenting throughout. Just couldn't put this book down."*

FINDING LOVE – *"I waited for this book because the first two was such good reads. This one didn't disappoint.... Judith Keim always puts substance into her books. This book was no different, I learned about PTSD, accepting oneself, there is always going to be problems but stick it out and make it work. Just the way life is. In some ways a lot like my life. Judith is right, it needs another book and I will definitely be reading it. Hope you choose to read this series, you will get so much out of it."*

FINDING FAMILY – *"Completing this series is like eating the last chip. Love Judith's writing, and her female characters are always smart, strong, vulnerable to life and love experiences."*

"This was a refreshing book. Bringing the heart and soul of the family to us."

THE CHANDLER HILL INN SERIES – Books 1 – 3

GOING HOME – *"I absolutely could not put this book down. Started at night and read late into the middle of the night. As a child of the '60s, the Vietnam war was front and center so this resonated with me. All the characters in the book were so well developed that the reader felt like they were friends of the family."*

"I was completely immersed in this book, with the beautiful descriptive writing, and the authors' way of bringing her characters to life. I felt like I was right inside her story."

COMING HOME – *"Coming Home is a winner. The characters are well-developed, nuanced and likable. Enjoyed the vineyard setting, learning about wine growing and seeing the challenges Cami faces in running and growing a business. I look forward to the next book in this series!"*

"Coming Home was such a wonderful story. The author has such a gift for getting the reader right to the heart of things."

HOME AT LAST – *"In this wonderful conclusion, to a heartfelt and emotional trilogy set in Oregon's stunning wine country, Judith Keim has tied up the Chandler Hill series with the perfect bow."*

"Overall, this is truly a wonderful addition to the Chandler Hill Inn series. Judith Keim definitely knows how to perfectly weave together a beautiful and heartfelt story."

"The storyline has some beautiful scenes along with family drama. Judith Keim has created characters with interactions that are believable and some of the subjects the story deals with are poignant."

SEASHELL COTTAGE BOOKS

A CHRISTMAS STAR – *"Love, laughter, sadness, great food, and hope for the future, all in one book. It doesn't get any better than this stunning read."*

"A Christmas Star *is a heartwarming Christmas story featuring endearing characters. So many Christmas books are set in snowbound places...it was a nice change to read a Christmas story that takes place on a warm sandy beach!" Susan Peterson*

CHANGE OF HEART – *"CHANGE OF HEART is the summer read we've all been waiting for. Judith Keim is a master at creating fascinating characters that are simply irresistible. Her stories leave you with a big smile on your face and a heart bursting with love."*

~Kellie Coates Gilbert, author of the Sun Valley Series

A SUMMER OF SURPRISES – *"The story is filled with a roller coaster of emotions and self-discovery. Finding love again and rebuilding family relationships."*

"Ms. Keim uses this book as an amazing platform to show that with hard emotional work, belief in yourself and love, the scars of abuse can be conquered. It in no way preaches, it's a lovely story with a happy ending."

"The character development was excellent. I felt I knew these people my whole life. The story development was very well thought out I was drawn [in] from the beginning."

A ROAD TRIP TO REMEMBER – *"I LOVED this book! Love the character development, the fun, the challenges and the ending. My favorite books are about strong, competent women finding their own path to success and happiness and this is a winner. It's one of those books you just can't put down."*

"The characters are so real that they jump off the page. Such a fun, HAPPY book at the perfect time. It will lift your spirits and even remind you of your own grandmother. Spirited and hopeful Aggie gets a second chance at love and she takes the steering wheel and drives straight for it."

THE DESERT SAGE INN SERIES – Books 1 - 3

THE DESERT FLOWERS – ROSE – *"The Desert Flowers - Rose, is the first book in the new series by Judith Keim. I always look forward to new books by Judith Keim, and this one is definitely a wonderful way to begin The Desert Sage Inn Series!"*

"In this first of a series, we see each woman come into her own and view new beginnings even as they must take this tearful journey as they slowly lose a dear friend. This is a very well written book with well-developed and likable main characters. It was interesting and enlightening as the first

portion of this saga unfolded. I very much enjoyed this book and I do recommend it"

"Judith Keim is one of those authors that you can always depend on to give you a great story with fantastic characters. I'm excited to know that she is writing a new series and after reading book 1 in the series, I can't wait to read the rest of the books."!

<u>THE DESERT FLOWERS – LILY</u> – "The second book in the Desert Flowers series is just as wonderful as the first. Judith Keim is a brilliant storyteller. Her characters are truly lovely and people that you want to be friends with as soon as you start reading. Judith Keim is not afraid to weave real life conflict and loss into her stories. I loved reading Lily's story and can't wait for Willow's!

"The Desert Flowers Lily is the second book in The Desert Sage Inn Series by author Judith Keim. When I read the first book in the series, The Desert Flowers-Rose, I knew this series would exceed all of my expectations and then some. Judith Keim is an amazing author, and this series is a testament to her writing skills and her ability to completely draw a reader into the world of her characters."

<u>THE DESERT FLOWERS – WILLOW</u> – "The feelings of love, joy, happiness, friendship, family and the pain of loss are deeply felt by Willow Sanchez and her two cohorts Rose and Lily. The Desert Flowers met because of their deep feelings for Alec Thurston, a man who touched their lives in different ways.

"Once again, Judith Keim has written the story of a strong, competent, confident and independent woman. Willow, like Rose and Lily can handle tough situations. All the characters are written so that the reader gets to know them but not all the characters will give the reader warm and fuzzy feelings.

"The story is well written and from the start you will be pulled in. There is enough backstory that a reader can start here but I assure you, you'll want to learn more. There is an ocean of emotions that will make you smile, cringe, tear up or out right cry. I loved this book as I loved books one and two. I am thrilled that the Desert Flowers story will continue. I highly recommend this book to anyone who enjoys books with strong women."

The Beach Babes

A Seashell Cottage Book

Judith Keim

Wild Quail Publishing

wildquail.pub@gmail.com
www.judithkeim.com

Published in the United States of America by:

Wild Quail Publishing
PO Box 171332
Boise, ID 83717-1332

ISBN# 978-1-962452-18-2

Dedication

This book is dedicated to women everywhere, honoring your strength and the ability to reach out to one another for help in times of need. I wish this kind of support for each of you and to know love, always love.

CHAPTER ONE

CATE

Catherine "Cate" Tibbs stared out the window of her home office at the pine trees lining the backyard of her upstate New York property, taking a moment to study the way the wind and the rain of the autumn storm were making the green-needled boughs sway like graceful dancers. The words she wanted to put on the computer screen for the new book she was writing were not coming easily to her. She knew why. She couldn't stop thinking back to the time she and her two best friends became The Beach Babes. They were such an odd trio of thirteen-year-olds, but somehow their friendship had formed and had endured through the years. Until recently, that is. She hadn't heard from either Amber or Brooke for several months now.

Cate sat back in her chair, made a few notes before moving away from her desk, and headed into the kitchen to make a cup of herbal tea. *Time to set things in motion,* she thought. She and her friends were all turning forty in the upcoming year, and she had a plan.

From the side of her refrigerator, she lifted her favorite photo of the three of them as young girls, back when their friendship was new. Brooke's family had invited Cate and Amber to visit their luxurious summer house on the Long Island shore for a couple of days. In the photograph, the three of them dressed in bathing suits were sitting in a line on the sand in front of the house holding hands and staring up at Brooke's father. They'd just named themselves "The Beach

Babes" and thought it was the coolest thing ever. Brooke's father was laughing with them while he snapped pictures.

Cate held the photograph up to the light. Brooke had found the original a few years ago and made copies for Amber and her. Brooke was the red-headed, heavy girl in the middle. Her green eyes bordered by brown-rimmed glasses, she wore braces and a smile that usually wobbled a little from insecurity, but on this day with her father present, her smile was wide. Amber sat on the right of her. Beautiful already, with naturally blond hair, blue eyes, and a tall, willowy figure, Amber had a brash style and sassiness even then that had intrigued Cate. It covered up a lot of hurt.

Cate's gaze settled on her younger self. Her long brown hair was tied back in a ponytail. Brown eyes stared out at the world with curiosity, her serious expression hiding a lot of shyness. Interesting, she thought, how different they'd grown and yet how much they'd remained the same.

After fixing her tea, Cate sat down at the kitchen table uncertain who to call first. Amber, who was the personal assistant for the owner of the Galvin Modeling Agency, sometimes modeled for one of their clients, a perfume company. She might be on a shoot with them. Without Amber's ability to join them, Brooke might not want to leave California. It had always been that way. The three of them or nothing. Maybe because they balanced one another.

Cate took a sip of hot tea and wondered about a perfect location for the meeting she hoped to plan. Then it came to her. Two years ago, when she was struggling to meet a publishing deadline, her agent told her about a place called the Seashell Cottage. It was a perfect spot for a retreat—on the beach along the Gulf Coast of Florida. Though it was called a cottage, it was an elegant house that had three bedrooms with en-suite baths, a modern kitchen, and a private, screened-in swimming pool and spa.

Excited by the possibility, Cate hurried back to her desk and pulled up the information on the cottage. Online, it looked as lovely as she remembered. She checked her calendar. The first weekend in November might work, she thought. Halloween would be over, and the Thanksgiving and Christmas holidays were far enough away that they shouldn't be a problem, even for a busy mom like Brooke. Amber usually traveled for the holidays to somewhere unique to keep from having to spend time with her mother. As for herself, she was available anytime. She had no family to speak of, her relationship with her long-time boyfriend was such it wouldn't be a problem for her to take off for a long weekend, and her next book wasn't due to her editor for another six months. For this book, the one she was working on, she knew pretty much what was going to happen—a benefit of writing a popular series in a world of her own creation.

Reminding herself that Amber would be glad to hear from her, Cate lifted her phone to call her. Amber was a little intimidating until they'd talked for a while.

When Amber's voice mail message came on, Cate was almost relieved. Amber was the city mouse compared to her country mouse. She was just about to click off the call when she heard a voice say, "Hello? Hello? Is that you, Cate?"

"Amber? Hi!"

"Hey, how are you, sweetie? It's been a while."

"I know," Cate said. "Too long. That's why I'm calling. I have an idea. I think we should get together to celebrate our coming birthdays. It's a big one for us. We can start celebrating early."

"Celebrate? In my business, being forty is like being eighty for anyone else."

"We're not all in the world of glamour," Cate said. "Besides, it will be good for you, Brooke, and me to get together whether we celebrate our birthdays or not. I've missed the two of you. It's been almost two years since we've been together, and we haven't talked for a while. We can't keep letting time slip by."

"So true," said Amber. "You are my best friends. Everything all right?"

"I have a lot of things to think about," Cate answered honestly. "That's why we need to get together."

"Oh, okay," Amber quickly replied. "Where? What dates were you thinking of?"

Cate told her about Seashell Cottage and the long weekend she hoped to book there.

"Count me in," said Amber. "Something in your voice worries me. You'd tell me if anything was seriously wrong, right?"

"Sure," said Cate. "Everything all right with you?"

"A lot of the same old stuff, but I could really use some input from the two of you. Let me know if Seashell Cottage is available, and I'll mark my calendar."

"Okay, I'll get right back to you. I'm calling them now."

Cate was on her desk phone talking to the rental agency when a call came through on her cell. She put that one on hold, quickly finished her discussion with the rental agency, picked up her cell, and chirped, "Hi, Brooke!"

"Hi, Cate! I just got off the phone with Amber. She told me what you have in mind. She also told me she was worried about you. Is everything okay?"

"Yes, but I've been missing you, and I think we should get together to celebrate our upcoming birthdays. Amber hates the idea of being forty, but I figure it's better than the alternative. Besides, our being together again is the purpose."

Brooke chuckled. "Well, you know how Amber is about her body. She has to look perfect, and turning forty is stressful in the fashion industry. What dates are you talking about?"

"It looks like the cottage is free the first weekend in November. Does that work for you?"

"I'll make it work," said Brooke. "It will do my heart good to spend some time with both of you. Send me all the information, and I'll see you then. Just four weeks to go. Can't wait!"

Cate heard the excitement in Brooke's voice and smiled. "Wonderful. I'll confirm everything, and we'll be set."

"Send me the bill. This will be on me," said Brooke.

"We'll see," said Cate, unwilling to accept Brooke's offer without Amber's input. Brooke was very generous, always had been. Sometimes, Amber found that uncomfortable. She'd grown up poor and worried about having others pay for her. Besides, they were now each capable of paying their fair share.

After making final arrangements with the rental agency, Cate sent out notices to Amber, Brooke, and her agent, and then called the airlines. She'd briefly thought of driving, making it a longer vacation, but after more consideration, she chose to fly, rent a car, and delay any decisions on extending the long weekend. The truth was, like she'd told Amber, she needed this time to think a few things over.

She heard the sound of someone entering through the back door and rose. Jackson Hubbard was the source of her worries. She went to greet him.

Her heart filled at the sight of the man standing inside her kitchen. He seemed to fill the room with his tall, broad-shouldered figure. The smile on his face crinkled the skin at the corner of his blue eyes and radiated his happiness at seeing her.

"Hi, sweetheart! How's the writing going?" he asked, slipping off his jacket and setting down a bag of groceries on the kitchen counter. "I bought some fresh pasta. How about my famous spaghetti tonight?"

"Famous, huh?" She laughed as she went into his arms and snuggled up against his strong chest. "It sounds perfect."

They broke apart and smiled at one another.

"How were the kids today?"

"Restless. Each year it gets harder to control the ones who are bored when they should be listening to their remarkable high school teacher talk about biology." He sighed. "Seriously, I'm ready for a break, and the school year is just getting underway. I have a feeling it's going to be a long, tough one."

"I'm sorry," she replied. "Speaking of breaks, I'm traveling to Florida for a long weekend at the beginning of November to meet up with Amber and Brooke."

"Nice. You haven't seen your best friends for a while, right?"

"It's been almost two years. I'll be anxious to catch up with them. A lot can happen in that time."

"Yes," said Jackson solemnly. "Like with us."

She nodded, too conflicted to say anything. She still had so many things to think about. He wanted marriage and babies, and she wasn't quite ready. What was simple and easy for him was a difficult decision for her.

Her thoughts flew to the aunt who'd been forced to take her in when her mother took off, claiming she'd be in touch. That didn't happen. Shortly after she dumped Cate with Aunt Margaret, her mother died in an automobile accident that left five-year-old Cate in the hands of a woman who hadn't wanted her. Raising someone else's kid wasn't for her, Aunt Margaret often grumped as she prepared meals for them in the evenings that stretched long and silent between them.

Jackson's voice startled Cate out of the old, sad memories that lingered in her mind. "I bought a nice pinot noir. Let's have a glass, and then I'll get started on the spaghetti sauce."

The sound of scratching at the door caught their attention.

He reached for the back door. "I'll let Buddy in. He was a good boy at doggy camp. They love him there."

A smooth-haired, black-and-tan dachshund burst through the open doorway, ran over, and stared up at her, wagging his tail so furiously his whole body wiggled. She chuckled and bent down to scratch his ears. "Hi, baby!"

She knew anyone overhearing her would laugh at the way she crooned to the dog, but she didn't care. Buddy was her baby. The only one she'd thought she wanted.

"It's great for him to get out with other dogs, but I miss him when he's gone," she said. "And this is one day when his antics wouldn't have bothered me. I can't come up with the motivation for Serena to fight for the Galeons' supremacy. It's got to be something different from the usual stuff. Even though it's science fiction, it has to make sense. And her feelings for Rondol are way too intense. It makes her seem weak."

Jackson handed her a glass of wine. "Passion isn't a sign of weakness, Cate," he said gently.

He was right. She knew it. She also knew he wasn't talking about characters in her book. She accepted the wine from him and waited silently for him to lift his glass in his usual salute to them before taking a sip.

The velvety wine slid down her throat, coating her tongue with a smooth, fruity finish. Jackson and she had met at a writing class seven years ago. They'd hit it off right away and had gone from friendship to lovers in a short amount of time. But now Jackson wanted more—marriage and children. And though she loved him, the thought of having children with him was frightening. She didn't think she'd be a good parent. Her mother and her aunt hadn't been prime examples for her to follow. She worried it was something in her genes, this lack of maternal love.

"I love you, Jackson, more than you'll ever know," she said, hoping he'd understand all she was trying to say.

"But not enough to marry me," he replied, a familiar frustration twisting his face. He set down his wine glass. "We're the best of friends and great lovers. At forty-six, I don't want to wait any longer to have kids. As it is, when any child of ours is ready to go off on his or her own, I'll be damn close to seventy. And that's if you got pregnant right away."

"And what if I had complications? That could be awful for both you and any baby we might conceive."

"As a biology teacher, I know how easily that can happen. But you are healthy and still young enough to have children." He wrapped her in his embrace. "Besides, I love you more than anything. I'll always take care of you."

"Love you, too," she murmured, feeling safe in his arms. He wouldn't ever let her down. If only she felt differently about the need to marry and have children. He was right, though. Time was running out for both of them.

CHAPTER TWO

BROOKE

Brooke Ridley Weston clicked off the phone call with Cate and stared out the kitchen window at the kids playing in the pool. Her oldest child, nineteen-year-old Paul, Jr., was away at college. Her twin daughters, Brynn and Bradley, were hosting friends for an after-school get-together. They were beautiful girls, carbon copies of one another, whose features were a mix of Paul's and hers. Their hair held a hint of red from her, heavily-lashed blue eyes from Paul, and classic facial features of both sets of grandparents. At ten, they were a social duo with lots of friends.

She was pleased to see them surrounded with playmates. Her childhood had been lonely until she'd been introduced to Amber and Cate. With their friendship, her world had opened up. But being bullied for her weight had already inflicted wounds on her. As outgoing as she seemed, she carried that hurt within her to this day.

As soon as the girls got out of the pool and lay in the warm California sun, Brooke told them where she was going, and wandered upstairs to the master bedroom to see what clothes she might want to pack for Florida. Cate had told her in a text that she hoped it would be a low-key, casual time, but Brooke wanted to look her best. She'd remarked that Amber was concerned with her appearance, well, so was she. In fact, that was the reason she'd elected to accept plastic surgery to reshape her nose as an early, high school graduation gift from her mother before her senior year of high school. That, a weight-loss program, Lasik surgery on her eyes, and caps on her teeth had made her more confident.

It was such a blessing when she met Paul Weston her freshman year in college. Besides her father and her two best friends, he was someone who loved her for who she was inside. She studied the large diamond on her left hand. Of the three Beach Babes, she was the only one to marry. Cate hadn't wanted to marry or become a mother. And who knew about Amber? She dated, but was careful about getting too committed to anyone and kept her personal life pretty private.

Brooke sighed. They all had their flaws, but she loved the idea of the three of them together. The ABC's her father had sometimes called them—Amber, Brooke and Cate—the terrifying trio. It had been a joke among them, one to inspire confidence. Oh, how she missed her father. He'd been such a support to her. Her mother? Not so much.

She glanced in the mirror. She looked pretty good for a woman approaching forty. The trouble was, you could change someone on the outside to look better, but it took a lot more work to make her believe it. And with Paul's unusual behavior lately, her self-confidence was at an all-time low.

"Hey, Mom! We're hungry!" cried Brynn, entering her bedroom like a whirlwind, displacing Brooke's musing.

"Yes, we kids need a snack," added Bradley, right behind her sister, wearing a pink bathing suit that brought back a memory of The Beach Babes wearing something like it one summer.

Brooke smiled at the daughters she adored with all her heart. "Let's get you all fed."

She followed them downstairs and into the kitchen. Automatically, she reached for apples, sliced them, and put them on a tray, along with chunks of cheese, a bowl of nuts, and an icy-cold bunch of green grapes. She kept her twins away from sugar as much as possible. On those occasions when it wouldn't work, she never mentioned sugar, weight, appearance, or regrets.

Their brother had no such worries. "P.J.," Paul Junior, looked a lot like his father—tall and thin, with craggy, pleasing facial features. But it was her own father's good humor in him that made Brooke love him so much. His impending birth had caused a major disruption in college, but she didn't regret having him. Being a mother and a wife was something she'd always wanted.

Her cell phone rang. *Paul.* She picked up the call. "Hi, honey!"

"Just giving you a call to say I won't be home until late. Go ahead with dinner without me."

"Another baby on the way?" As the wife of an Ob-Gyn doctor, she was used to his erratic schedule.

The click signifying the end to their call sounded in her ear. She frowned. It wasn't like Paul to be rude like that. And yet again, he hadn't answered her question.

CHAPTER THREE

AMBER

Amber Anderson studied the information on the screen of her computer and uttered a sigh of relief. The list of details from Cate was just what she needed. A chance to be with true friends who would understand her dilemma. At almost forty, all the good genes in the world might not help her. In her business, she could soon be out of a job.

Many times, she'd silently vowed not to be like her mother, had promised herself she'd be better, stronger, nicer, more careful. But she was in a mess typical of one her mother might have made. And all because she'd thought she'd fallen in love. Another thing she'd promised herself would never happen.

"Amber?"

The strident voice calling to her jerked her out of her thoughts. She jumped to her feet and faced her boss. "Yes, Belinda? What is it?"

A tall, thin, striking woman with steel-gray hair studied Amber with dark, cold brown eyes that reached deep inside her, forcing Amber to swallow hard. Belinda "The Bitch" Galvin was a woman who'd scrapped and fought her way to the top of the modeling agency she now ran. No one went against her wishes. Those who dared to question her suffered from the terrible verbal lashings for which Belinda was known. Amber had worked for her for three difficult years, and yet, though there was a lot she didn't like about her boss, she respected Belinda for being the strong, in-charge woman she was.

"I need you to make sure Jesse Carpenter's entire crew is scheduled for the shoot in Antigua, and that they will give us four days, not three, for the perfume commercial you're doing for us with *L'eau Ange*. Understand?" Belinda frowned. "Jesse is excited about shooting it with you. Be your best, Amber. Remember, this is a big account for us. It's unusual for someone like you, working as my assistant, to be included in a photo shoot."

"Yes, I know," Amber said to Belinda's back. Not one to hang around and chat, Belinda had already walked away.

Amber called Jesse's studio, talked to Gayle Nickerson, the assistant he'd used for years, and confirmed the arrangements.

"Should be a nice location for you," said Gayle. "It's been what? Three years of filming for this company for you?"

"Yes," said Amber. It had been such a coup for her to get the contract. If Jesse hadn't insisted on it, Belinda wouldn't have agreed.

"Time flies," said Gayle. "I can't believe I've been with Jesse for twelve years now. I remember when you went to work for Belinda. I didn't think you'd last, but you've managed to work with her when a lot of people haven't. How do you do it?"

Amber laughed. "By keeping my mouth shut and wanting to prove to my mother I could make it on my own."

Gayle chuckled softly. "Good enough reasons. I'll tell Jesse you called and that Belinda needs everyone there for a day longer."

"Thanks," said Amber. "I'll see you then." Quickly, while Belinda seemed to be in a good mood, she emailed her a request for the two days off she'd need in order to meet her friends at the Seashell Cottage. She needed to be there. They were the only two people in the world she trusted to help her out of the mess she was in.

CHAPTER FOUR

CATE

Frustrated by how her writing had stalled, Cate got up from her desk and paced her office. At one point, she picked up the lightweight wooden sword Jackson had made for her in woodworking class and swung it back and forth, prompting piercing barks from Buddy.

"It's okay, Buddy boy," Cate said, assuming a fighting stance. "It's just Serena. She's come upon her arch enemy and needs to fight her way out of a touchy problem. I'm just trying to get the right movements down for my book."

Cate set the sword on her desk and picked up Buddy for a quick snuggle. "Maybe Serena needs a new guardian dragon. Her faithful companion was injured in the last book."

Buddy licked her face as if he agreed.

Laughing, she set him down. "Okay, I'll come up with a new one."

She sat in front of her computer again and tried to focus on the world she'd created. She'd been surprised when book one of the Galeon Wars series was so successful. But then, Serena was a compelling character—everything Cate was not. Big, brave, and strong, Serena was unafraid to tackle any problem, take on anybody, expose herself to any danger imagined or real.

Funny, few suspected how much Cate loved the world Serena lived in. Writing about that world allowed her to feel free in a way she'd never been allowed.

The need for Cate to be quiet, restrained, and all but hidden had begun with her moving in with her aunt. The less her aunt saw or heard from her, the better it was. It became even worse when Aunt Margaret went to work for Mr. Ira Pennyman, a neighbor of Brooke's family. Deceased now, her aunt, a nurse practitioner, had admired the older gentleman she took care of six days a week. In a wheelchair from an auto accident that had crushed his back, paralyzing him from the waist down, Ira Pennyman was a demanding man in his seventies who didn't like children. Something both he and her aunt agreed on.

He'd met Cate a few times and only by accident. Her aunt repeatedly told Cate to be quiet and stay out of his sight, that he might fire her for having a child around and she couldn't find another job as good as this.

It was while Cate was playing quietly in the spacious yard at Ira's house one day that she saw Brooke next door and made friends with her. And when Amber met them at the neighborhood park one morning, the twosome became a threesome—three girls from different backgrounds brought together by loneliness and fate.

Buddy barked, jarring Cate out of her wayward thoughts.

Concentrating on her book once more, Cate decided Buddy was right. Serena needed a new dragon. She quickly went through names in her mind and settled on Condora. She could imagine the little creature already. She began to describe the battle and how a young dragon appeared by Serena's side, helping to save the moment. She was so lost in the story it took several moments before she realized her cell phone was ringing. Jarred by the change in setting, she picked up the call. *Abby Francis, her agent.*

"Hello?"

"Hi, Cate. Abby here. I've found an opportunity for you to speak at a small bookseller's convention the first weekend in November. Sales have been lagging a bit. I think you need to do it."

Cate swallowed hard. She hated to disappoint Abby, who'd been her staunch supporter from the beginning. "I'm sorry, Abby. I can't. I have some personal time set aside for that period."

"Don't tell me you're finally going to marry that hunk of yours," Abby replied.

"No, no, nothing like that. I'm meeting my two best friends in Florida. It's very important to all of us."

"Are you sure you can't change it?"

"Positive," Cate said firmly. Getting the three of them together wasn't easy. She was lucky they'd agreed to find the time to join her.

"Okay. I'm disappointed, but I understand. You usually don't let me down. I'll allow this one opportunity to pass, but remember how important book five is to your career. The publishing house should be coming up with the cover soon, and then you'll have to begin your part of promoting it."

Cate sighed. "I know. Not one of my favorite things to do. Is there any way you can get more money out of them for advertising and promotion?"

"I wish," grumped Abby. "Each year it gets harder and harder. That's why we have to keep your sales figures up. It's such a numbers game. But don't worry. I'll try. Your readers have been waiting for this one."

"I know. I'm working on it now."

"Well, give yourself a break and then get a draft to your editor pronto. The early bird gets the worm and all that."

Cate laughed. Abby was often coming up with little sayings like that. "Serena is getting another dragon. A cute little girl this time."

"Nice. I like that angle. Talk to you later. I've got another call coming in."

Cate clicked off and wondered what she would have done without Abby. She'd been so green, so naïve about the publishing business when she'd first started that she might have failed if Abby hadn't stepped in. Now, after a lot of missteps, hurt feelings, and determination, Cate had built an imaginary shield around herself to get through the process of dealing with the publisher and her editor. The book business was not for sissies.

She got up, went into the kitchen, and fixed herself a cup of tea, her mind whirring with ideas about where to take the plot of the book. She hoped to get most of the first draft of the book done before she left for Florida. She had a feeling that the weekend with her friends was going to be full of surprises. It usually was that way when they got together. She could hardly wait!

The days alternately flew by and dragged as Cate worked on her book. Even though she knew it would need lots of editing, she pushed herself to get words down.

Finally, the day came when Cate packed her suitcase, bid Jackson a heartfelt goodbye, and headed to the airport. Rather than go into the city, she drove to the Westchester County Airport in White Plains to catch a flight to Tampa. Most of the flights from there required a change of planes, but Cate was able to get a seat on the non-stop flight. It was much easier than driving into the city and dealing with the hassles of the traffic on the way to either LaGuardia or Kennedy Airport.

Once past security, she waited to board and then settled in her seat, feeling like a child before her birthday party was about to begin. She could hardly wait to see her friends, hear what they'd been up to, what plans they had for the future.

Fortieth birthdays were called milestones for many reasons. It used to be that at age forty, one was considered half-way through her life, and that was if they were lucky. Nowadays, forty was the new thirty, but still meant a milestone.

Aloft in the plane, she stared out the window watching the miniature towns below. Large, puffy white clouds drifted lazily in the air, creating shadows on the land beneath them before floating away.

As they headed south, Cate's spirits lifted. She needed this time away from work and the worry about the decision Jackson was placing upon her. This, she decided, would be her time to let loose in a way she hadn't allowed herself in a long while.

She lay her head against her headrest, pleased she'd booked a seat with extra space. It wasn't elegant, but it was better than being in the back of the plane.

The next thing she knew, the pilot's voice was announcing their approach to Tampa International Airport. She checked her watch. 11:40 AM. Perfect, Amber's plane was due in at noon. Together, they'd head down to the cottage and get it ready for Brooke's arrival that afternoon.

At the signal to release seat belts, Cate got to her feet, and waited for the exit door to open, wanting to dance with impatience. She'd brought only a small carry-on bag onto the plane, which made things easier.

Exiting the plane, she joined the throng of passengers moving toward the tram to the main terminal and the baggage claim area. She'd agreed to meet Amber there. Thinking of her, Cate automatically brushed her hand over a wrinkle in her slacks. Amber looked put together in a way Cate could never achieve, not against Amber's figure and sense of style. If she was having a good writing day, Cate sometimes worked at home in her pajamas for the entire time.

She found an empty seat and sat, watching people. It was as good a sport as any other for her. Observing strangers, studying what they were wearing, overhearing conversations, her quick mind easily made up stories about them. Though she lived vicariously in a world of her creation, it didn't stop her from envisioning other stories—contemporary ones placed in the real world. So far, she hadn't switched genres, but one day she might choose to write a contemporary fiction novel under a pseudonym.

When at last her attention was drawn to a tall blond heading her way walking with a model's sway to her hips, Cate jumped to her feet. Dressed in white jeans and a flowing, turquoise sweater, Amber looked every bit the beauty she was and always had been. But as her friend crossed the space between them, Cate filled with dismay. Dark circles under Amber's light-blue eyes marred her face. She held back a gasp. Amber looked ... well, terrible.

"Hey, Cate!" Amber said. A smile broke out, lighting her flawless face, making her seem more like the old Amber. She held up her hand to block conversation. "Don't say anything about it. I know I look awful."

Cate wrapped her arms around Amber and hugged her tight. "No matter what, you're beautiful."

Amber stepped away and gazed at her, missing nothing. "You look spectacular. Jackson must be treating you well. Very well."

Thinking of their lovemaking last night, Cate felt heat creep to her cheeks. Jackson was a wonderful lover—passionate and generous. And he'd made it clear that he would miss her, even if she was going to be away for only a long weekend.

Amber laughed. "I knew it!"

"Do you have luggage?" Cate asked, quickly changing the subject. She wasn't ready to talk about Jackson. Not until

Brooke was with them.

"I do have one suitcase," Amber admitted.

"Large, no doubt," teased Cate.

Amber shrugged. "A girl has to be ready for anything. Right?"

Cate grinned and shook her head. Amber seldom traveled light. Why should she? Her collection of designer clothes was suitable for a princess.

After they picked up Amber's oversized suitcase, they wheeled it toward the car rental desk. Out of the corner of her eye, Cate studied Amber as they walked. She'd usually been the one to join in on any adventure, but today she was looking and acting like that might not happen.

CHAPTER FIVE

AMBER

"Are you all right?" Cate asked her, unable to hide the concern in her voice.

"Let's wait until Brooke is here, and then I need to talk to both of you." Amber's eyes welled with tears. "I'm in such a mess."

"Oh, but ..." Cate looked stricken.

Amber drew a breath and straightened, stuffing the helplessness she felt into a safe spot within her. "Sorry. I'll be all right. This get-together is the best idea ever, Cate. What would we Beach Babes do without you to guide us?" Kind, sweet, and with a natural, quiet beauty, Cate was the one who kept them together.

Cate's smile filled her face, lighting her brown eyes. "I'm delighted you and Brooke could make it. I've missed the two of you so much. C'mon. Let's get our car and be on our way. I want everything to look nice for Brooke. You know that means a lot to her."

"As if she ever had to worry about things being nice," Amber said with a slight edge to her voice.

At Cate's look of surprise, Amber felt heat reach her cheeks. "I'm sorry I said that. Brooke might have had all the financial advantages in the world, but her life wasn't easy growing up with a mother who constantly found fault with her."

"Thank goodness, Brooke's father adored her," said Cate. "Still, a mother's rejection is something no child ever gets over. I know that all too well."

Amber put an arm around Cate's shoulder. "Mothers. Who needs them?"

Cate chuckled. "I'd say the three of us."

They chose to rent a red convertible for a premium fee.

"This one is on me," Cate said, pulling out her wallet from her purse. She didn't often talk about numbers and her success, but Amber knew she enjoyed a nice income from her books.

They loaded their luggage into the trunk of the car, put the top down, and with Cate driving and Amber guiding them, they left the airport.

As they drove on the causeway across Tampa Bay and then south along the coast, silence reigned in the car. With the air blowing around them, whipping their hair about their heads, conversation would have been difficult at best. Better to leave it this way, thought Amber. Once she started talking, she might not stop.

When Cate pulled into the driveway of the Seashell Cottage, Amber gazed at it and let out a sigh of contentment. It was as lovely as the pictures online.

"We're here!" Cate cried joyfully, beaming at her.

"Thank God!" Amber said, quickly unbuckling her seatbelt. "Hurry and unlock the door."

"Hold on! I've already memorized the code." Cate climbed out of the car and rushed over to the lockbox hanging on the front door knob.

As soon as the door was opened, Amber rushed through the doorway and disappeared down the hallway off to one side.

Moments later, she returned to stand beside Cate in the entry way and studied her surroundings. She knew from online research that one of the bedroom suites lay to her left, facing the Gulf waters. The two others, overlooking the courtyard and pool, were located off the hallway where she'd gone. Ahead of her, the living room was filled with comfortable furniture. Beyond that and behind the one front bedroom was the large, modern kitchen. All in all, it was everything Amber had seen on her computer screen.

She smiled. "Wow! This is great! It must have cost us a pretty penny."

"Well, Brooke has offered to pay for it," said Cate. "I think we should let her. You know how it pleases her to treat us."

Amber rolled her eyes. "Like usual, huh?" She hated to be beholden to anyone. It went back to her not having money to do the same for her friends.

"She means well, Amber. I, for one, will eternally be grateful to her for taking me in, showing me new things, and sharing new experiences. She's a generous person."

"You're right," said Amber, wondering why she was acting this way. Was it the hormones she felt raging inside her body? Or her lack of sleep lately? She cleared her throat and fought tears. "Brooke has been good to me too. Both of you have. Before you two, I had few friends, mostly because I couldn't bring anyone home. The only times I did, the girls' mothers made sure they didn't come back. And why not? I never knew what man my mother might be entertaining next."

Cate didn't respond. She didn't need to.

Amber's mother, Tessa, was a single mom who was constantly forming a new romance with an unsuitable guy who sometimes showed an unhealthy interest in Amber. It was why she still stayed away from her mother as much as possible. Bad energy between them.

"Let's bring in our suitcases and then take a stroll along the beach," Cate suggested. "Brooke won't be here for a while, and we have time for a quick walk before we need to go shopping for groceries and grab lunch."

"I choose one of the rooms down the hallway," said Amber.

"And I'll take the other," said Cate. "That will give Brooke more privacy and a room looking out at the water. If she's paying, she deserves it."

They each got organized in their rooms and then met in the kitchen.

"I've started a list of the things we need to buy. Even if it's just for a few days, I want to make sure we're well stocked," said Cate.

Amber nudged her. "You're our organizer."

Cate laughed and took hold of her arm. "Okay. Let's take that walk. We'll talk later when Brooke is here. I don't want to leave her out."

They left the house and stood a moment in the yard, staring out at the blue waters of the Gulf of Mexico. Amber breathed in the salty air and felt a smile cross her face as satisfaction filled her. There was something almost magical about the smell of the fresh air, the way the gentle onshore breeze caressed her cheeks, and the sound of the water rushing to shore and pulling away again in a dance as old as time. She looked up to the sky as seagulls, terns, and other birds circled, the color of their white wings striking against the deep blue of the sky.

"Nice, huh?" said Cate, standing beside her. "I sometimes forget to take the time to see the beauty around me."

"I know. I just returned from the Caribbean, and I swear, I hardly knew I was there. It was all business."

"Another photo shoot?" Cate asked.

Amber nodded solemnly, and for a split-second her lips trembled before she got control of them. "Might be my last. We'll see."

"Oh, hon! You're upset. When Brooke gets here, I want to

know every last detail of what's going on with you," said Cate, studying her.

Amber told herself to suck it up and be strong. "C'mon, let's go. I can use the exercise."

Thinking how good it felt to be here, Amber moved swiftly across the grass toward the beach.

Cate eagerly ran to catch up to her long strides.

The packed sand along the edge of the water felt firm beneath Amber's turquoise sandals. She took them off, held the shoes in her hand, and began to run, wishing she could lift wings and fly away from all her problems.

Cate kept pace beside her.

When they stopped, Cate smiled at her and, between breaths, said, "It's so good to be away from home and the endless plotting and writing of a new book. I wish I was one of those novelists who carefully outlined each book. But I'm what is called a 'pantser,' letting the story unroll from my heart as new twists and turns come to me."

"That's why everyone loves your books. They're written from the heart," Amber said, smiling at her with affection. "And your heart is as big as your smile."

"Aw, thanks," Cate responded shyly. She pointed down the beach a short way from them. "Race you to the pier."

They jogged side by side and then slowed as they neared the wooden pier. It reached into the cool water like a tentative finger about to test the water's temperature.

"Ah-h-h, that felt good. I realize I need to get out and exercise more," Cate said, working to catch her breath as she lowered herself onto one of the wooden benches that lined both sides of the pier.

"You should try to run outdoors or go to the gym as much as possible," prompted Amber. "I long for the day when I won't give a damn about staying so thin, but then what would

I do? Part-time, low-key modeling and working in fashion in New York are what I've always done."

"Turning forty is making me wonder about a lot of things too." Cate checked her watch. "We'd better head back. We have to grab lunch and go grocery shopping before Brooke arrives. Can't wait to see her."

"I wonder what her new look will be," said Amber. "She's constantly trying to change her appearance."

"It's an old habit, even though she's perfectly fine as she is. No matter how good she looks, she doesn't believe she's attractive. Her mother really did a number on her." A bitter snort erupted from Cate, surprising Amber. "In some ways I suppose she was lucky. I had to fight for any attention from my aunt and that didn't usually end well."

"Yeah, I remember," Amber replied with genuine sympathy. "It was like you didn't exist to her. Later on, her cat got more attention than you ever could."

They returned to the house and because of the time, decided to grab a salad at the grocery store while shopping rather than take a chance on not getting back to the cottage before Brooke got there.

At lunch, Amber carefully removed any topping that might have unwanted calories and dutifully set aside the container of salad dressing.

Cate watched her. "I hope you're going to enjoy our time together. Eat, be merry, and all that."

She grimaced. "You're right. I'll watch what I eat, but I won't be ridiculous about it." She opened the salad dressing and drizzled it on top of the lettuce. "See?"

"I didn't mean to make you uncomfortable," said Cate. "I know it's all part of your job."

Amber didn't respond. Cate had no idea how competitive her situation was at work.

CHAPTER SIX

CATE

Back at the house, Cate sat in a rocking chair beside Amber on the front porch, moving back and forth in rhythm with the sound of the waves kissing the shore with a smack and pulling back for more like a greedy lover. She closed her eyes and listened to the whispering of the palm trees nearby, their fronds swaying in the breeze, telling secrets of their own.

"I heard a car pull in," cried Amber, jumping to her feet. "She's here!"

Cate followed Amber off the porch and around the house to the driveway, where a white limousine was idling.

The driver got out and opened the back door.

Cate held her breath as she waited to see Brooke. At the sight of her, her hair with its natural red curls, she released a sigh of relief. It appeared Brooke was okay. When things were bad, Brooke did outlandish things with her hair. She'd gone for months with her hair dyed an Irish green after the twins were born, and she hadn't yet lost weight following their births.

Smiling, Brooke moved toward Cate and Amber with outstretched arms. "It's so good to see both of you! Couldn't wait to get here!"

After hugs had been exchanged all around, Cate stood back and studied her. Brooke was taller than she but was overshadowed by Amber, who was the tallest by far. Plastic surgery had straightened a nose that had once featured a bump, and shaped the area around eyes that had been corrected with Lasik surgery. But the white, straight-toothed smile she was shining on them was genuine and held a little bit of the insecurity that was part of her nature.

While Brooke paid the driver, Cate gathered the suitcase he'd set on the driveway and waited to roll it away. Amber took hold of the large carry-on satchel.

"All set?" Brooke said, turning to them.

"We've got your stuff." Cate headed for the house.

Amber and Brooke followed behind.

Inside, Cate lead Brooke to her bedroom and then gave her a quick tour of the house.

"This is perfect," said Brooke. "And, boy, do I need this break." She paused and then blurted, "I'm thinking of leaving Paul."

Stunned silence followed, broken by Cate's high-pitched cry. "Paul?"

Brooke nodded. "He's been acting weird lately, and I've gained a few pounds, in case you haven't noticed."

"Whoa! You look terrific," Cate said. "By Los Angeles standards you might be a little heavy, but by ordinary standards you're thin. Maybe too thin." She wouldn't mention that there was a skeletal tightness to Brooke's face that happened when she dieted too strenuously.

"Paul is a good guy," said Amber. "There was an incident with a patient a couple of years ago, but what has he done to make you think he's cheating?"

Brooke sighed. "Let me get changed into something more comfortable. Then we'll sit and talk. And while you're at it, open a bottle of wine. It's got to be cocktail time somewhere and we're here to celebrate our upcoming birthdays, even if we're months ahead of time."

"I'll open a white wine," Cate said.

"And I'll fix a plate of nibbles," offered Amber.

After Brooke left them, Cate turned to Amber. "I can't believe she'd think of leaving Paul."

"Maybe she's just tired of worrying about him, wondering if another episode with a patient is going on. She told me he's never home," Amber said.

Cate opened the promised bottle of wine and got out three glasses. Five o'clock wasn't that far off.

When Brooke emerged from her bedroom, she was wearing black capri pants and a black and white striped shirt that showed off a fine figure.

"You look great," Cate said, meaning it. She'd often thought Brooke was the cute one.

"Thanks. I've been working at it. The weather has been cooperating. I've been able to use the pool in the morning for exercise after the girls have gone off to school."

"And how's that handsome boy of yours?" Cate asked. She was P.J.'s godmother and relished the role.

Brooke's face lit up. "He's doing great. He might even make Dean's List at the rate he's going." She accepted the glass of wine Cate offered her. "I want to hear all about the two of you." Her gaze settled on them, her expression sobering as she focused on Amber.

Amber lifted a plate of fruit, olives, and nuts. "It's nice out on the porch. We can talk there."

"And if we're lucky, maybe tonight we'll see the green flash everyone talks about," said Cate. "If you catch sight of the sun at the exact moment it slips behind the horizon and the temperature and humidity are just right, a green flash of light appears. I haven't observed it, but I look for it every time."

"Let's hope we do. It might be a good sign of all of us," said Brooke.

They went out to the porch and formed a circle with

rocking chairs. A small table sat in the middle holding the appetizers, but no one reached for any. Too many unsaid words floated in the air like feathers drifting around them.

"Okay, Miss Brooke," said Amber. "What's going on with you and Paul? Are you really thinking of leaving him?"

Brooke set down her wine glass and shook her head. "I don't know. I've decided to confront him when I get home, and if he's fooling around, that's it for me. I can live on my own comfortably."

"But you'd be giving up a lot—a close family unit, maybe your house, and some of your family money. Divorce in California isn't cheap," said Cate.

"Believe me, it would be worth it. I can't stand wondering any longer. He's just not been himself lately, and you know what they say on all those afternoon television shows. It's a sign that something is going on with him."

"Any perfume or lipstick on his shirts?" asked Amber.

"No, nothing like that. It's just that things aren't right. You know? He used to greet me with a kiss at night and leave me with a kiss in the morning." Her eyes welled. "Now he hardly speaks to me."

"The important thing is to prepare yourself mentally, physically, and emotionally for such a drastic decision as separation and divorce," Cate said gently. "Have as much as possible in writing."

"Why don't you hire a detective?" said Amber. "Make sure that's what is going on, have proof. Paul isn't that kind of guy. So, he screwed up once. He admitted it was a mistake, and it wasn't an affair, just a kiss to comfort a patient who'd lost a child."

Brooke sat back in her chair, looking miserable.

Cate's heart went out to her. "I can't imagine Paul doing this to you, but if he is, you're strong and capable."

Brooke covered her face with her hands. After a few moments of silence, she straightened in her chair. "Damn right. Thank you, Cate. You make me feel better." She picked up her glass of wine. "Okay, enough about me. What's happening with the two of you."

"Are you ready to talk now?" Cate said to Amber. She then turned to Brooke. "We decided to wait until you arrived before we got into any deep discussions."

Amber sighed and shook her head. "I'm in a mess. You both know how difficult my boss, Belinda Galvin, is."

"She's legendary," said Cate.

"Yeah, a real bitch," agreed Brooke.

"She's a powerful figure in the fashion business and used to getting her way with everybody and everything. It's taken a lot of swallowing of pride for me to get along with her. It isn't easy, but it's been worthwhile for me to work for her. Not only for the money, but to learn the business. Outside the office, I've got a beautiful condo, an interesting life, and everything one could wish for."

"But?" Cate's gaze rested on her, seeing misery.

"But I've made a mess of it by falling for the man Belinda claims is her boyfriend, even though he denies it and has told me he dated her only a couple of times before he ended it."

"So?" said Brooke. "That shouldn't be too bad. It happens all the time in Hollywood."

"This ain't Hollywood, though it could be," said Amber, in a tough voice nobody believed.

"What's the problem?" Cate asked, knowing there had to be a lot more to the story.

"The problem is that Belinda says she still wants him after just a couple of dates, sends him flowers, sets up business meetings with him, and makes all kinds of moves toward him. He told me he broke it off with her several months ago, but she won't give up on the idea of getting together with him."

"Who is this guy?" Brooke said.

Amber's cheeks turned pink. "Jesse Carpenter."

Cate's eyebrows shot up with surprise. "Jesse Carpenter? The guy who's famous for his photography work? He recently released a book of photographs of people in different parts of the world that is receiving rave reviews. Some even call him the Ansel Adams of people, with stunning work in both black and white and color."

"Yeah, that's him. A real sweet guy. I've known him casually for a long time. We got to know one another much better when I began shooting for the perfume company a couple of years ago. if Belinda ever finds out about me and Jesse, I'll lose my job."

"And how is she going to find out?" asked Brooke.

Amber's face crumpled. Tears slid down her face. "Because I'm pregnant."

The gasps from Brooke and Cate hung in the air like helium-filled balloons floating above them.

"See? I knew you'd be as shocked as I am. I figure I'm only about eight weeks along. We've been dating only a few months, and I'm very careful. You know how I feel about kids. I like 'em, but I don't want any of my own. You understand. Right, Cate?"

Cate slumped in her chair. "That's what I needed to talk to you two about. Jackson doesn't want to wait any longer to start a family with me. I told him I need time to think about it."

"Think about it? My God, Cate, you two together are better than an old married couple," Brooke declared with feeling. "You'd be a fool to let go of that. Besides, you'd make a great Mom. Look how you are with Buddy! And he's just a dog."

"Not just any dog. A dachshund," Cate reminded her. She

caught the corner of her lip, unable to speak at the moment. "We're all in a mess, aren't we?" She lifted her glass. "Here's to us!"

Amber lifted her glass and set it down. "I can't drink. Remember?"

"Hold on," said Brooke. She ran into the house and returned with a wine glass full of iced tea. "Okay. Here's to us! All of us!"

"The Beach Babes!" cried Amber.

They clinked glasses together, but the sound of it did little to cheer Cate. She hadn't imagined all the trouble they'd be in.

A little later, the three of them stood together on the sand, facing the setting sun. The glowing orb of the sun slowly slid below the horizon. Out of the corner of her eye, Cate studied the women beside her and noted the hopeful look on their faces. But when the sun was entirely hidden behind the horizon of gray clouds, no one shouted that they'd seen the green flash.

CHAPTER SEVEN

BROOKE

The next morning, Brooke lay in bed thinking about her friends and the issues they all faced. There would be a lot more talking, but the fact remained that it would take more than talk to make these predicaments right.

She got out of bed and peeked out the window. The blue skies and sun that greeted her lifted her spirits. They were strong women, smart. Together they'd come up with ideas and plans. One thing was for sure. In the days ahead, they'd need to be there for one another.

She dressed in shorts and a T-shirt, tiptoed out of her room, and quietly left the house. She needed a sense of nature to calm her troubled soul. She'd told the others she would be quick to divorce Paul, but the truth was, it would break her heart. As Cate had mentioned, he'd loved her as she was from the beginning. They'd met her first year of college and his last year in med school. An only child of older parents, he wasn't afraid to be a non-cool kid, a geeky sort who'd grown up wanting to be a doctor. It was after she became pregnant with his child that he decided to go the Ob-Gyn route.

She saw Amber in the distance and walked to meet her.

"What are you doing up so early?" Brooke asked, approaching her.

Amber gave her a sheepish smile. "Trying to figure out how to handle things. As I told you and Cate last night, Jesse doesn't know about the baby. I'm not sure he's going to be happy about it. He made it clear to me that after his divorce six years ago, he has no desire for a long-term relationship with anyone else. He has two kids in college, and I can't imagine him wanting to start all over again. Besides, he travels for his work."

"Still, he has a right to know," said Brooke.

"Yes, I'm aware he needs to be told." Amber's voice held a snappishness to it, but Brooke didn't mind. She knew Amber disliked the idea of losing her independence, especially when it came to a man. Shades of her childhood.

"I'm trying to think of a way to tell Belinda I need personal time off in a few months when I'm scheduled to have the baby."

"And afterwards?" Brooke wondered if Amber realized all the changes that were coming her way.

Amber shrugged. "That's the part I'm unsure of. There are so many things to think about."

"Good morning, dear friends," said Cate joining them. "I want you to know how happy I am that we're together again. Even as I tossed and turned last night, I know that no matter what happens to each of us, we'll remain the best of friends and help one another out."

"You got that right," said Amber, giving Cate a quick hug.

"What have you two been talking about?" Cate asked.

"I'm trying to come up with a plan to keep my job and still be able to ask Belinda for time off to have the baby."

"Look, if you need a place to stay while you wait for the baby or afterwards, you can come to my house. Jackson spent most of his summer break renovating the old cabin on the property as my personal space, like a "she-shed." Finishing touches need to be completed, but it's gorgeous. In addition to my office, it has a bedroom, bath, and kitchen."

"More like a guest cottage," said Amber. "Thanks. I might take you up on that."

"It's not so simple. There are going to be a lot of changes in your life," Brooke said to Amber. "And the same for you, Cate, if you decide to go ahead and have a baby with Jackson."

"Yes, that's one of the things I'm worried about," Cate quickly agreed. "I remember how much my aunt resented the care of me. Any child of Jackson's and mine will be my concern for the rest of my life. That thought scares the heck out of me. What if I turn out to be as uncaring and cold as she was toward me? I wouldn't ever want to do that to a child. It was awful."

Brooke studied her. "You're nothing like your aunt."

"But both she and my mother were like that. What if it's in my genes?" Tears moistened Cate's eyes.

"Oh, hon," said Amber. "You're such a sweet person, I don't see that happening."

"It's a big worry of mine," Cate admitted. "But I don't want to lose Jackson. He's the best part of me."

"No way. You're the best part of him." Brooke grinned and elbowed Cate. "Remember what we talked about last night. It's time for The Beach Babes to take charge, live life fully, and be strong."

They lined up along the beach, facing the water. It seemed right that in front of them a trio of pelicans skimmed the surface of the water looking for food, resembling fighter jets in formation, as vibrant as the three women watching them.

At lunch, Brooke sat with Amber and Cate at an outdoor table at the Purple Pig. New to the area, the bar was known for serving excellent food and fancy margaritas. Normally, Brooke didn't drink during the day, but when Cate asked her to join her to celebrate their birthdays, she couldn't resist ordering a Texas margarita. She pushed her circumstances at home to the back of her mind. It was more important to spend time with her friends and help them decide what to do about their futures. As for herself, she'd listen to any advice they wanted to give her. Except for Paul, they knew her best.

As Brooke sipped her drink, she took a moment to look through the open sliding doors to the inside of the building. The interior walls were painted a plum purple and served as a nice background for the comical pig prints that covered a good portion of them. Purple linen cloths covered the tables and were offset by pale pink napkins and sparkling glassware. A crystal stem vase held a purple-accented white orchid. Funky but cute, the bar turned out to be a nice surprise.

During their meal, Brooke said, "Let's go shopping. It's been a while since I've needed baby stuff and there are so many terrific new things out now, I'd like to see what's there. Amber, you'll need to know about them and, Cate, if you're thinking about a baby, you might want to check them out too."

Amber and Cate exchanged glances.

"Okay by me," Amber said. "It's a world I haven't been part of and, heaven knows, I'm going to need all the help I can get."

"Me too." Cate hugged herself. "I can't imagine me with a real baby."

"I hope you decide to go ahead with it. Motherhood has been a pleasure for me. P.J., Brynn, and Bradley are my pride and joy." Brooke paused, momentarily overcome by sadness. "And for Paul too. He's a good father. I'll give him that." She took a last bite of her grilled salmon Caesar salad. "Delicious."

"Ready? I'm going to pay for lunch." Amber held up the tab the waitress had placed on the table. She pulled some bills out of her purse and tucked them underneath her plate. "There. We can leave now."

Brooke watched her, amused by the determined pat Amber gave the bills. Amber was sensitive about money, mostly because she hadn't had any growing up.

They left the restaurant and drove to a big box store where every imaginable thing needed for an infant was displayed.

Seeing all the colors, baby equipment, and tiny clothes, Brooke clasped her hands. It brought back so many memories. Sadly, she'd been so busy with the twins she hadn't had time to enjoy them as she had with P.J. She turned to Amber. "You said you're eight weeks along, which means you're going to have a spring baby. Spring is a good time for a little one. You'll be able to take walks with her and ..."

Amber raised a hand to stop her. "Wait a minute! Her? I might be having a boy. I hope so."

Brooke laughed. "Okay, time to walk with *him* and be outdoors. Let's take a look at strollers here and then do research online."

"Look at this." Cate held up a tiny pajama outfit. In white, the footed pajamas sported a pink, three-dimensional cloth butterfly on the upper left shoulder. Embroidered nearby, a ladybug appeared ready to go exploring.

"That's adorable. Okay, I'll start a list of the things you'll need," said Brooke, taking a piece of paper and a pen from her purse. "Then you won't be so confused."

"I can't imagine raising a child in New York City, especially in my small condo," said Amber. "But I guess I'd better start thinking about it."

"Remember, you have space at my house if you need it," Cate said.

"Or at mine," Brooke piped up.

"I hope it won't come to that," said Amber. "Let's keep going so I have a better understanding of what will be needed. My mind is spinning. Each bit of clothing looks small enough for a doll, and each piece of furniture looks enormous. What am I going to do? My life, my space, my time will be completely upended."

"One day at a time," Brooke said.

Cate trailed after them as Brooke led Amber from one section to another. They all stopped where musical mobiles were displayed. The tinkling sound of music made Brooke smile. She watched as a cow, a plate, and a spoon circled above a crib—intriguing shapes and colors to entertain a baby, and she felt her heart warm at the memory of her girls. Lying side by side in a crib, they'd reach for the same things on the mobile above them at the same time. She'd been fascinated by how connected they were.

At the sound of a sob, Brooke turned to Amber. The anguish on her face frightened her. "What's wrong, hon?"

"What if the baby's a girl? How will I ever be able to protect her? Or even a boy?"

Brooke placed an arm around her. "I'm sure you'll take good care of your baby."

"You're going to be a good mother, Amber," said Cate.

Tears rolled down Amber's cheeks. "You don't understand. I haven't told you before, but there was one time when no one protected me."

Cate looked as sick as Brooke felt. She knew Amber had felt threatened by her mother's male friends, but she hadn't realized it had ever gone beyond that.

"Oh, hon!" Brooke wrapped both her arms around Amber and hugged her tight. "I'm so, so sorry. I wish you'd told us."

"I couldn't ..." Amber said. "It wasn't until recently that I've addressed a lot of issues. That one included." Tears spilled down her cheeks in a steady stream.

"C'mon, sweetie, let's get you out of here," said Cate, her eyes filling.

Stemming her own tears, Brooke took one arm; Cate, the other, and they left the store.

CHAPTER EIGHT

CATE

While Cate drove, Amber and Brooke sat in the backseat. The only sounds inside the car were Amber's sobbing and Brooke's murmurs of sympathy.

When they returned to the cottage, they gravitated to the porch and took seats there.

Cate's mind was still spinning with thoughts of Amber being sexually abused. The thought made her nauseous. "I didn't realize ..."

"Realize how bad things were, living with dear old Mom?" Amber said with a harshness Cate understood. "At the time, I didn't dare tell anyone else, but I might as well talk to the two of you about it now. This seems to be a time to deal with a lot of stuff—old and new."

"If you don't want to discuss it, don't," Cate said. "We're here for you no matter what."

"Right," said Brooke. "I knew the relationship with you and your mother wasn't good, which is why I kept inviting you to my house. But I had no idea how bad it actually was."

"Yeah, it wasn't great. I knew if I said anything to anyone, I might be placed in foster care which would have been even worse. That's why I pretended things were okay."

"How awful," said Cate. Her heart ached for Amber.

"After working with Belinda for a while and trying to deal with her difficult management style, I uncovered a lot of feelings I had about my mother. I sought counseling last year and finally told a professional counselor what happened to me." Amber sighed. "After several attempts to reconcile with my mother, I spoke to the counselor, and she agreed I should stay away from such an unhealthy relationship. That's why I don't have anything to do with my mother."

"I'm so sorry," said Brooke.

Amber smiled at her. "Staying with you was, for me, like living in a fairy tale."

Brooke shook her head. "My mother adored you. Why wouldn't she? You were beautiful, everything I wasn't. And, Cate, on top of being so pretty, you were smart, and kind, and polite. You have no idea what it was like living in my house with Diana Ridley as my mother. But, Amber, I didn't have to put up with the kind of stuff you had to deal with. And, Cate, my mother at least spent time with me, while yours left you."

"Still, your mother wasn't easy," Cate said.

"She and I see each other quite often now with both of us living in California, but it's not pleasant for me. I do it for my kids, though. The twins love her, and she adores them. So, I guess I did something right."

"Your children are wonderful, Brooke," Cate said, quickly coming to Brooke's defense.

"Thank God they didn't get my bumpy nose," Brooke said, and suddenly the three of them were laughing—great belly laughs which helped to relieve the tension of the moment.

"I think it's time for a glass of wine," said Cate, getting to her feet. "Should I fix you an iced tea?" she asked Amber.

"Thanks. That sounds refreshing," said Amber.

When Cate returned, she handed out the drinks and then took a seat. Staring out at the water, she felt her body relax. She'd been terribly shaken that neither she nor Brooke had known what Amber had gone through alone. But then, even the closest of friends hid some secrets.

Brooke's cell rang. She checked it and left the porch.

"Have you decided what you're going to do?" Amber asked Cate. "If you get pregnant soon, our babies could become friends."

"That would be sweet, but I'm still not sure if I should go ahead with such an idea. There are so many things to consider. Still, you two have made me start to think seriously about it."

Amber took hold of Cate's hand. "I know you're not much of a risk taker, but life is full of opportunities. If you don't grab hold of them, you'll have lived only a part of it."

Cate sat back and stared at her with amazement. "When did you become so philosophical? I like it."

"Guess it was that good shrink of mine," said Amber, giving Cate's hand a squeeze before letting go.

Brooke emerged onto the porch. "Sorry to take so long. That was Paul." She sank into a chair. "He told me that when I get back home, we have to talk."

"About what?" Cate said.

Brooke shook her head sadly. "He wouldn't explain, but said it was important." She stared into space, her eyes welling with tears. "He sounded stressed. It has to be about another woman."

"Don't be too quick to judge. Maybe it's something quite different," said Amber.

"I can't put my finger on it, but he's become so quiet, so private that it scares me. We usually talk about everything," Brooke responded. "Or we used to. I've given up trying."

Cate studied her friends and fought for a brighter mood. "A certain wise person told me that life is full of opportunities. Our being together in Florida is a chance to put aside our worries and have fun. This evening let's get dressed up and go out to dinner. I hear Gavin's at the Salty Key Inn is wonderful, and it's close by. In the meantime, let's swim."

"You're right," said Brooke, nodding emphatically. "We need to have fun. My crying now isn't about to change a thing."

"I agree," Amber said. "Let's enjoy this time together. But after this weekend, we need to be in touch more often. Everyone okay with that?"

"Yes," Cate and Brooke said together.

"Sounds like a plan," said Amber.

"A good one," Brooke said, getting to her feet. "It's a beautiful day. Last time I checked the pool was at eighty-eight degrees."

Cate went inside, made dinner reservations, changed into her bathing suit, and went outside to join her friends. They were stretched out on chaise lounges, relaxing.

Brooke might complain about being heavy, but she was cute with a few curves that men seemed to like. Or maybe it was her red hair, a feathery crown above her face that caught their attention. She couldn't imagine Paul getting into another sticky problem, but she also knew some men strayed. If he'd come close once, would he do it again?

Her attention turned to Amber. How would she handle all the changes that were bound to happen to her body? Her self-worth had forever been tied up in her appearance. Even now, that's how she survived—by working in the fashion business and doing some part-time modeling.

Cate thought of how burdened many women were by trying to look like something they saw on television or in the movies, and she wondered why in the world she and other women fell into that awful trap. When she'd complained about something she wore or how she looked, Jackson had told her on more than one occasion that to him she always looked beautiful; he loved her. *Jackson is such a good man! He'll make a great father if I have the courage to go forward.*

Brooke and Amber turned to her, and Cate realized she'd spoken her thoughts aloud.

"Sounds like Cate is getting close to making a decision about having Jackson's baby," said Brooke, giving her a thumbs up.

Cate chuckled. "Closer." Her heart filled with love for Jackson. It was true. He was a wonderful man who'd make a great father. Did she owe them both the opportunity to become parents?

Cate's excitement grew as they drove into the Salty Key Inn. She'd forgotten how much fun it was to get dressed up for dinner at a nice restaurant. All reviews indicated Gavin's was one of the best. Though she and Jackson had many opportunities to go out, they tended to stay in so he could cook a gourmet meal for the two of them.

"There's such a cute story behind the inn and restaurant," said Brooke. "I once read about it in a magazine that showcases people and places."

Cate pulled up to the valet service spot. "Tell us at dinner. I'd love to hear about it."

"This place is packed. It's a miracle you were able to get reservations," said Amber, climbing out of the backseat of the convertible, while a young man held the door for her and offered her a hand as well.

"We're a little early." Brooke stepped onto the sidewalk and turned to them. "We can wait in the bar if we have to. You don't mind, Amber, do you?"

"No. I'm not used to drinking anyway. Belinda's rules. No fat person is allowed to work in Belinda's office. Me, most of all."

"That's awful," said Cate. "I wouldn't make it in her office.

Not as long as I enjoy Jackson's cooking."

"The policy hasn't ever been stated as such, but it's true," said Amber. "That's one of the things I've been worried about. Chances are, by becoming pregnant, I'm going to lose my job."

"That would be grounds for legal action," Brooke said, taking hold of Amber's arm and turning to Cate. "Isn't that right?"

"Not necessarily. But if all the stories I hear about Belinda are true, it wouldn't matter. She'll find a way to get rid of her," Cate replied, giving Amber a sympathetic look.

"She's careful about those things. I'll be given a job out of sight and will have less and less influence until I finally give up and quit."

Their conversation ended as they walked into the restaurant. Cate stood a moment to take in her surroundings. Rich, dark-wood paneling lined the walls, softly lit by crystal wall sconces. Crystal chandeliers cast light from the ceiling above. Crisp white tablecloths covered tables, and crystal wine glasses and water goblets reflected light, lending a shimmery feeling to the room. Silverware sparkled at each setting. A simple, flower-shaped holder with one bright hibiscus bloom in the middle of each table was the perfect finishing touch.

"It's lovely," said Brooke, smiling. "I hope the food is as good as they say. If so, I may not leave. As we've all agreed, we're going to have a good time."

The hostess approached, took their names, and handed them over to the maître d' to be seated.

They were shown to a table in the corner of the main room. Though the restaurant was busy, their table was situated to allow them a sense of privacy.

"Stephanie will be serving you tonight, with the assistance of Mark. Enjoy your meal. We're delighted you're here," announced the maître d' before leaving them.

"Brooke is right. We're lucky to be here," said Amber, gazing around. "How did you manage it?"

A stunning red-haired woman approached their table. "Catherine Tibbs? Hello, my name is Darcy Sullivan Blakely, one of the owners. When I saw your name on the list, I had to come say hello. I love your books. At one time I thought I'd become a writer, but then life happened. I haven't given up; I'm just devoting time to my growing family."

"I've read about you and your sisters," said Brooke, beaming at Darcy. "This place is spectacular."

Darcy smiled. "Thank you. My sisters will be glad to hear it. It's dedicated to my uncle, for whom it's named. Enjoy your dinner. I'm so happy you all could join us."

After she left the table, Amber nudged Cate. "Now we know how we got last-minute reservations. A certain owner is also a fan of a famous author."

Cate laughed. "Me? The famous author? Not likely. But it's nice when a reader likes what I do. Makes all those hours working alone worth it." She turned when the wine steward approached the table.

"May I offer suggestions for wine tonight?" he asked them.

"You bet," Brooke answered, and Cate was pleased to see that the gloomy look Brooke had worn earlier was gone.

After they placed an order for what the wine steward called a lovely, light pinot noir from the Chandler Hill Inn and Winery in the Willamette Valley of Oregon, Brooke told Cate and Amber all about the three Sullivan sisters who'd inherited the Salty Key Inn when it was a dump and how they'd converted it into something so nice.

"I love hearing stories about strong women," Cate said.

"I've decided that if Paul is having an affair, I'm not going to wait, I'm going ahead with a divorce. I don't want to be like some of the people I know who turn a blind eye to their husband's roving because he provides her a nice living style. I don't want my son or the girls to think it's right. Paul and I worked hard to smooth things out and make a stronger relationship after the incident with one of his patients, but I'm not going to do it again."

"Whatever happens, we'll be here for you," said Cate, worried about the look of sadness that filled Brooke's eyes. With her history of never measuring up to her mother's expectations, Brooke would suffer more than many people at being betrayed by Paul.

When it came time to order dessert, the waitress asked if anyone would care for coffee or something else to drink, that dessert had been specially ordered for them.

Amber and Brooke turned to Cate.

Cate grinned. "I told them it was our birthday celebration."

Smiling, they placed their orders for coffee and tea.

After the waitress left, Brooke patted her stomach. "I don't care how full I am, I'm having my share of dessert. Celebrating our birthdays together is the best idea ever." She raised her wine glass. "I love you both."

"Here's to us," Cate said, pleased their time together was working so nicely.

When the waitress returned, she was followed by a young man wearing a white chef's jacket and black-checkered pants, carrying a cake on a plate.

"I understand we have not one, but three birthdays to celebrate. Best wishes to each of you. Enjoy!"

He placed the plate in the center of the table. "It's our lemon-chiffon cake. And per your request, we've kept to a beach theme." The white-icing covering the cake was decorated with a small scattering of seashells and a single pink hibiscus blossom.

Delighted, Cate clapped her hands. “It’s beautiful! Thank you so much!”

“Yes! Thank you!” echoed Amber and Brooke.

Moments later, as Cate took the last bite of her slice of the small, lemony cake, she moaned softly with satisfaction. “This has been the best meal I’ve had in a long, long time. I don’t know how they did it, but everything was perfect—from the steak tartare, to the sole almondine, to the best dessert ever.”

Since living with Jackson, she’d come to appreciate good food. He loved to try new recipes, but his old, tested ones were fine, too. Still, she’d tell him about the food they’d eaten and the lime dressing on the salad. It was especially good with the sprinkling of zest throughout.

“My lamb was to die for,” said Brooke.

“The seared scallops were as tender as I’ve ever had them,” said Amber. “Not that I have them often, with all that butter.”

“Now that you know you’re pregnant, your diet will have to change some,” said Brooke. “You can’t deprive your baby out of fear of gaining weight.”

A dark cloud seemed to cross Amber’s face. “I know. I know. I can’t imagine what the next few months will bring. I don’t blame Jesse for not wanting children.”

Cate couldn’t stop herself from saying, “Hold on! Why would you say that? You haven’t even told him about the baby.”

Amber lifted her glass of water to her lips and set it down. “It’s what I haven’t told him that’s the problem. It’s something I’ve never said to a man.” Her eyes shimmered with tears. “I think I’m in love with him.”

Cate and Brooke exchanged looks of surprise.

“Whoa! This is a whole different ballgame,” said Brooke.

“Do you want to talk about it?” Cate asked.

Amber shook her head firmly. “No, I don’t.”

CHAPTER NINE

AMBER

After they all walked into the cottage, Brooke said, "Let's watch a romantic movie, something that makes us cry. We can get out a lot of our feelings that way."

Amber knew Brooke was trying to help her and was touched by her effort.

"It'll do all of us good, and, later, if you want popcorn, I'll make some," said Cate with an impish grin.

Amber laughed. "Your burnt butter kind?"

The three of them chuckled at the memory of fourteen-year-old Cate burning the butter in the pan before throwing in the popcorn during one of her first attempts to make it. But with a little adjustment of butter and oil, Cate's popcorn had become their favorite—a tradition when the three of them were enjoying a sleepover at Brooke's house.

Brooke gave them a mysterious smile. "Before we start, I'm going to get into my pajamas. Wait here. I have a surprise for you!"

She left the room, giggling.

"Wonder what she's up to," said Amber.

Smiling, Cate shook her head. "I don't know, but it sounds like old times. Do you remember how often she used to do something like this?"

"Remember the time she made us put on fake tattoos?" Amber said.

Cate clapped her cheek. "Oh my God! When my aunt finally noticed, she was furious. She called me a little tramp."

Hearing Brooke's "Ta-dah!" Amber and Cate swiveled around.

Brooke struck a pose for them. Wearing a sleeveless, low-cut pink top with a drawing of a naked woman across the front and the words "Beach Babe" scrawled beneath the picture, she wiggled her hips. Pink, silky shorts dotted with red hearts and edged with lace completed the outfit.

"What do you think?" Brooke swiveled her hips and arched her body so her boobs stood out.

Amber laughed. "It's as cheesy as you can get."

"Yes! Perfect," cried Cate.

Still chuckling, Brooke handed each of them a package.

"I'm going to put mine on right now," said Amber, working to keep cheerful as she left the room with her package. The outfit was something her mother would have loved.

In her bedroom, Amber pushed aside thoughts of her mother and slipped on the pajamas. In front of the mirror, she noticed the slight curve of her usually flat stomach and shuddered at the thought of what a baby would do to her figure. She told herself she was being foolish, but then, her thin body was part of the reason she'd been successful modeling. Maybe having a baby would force her to rethink her life.

Her thoughts flew to Jesse. Perhaps because he worked with models all the time, he was the one man in her life who had made her feel special in a way that had nothing to do with her looks. They enjoyed talking about music and art and met at the Museum of Modern Art on several occasions before quietly having a meal in nearby, offbeat places. She'd even thought of taking art courses so she could add more to their conversations.

A knock at the door ended her musing.

"Are you ready?" Cate called, opening the door a crack.

"Brooke wants to get pictures of the three of us."

"All set," said Amber. She slinked down the hallway, exaggerating a model's gait.

"My God! You make even this outfit look fabulous on you!" said Cate, chuckling.

From the end of the hallway, Brooke looked at them with approval. "I knew it! This is just what this party needed! The two of you look gorgeous!"

"So do you, dahling," Amber said. She held out her arms and twirled, feeling more like the hopeful young girl she used to be. It felt so good to be a Beach Babe.

CHAPTER TEN

CATE

Cate was lost in the movie, following each plot line carefully, seeing what worked and how it might unfold, when Brooke shook her shoulder. "Cate? Did you hear me?"

She startled. "What?"

"Your phone is ringing. You must have left it in your bedroom."

Cate cocked her head to listen. It was Jackson's ring tone. "Be right back!" She hurried into her bedroom and snatched the phone from the bureau top. "Hello?"

No answer. He'd already hung up.

She punched the button for his number and waited.

"Hey, there!" Jackson said. "I just tried to call you."

"I'm sorry. I couldn't get to the phone in time. How are you? And how's Buddy?"

"We're fine. Just hanging out together, missing you."

"I've got an idea. I know how much work it is to prepare for a substitute, but can you take a couple of personal days off? Seashell Cottage is available for a few days after Amber and Brooke leave. Why don't you meet me here? We need to have some quality time together."

"What's going on? Is this about the talks we've been having about a family of our own?" Jackson said, his tone wary.

"That, and more. We need time to ourselves away from work, just the two of us in a romantic setting. After being with Amber and Brooke and knowing what each is going through,

I realize how important it is for us to do this."

"Hmmm, you're asking me to join you for what you promise will be a sexy getaway? Is that it?" he teased.

"I hope so," said Cate, laughing at his description. She loved Jackson at his most playful.

"I'll make it happen," Jackson said with determination. "Amber and Brooke leave on Monday, I'll be there Monday night. You're right. This is something we've needed, Cate."

"That's why I'm inviting you here."

"Anything you want, dear," he said, playing a game with her. But Cate heard the happiness in his voice and knew it was a good thing to do at this point in their relationship.

When she returned to the living room, Amber and Brooke studied her.

"You're smiling," said Amber. "Spill."

"Jackson is going to join me Monday night."

"And?"

"After thinking it over, being with the two of you and hearing what you have to say, I'm pretty sure I've decided to tell him I'll marry him."

Amber gave her a thumbs up. "It's about time. You two are dynamite together."

"I'm so happy for you," cried Brooke, jumping up from the couch and giving her a hug.

Cate knew it wouldn't be as simple as everyone thought. She and Jackson were independent people. Marriage and a baby would change so many things.

As the ending of the movie faded from the television screen, Cate dabbed at her eyes with a tissue. "That was wonderful, just what I needed." She loved a movie with a happy ending, even when it made her cry. It's why Serena and

Rondol would find happiness together at the end of her book series.

Brooke stood and faced them. "I've got to get some sleep. Or try to, anyway." She padded off to her bedroom.

Amber turned to Cate. "I've never seen Brooke so self-contained, so determined to resolve the issue with Paul. I don't know whether to applaud her or worry."

"I think of what divorce will do to her family. Her girls love their dad."

"It's not like Brooke to act so impulsively. Maybe there's something to the saying that life begins at forty. It seems like the three of us have a whole new period ahead of us in our lives."

"I just hope we make the right choices," said Cate, feeling uneasy about Brooke. She recalled how quiet, how uncertain Brooke had been when they'd first met. If it hadn't been for the way her father adored her, she'd be totally broken by trying to please her mother.

"Ready for bed?" Amber asked. "I'm so tired I feel as if I could sleep for months."

"Tomorrow, our last full day here, we can make it a lazy one. Rest will be good for all of us." *And maybe it will give me time to talk to Brooke.*

The sound of raindrops hitting the glass of her bedroom window encouraged Cate to nestle under the covers. She peeked out at the early morning light. Gray skies offered little brightness. *A perfect day to be lazy. A perfect day to dig deeper into her dearest friends' troubles.* She'd do anything to help them. Seeing her friends again had filled her with affection for all they'd shared, all they meant to her.

When she finally arose, she slipped on a white, terrycloth

robe provided in the room and made her way into the kitchen. The smell of coffee was too enticing to linger any longer.

Brooke was sitting at the kitchen table. She smiled. "Morning."

Cate smiled. "Good morning." She filled a cup with coffee and sat down opposite Brooke.

Brooke reached over and patted her hand. "I'm glad you've made the decision to marry Jackson. I know it might seem odd coming from me when I might be about to end my marriage, but it's right for you and Jackson to be together and to start a family. The two of you are perfect for one another."

"Thanks," said Cate. "I'm becoming less nervous about the whole idea of it. I have to be a lot more like my character Serena and just go ahead and do it."

"How is your latest book coming?" Brooke asked.

"Limping along. I thought I had it all planned out, but I've rethought a few essential things and will now have to go back and edit before I can move forward. This process is nothing new, but it's sometimes discouraging." She set down her coffee cup and studied Brooke. "What's going on with you? You and Paul have had such a strong connection, I can't imagine his straying."

Shaking her head, Brooke shrugged. "I can't figure out why he won't talk to me or tell me where he's going when he says he has business to take care of. It has to be another woman. I can't come up with anything else. And as I mentioned, after a while the magic of marriage can disappear. It sure has in our case. The last few months I feel as if I have a roomie, nothing more."

"Do you have any idea who it might be? As a beloved Ob-Gyn doctor, he's adored by his patients. I remember my agent telling me she fell in love with her doctor when she was pregnant with her last child. She said he was the only man who understood what she was going through, that her husband had no clue why she was so emotional and what her needs were."

"Did she end up getting a divorce?" Brooke asked, her eyes wide.

Cate shook her head. "No, of course not. But she still thinks he's the greatest doctor ever."

Brooke sighed. "Paul's a wonderful doctor."

"After the incident a few years ago, Paul has dedicated himself to you and the family. I think there must be a lot more going on than you think. Don't rush into anything, Brooke, until you're sure."

"I think I'll take Amber's suggestion and hire a private detective after I get home."

"What else is going on with you?" Cate said, pushing her friend to talk about it. She knew Brooke well enough to realize something else was making her unhappy.

Brooke looked away and then back again, her face a mask of uncertainty. "The idea of turning forty has hit me hard. Unlike you and Amber, I don't have a career. I'm Paul's wife, and P.J.'s and the twins' mother. I've become lost. And don't even get me started on all the physical changes in my body. I've always had body issues, and not even additional plastic surgery is going to help. Besides, I don't want to become one of those full-cheeked women who'd do anything to hide a wrinkle or two."

"What about your watercolors? You used to love to paint."

"I haven't picked up a brush in forever. The girls keep me so busy, how would I ever find the time?"

"Brooke, you have to find your own happiness," said Cate. She spoke softly but she meant every word. "You may have to be creative about coming up with a schedule that will allow you time to yourself, but it's important for you to do it."

"Do what?" said Amber coming into the room.

"Find time for herself," Cate answered promptly.

Amber yawned and sat down at the table with them. "Cate's right, Brooke. It's great that you have a family, but you can't let them bury you with their demands. Have you painted anything lately or started that book club you talked about?"

"Not you too," groaned Brooke. "No, I haven't." She sighed and waggled a finger at Amber. "When was the last time you did anything for yourself?"

Amber looked at the two of them. "Not until now. There's a lesson here for us, ladies. We need to do this a lot more often."

"Agreed," said Cate. "Let's start a tradition of meeting every few months. Why don't the two of you come to my house after the holidays? By then, we should have a lot of answers."

"Deal," said Brooke.

"Count me in," Amber said. She patted her stomach. "Maybe I should say, count the two of us in." Her eyes filled. "I still can't imagine what lies ahead."

Brooke took hold of her hand and then Cate's. "Here's to The Beach Babes!"

"Such as we are," commented Amber, wiggling her shoulders, making the naked woman on her top shimmy.

Cate laughed with the other two, but she knew real challenges lay ahead. When developing characters for her books, she learned that each one had many layers. In the case of The Beach Babes, they all had issues from the past that were catching up to them.

CHAPTER ELEVEN

BROOKE

After the day turned sunny enough for a late-morning swim in the pool, Brooke lay in the sun with Cate and Amber, letting her mind wander. Those two were right. She needed to do something for herself. She used to enjoy painting. It was a great way for her to express herself, and people seemed to love the flowers and beach scenes she painted. At one time she'd even contemplated having an art show of her own. But before she could even get started on plans for it, she discovered she was pregnant with the twins. Fighting her way through months of not feeling well, she gave up the idea. After the girls were born, life picked up speed.

"Do you remember the camp song you taught us?" Amber asked her, her voice soft and dreamy as she lay back in the chair.

"The one about the moon?" Brooke replied. She sat up and burst into song. "I see the moon ..."

Amber and Cate joined in, laughing when she began another about beer bottles on a wall.

When the song ended, Cate turned to her with a smile. "Every summer I used to wait for you to return from overnight camp. It wasn't the same without you."

"Even though I had fun, I wished I were back in New York with you two. Mother wanted me to go to Cape Cod for the entire summer, but Dad helped me convince her that four weeks was enough."

Amber rolled onto her side on the lounge chair to face

them. "Even when you were away, Brooke, I trusted you'd come back, and Cate and I would be with you again. Cate and I made you swear it in blood. Remember?"

"Yeah, The Beach Babes days were the best," added Cate, smiling with affection at her.

Brooke grinned. "That was then. What about now?" She jumped to her feet, fiddled with her phone, found some music, and pulled Cate and Amber up onto their feet.

Laughing, the three of them lined up and began the moves of the Electric Slide.

"We're still pretty good," Brooke said as the song finished and they came to a stop. She hugged Cate to her and turned to Amber for another quick embrace. "I hope my daughters find friends as precious as the two of you are to me."

"Me too," Cate said.

"Hey, I'm going in and lying down for a while. I'm suddenly tired," said Amber.

"You okay?" Brooke asked.

Amber sighed. "Just a bit pregnant."

After she left, Brooke turned to Cate. "I wish she'd talk more about it. But you know Amber. She keeps a lot inside until she can't hold it in any longer."

Cate nodded. "She has a lot on her mind, for sure. We all do."

"I wish my father were here. He'd help figure things out. He's the only one who could get my mother off my back when she didn't like what was happening. And she won't like my leaving Paul."

"Your father was the best," Cate said. "Without his help, I wouldn't have received a scholarship to Columbia University. He's the one who contacted the school for me and helped me fill out all the paperwork. I dedicated my first book to him, but it couldn't begin to express my gratitude fully. If not for him,

I might not have been accepted into a creative writing program."

Brooke smiled at the memory. Richard Ridley, Brooke's father, had taken both Cate and Amber under his care. "He knew how smart you were, how talented. He also told me to trust you, you weren't like the girls at school, and you would remain loyal to me."

"Really?"

Brooke nodded. "I was a pretty lonely kid with a lot of people willing to make fun of me."

"They should see you now," Cate said. "But then, you've always been just fine."

"Bradley and Brynn have a tendency to gain weight, but I haven't said anything to them about it. I watch what they eat, but I'm not going to do to them what my mother did to me, with all her putdowns. Thinking back on it, she was cruel."

"Yes, she was. I remember how she fussed over Amber, telling her how beautiful she was in front of you and me, making sure we knew she liked Amber best."

"The sweetest revenge I have is not to act like her. Both of my girls are beautiful just the way they are. My mother tried to tell them they needed to do something different with their hair, and I made it clear that she was not to discuss their looks with them again." Brooke chuckled softly. "I was so angry I actually scared her."

"Good for you." Cate paused and studied her. "What is divorce going to do to the girls and P.J.?"

Brooke gazed into their surroundings, her heart fragile. "I don't know. They adore their father, and I don't want to damage that." She ran a hand through her red curls. "I'm so confused right now. You and Amber seem convinced Paul wouldn't ever cheat on me, but I've gone over the past several months in my mind and don't know what else it could be."

"One day at a time, remember?"

"I'll try. I need proof before I take action. In the meantime, I can hardly speak to him without wanting to cry."

CHAPTER TWELVE

AMBER

Amber lay on her bed and hugged one of the pillows close to her, remembering the romantic times she'd shared with Jesse. He was such a kind, understanding person. They'd known each other for almost three years before they dated. And even then, there was no rush to get into bed. He was one of the few people with whom she'd discussed her abusive background. She'd surprised herself by doing so, but then, traveling for photo shoots and working intimately together had made her feel comfortable with him.

More than that, she felt safe with Jesse. Something that mattered a great deal to her. It was the defining reason why she'd even considered going to bed with him. She knew he wouldn't hurt her.

She patted her stomach. She was almost embarrassed to tell him about the baby because he'd been upfront with her from the start, explaining he still loved his wife and hoped to get back together with her one day. In return, she'd told him she had no expectations beyond a special friendship, that she wasn't eager to give up her independence. Though she kept her word to him, she quickly understood their relationship was complicated by her growing feelings for him.

Thinking of it now, she wished she'd had the guts to tell him how she truly felt. Brooke and Cate were right. She needed to be open and give him the opportunity to choose to be involved with the baby or not.

She caressed the spot that would soon enlarge to give

protection to the baby she hadn't planned on. Her thoughts flew to her mother—such an egocentric nymphomaniac, forever measuring her worth by the amount of a man's attention to her.

A shudder went through her. She hadn't ever wanted to be like her mother. Others might think her mother was beautiful, but Amber knew better.

The other two in The Beach Babes trio were naïve compared to her. Amber hoped they would stay that way. They'd pulled her through a lot of low moments.

CHAPTER THIRTEEN

CATE

The next morning, clouds played peek-a-boo with the sun, casting shadows and then dancing aside to let sunlight brighten the day. These changes matched Cate's spirits. She was sad to see The Beach Babes' weekend come to an end, but excited to have Jackson here in Florida with her. She hoped their time together would be everything she wanted in a romantic retreat.

Cate stood in the driveway with Amber watching the limo Brooke had hired pull out. Earlier, there'd been tears as they said goodbye to her, but now Cate forced a brave smile. She could see Brooke waving at them through the back window of the car.

As the limo disappeared from view, she sighed and turned to Amber. "We all need to keep in touch. There's no way I want to let this much time get away from us again."

"That would be great," said Amber. "I'm so glad you arranged this weekend for us. I'm going to need a lot of support in the coming months."

"Are you going to be all right?" Cate asked.

Amber studied her. "I honestly don't know. That's what makes this so difficult. It's a good thing I'm not showing yet. It gives me a little time to decide how best to handle things."

Cate saw a new vulnerability in Amber. Usually self-confident, almost cocky, Amber liked to be in control. The next months would not be easy for her.

"Remember, if you need a hideaway, you've got my place in

Ellenton. I'd love to have you."

"Thanks, hon. You don't know how much that means to me. Now, I'd better go get organized for my trip back home this afternoon."

After Amber went inside, Cate walked onto the beach, eager for time alone. She strolled along the sand wondering what any baby she and Jackson might have would look like. One of four boys and two girls in his family, Jackson was a handsome man. His female high school students thought he was cool, though he was careful not to respond to such talk. But with his chestnut-brown hair, blue eyes, and chiseled features, he was worthy of their comments.

As she strolled along the water's edge looking for shells, she imagined holding a pink-cheeked baby with blue eyes and brown hair a shade between Jackson's and her lighter-brown locks. She heard a baby cry and looked up to see a woman walking toward her carrying a baby in a sling of some kind. Studying her out of the corner of her eye, she watched the woman calmly pat the baby and restore peace. Self-doubt tugged at Cate. Other women made it seem so easy, but she had no real experience with babies.

Her cell phone rang. She lifted it from her pants pockets and studied the screen. *Jackson.*

Pleasure rolled through her. "Hi, sweetheart! How are you?"

"Ugh. Not so good. I'm getting over the flu that's been going around the school."

"Oh, no! Are you going to be able to make the trip?" He sounded awful.

"I'm still planning on catching my afternoon flight. It's just a 24-hour thing."

Cate hid the deep disappointment she felt. "I'm so sorry. I'll have something bland for you for dinner and you can rest up here in the sun."

"I'll make it up to you another time. See you this afternoon."

Cate clicked off the call and let out a sigh. There went her romantic interlude this evening.

As she began walking again, she wondered if it was a sign she shouldn't go forward with her plans. She came to a sudden stop when she noticed a beautiful, pinkish, fan-shaped shell lying in front of her. She picked it up and studied it. A perfect gift from the sea. She clutched it in her hand and lifted her face to the sky, reminding herself to take things one step at a time.

The cries of the birds circling above her, the shorebirds running along the water's edge searching for tidbits, and the rhythmic sound of the waves gave her a sense of peace. She was more of a spiritual person than religious, and in enjoying this moment, she found the answer she was looking for. Scary as it sometimes seemed, she was ready to begin a new phase of her life.

Her early morning resolution lifted Cate's spirits even as she hugged Amber goodbye at the airport, sad to see her go. "Safe travels," she said to Amber, offering words that were meant for so much more than a mere flight.

"Thank you for everything," Amber replied, her eyes filling. "I'll definitely be in touch."

When at last Amber disappeared through the entrance to the terminal, Cate got into her rental car, eased away from the curb, and drove into the parking garage in the middle of the airport. Jackson's flight was due to arrive in an hour.

Inside the terminal, Cate was content to observe others around her. As usual, her imagination was sparked by the people she saw and the conversations she overheard. Readers often asked her where she got ideas for her stories. Like so many other authors, her reply was simple: "They're all around me."

She was busy watching a mother struggle with a toddler when she felt someone's presence and looked up to see Jackson walking toward her. He looked great in a pair of jeans and a black turtle-neck sweater that showed off his trim body. But it was the way he was smiling at her that filled her with joy. She knew then she couldn't ever let him go. She jumped to her feet and ran up to him. "Hi! How are you feeling?"

He gave her a wide grin and hugged her to him. "Much better. This morning I wasn't sure I'd make it, but I'm glad I did. It's raining and gray at home. I'm looking forward to a little sunshine and," he winked at her, "being with you."

She took hold of his hand and smiled up at him. "Me, too. I want this to be a special time for us. I know how tense the last few weeks at school have been."

"Yeah, don't know what it is, but the groups of kids in most of my classes are tough this year." He placed an arm around her shoulder. "C'mon! Let's grab my bag and get out of here."

Nothing sounded better to Cate. He was back to normal, and she'd made her decision.

Cate pulled into the driveway of the cottage and turned to Jackson with a grin. "We're home!"

"Nice! I think I'm going to like it here," he responded, looking around them with a smile that brightened his face.

Cate got out of the car. "I'll give you the grand tour, and then let's take a walk on the beach. It's a lovely time of day to do that."

"Sounds good." He got out of the car and sniffed the salty

air. "I love being at the beach."

She observed his enjoyment and wondered why they hadn't done more traveling together. Maybe this summer, they could go to Europe. Then she remembered. She might be pregnant and unable to travel. It was new—rearranging plans to accommodate a baby.

"Let's see the inside," said Jackson, lifting his suitcase out of the car.

Cate led him into the cottage and showed him around.

"Very comfortable," he said, pulling her into his arms. "I intend to enjoy being here."

"Me too," said Cate. She nestled against his solid chest, enjoying the sense of peace that washed over her whenever she was in his arms. Though a part of her wanted to blurt out her intention to go ahead with the idea of marriage, she decided to let things unfold naturally.

"Are you feeling well enough for dinner?" she asked. "We can order in, or I can make you an omelet or anything you want. You decide."

"An omelet and an evening with you sound perfect," he said, leaning down and kissing her on her forehead. "I'll be ready to rock and roll tomorrow."

"Great. The salt air and the sound of the waves will lull you to sleep and give you a chance to rest."

"Or something else. We'll see," he said, giving her a sexy grin.

She laughed. After being together for seven years, they were comfortable enough with one another to know when they were just playing around. She loved that about him.

He got things settled in their bedroom and held out his palm. "Ready for that walk?"

She clasped his hand in hers and they walked out to the beach onto the hardpacked sand. They stood there for a moment facing the water.

"When I was a kid, I used to go to the Jersey shore in the summer with my family. My grandparents had a house there. It was a circus with all of us kids running around, but I loved it. But this," he indicated the space around them with a sweep of his arm, "is spectacular."

"I love the palm trees and the colorful flowers."

"And the birds," he said, pointing to a group of sandpipers and other little shore birds scurrying by them as if they were in a race to see who could find the first tidbit.

"Look there!" whispered Cate, elbowing Jackson. A cattle egret was wading in the water to their right. Its white feathers against the blue water caught her attention as the long-legged creature bent down, struck at the water with its orange beak, and snatched up a wiggling, silvery fish.

Jackson gave her a smile. "Great idea to come here."

They strolled down the sand hand in hand. Though he stood over six feet, he measured his steps to match her smaller ones. He was considerate that way.

Cate thought of his childhood, so different from hers. He had two older sisters, and of the four boys in the family, he was second in line to Jake, the oldest. Two younger brothers, Jon and Jerome, followed him. They were a kind, loving family that was scattered now. She adored his parents and eagerly joined Jackson on any trip to visit them in North Carolina where they were now living. She hadn't met his maternal grandmother, but Jackson had inherited some money from her.

Filled with deep affection for him, Cate pulled him to a stop and threw her arms around him. "I love you, Jackson Hubbard."

"Enough to marry me and start a family?" He smiled down at her. It was a line he'd used before.

Heart pounding at finally making this commitment, Cate smiled at him. "Yes, Jackson, I will marry you and have your babies. You know how much I love you, how happy I am with you. And now, after having given it more thought while I've been away, I've decided I want to try to be a good wife to you and mother to our babies."

Jackson's look of surprise changed to one of tenderness. "You mean it?" He pulled her closer. "Ah, Cate, you don't know how much that matters to me."

Tears of happiness filled her eyes. "Oh, but I do," she whispered. "You're the best thing that's ever happened to me, and I want to make you happy."

He frowned. "Whoa! You're doing this for yourself too, aren't you?"

"Oh, yes! I've been afraid I'd turn out to be like the other women in my family. Neither my mother nor my aunt was a good example of a mother to me. But then, I realized with you by my side, guiding me, I honestly think I'm ready for this."

"God! I love you so much." Jackson lowered his lips to hers and kissed her with such tenderness, she felt the sting of fresh tears. His kiss deepened, sending shivers of delight through her.

When he pulled away, he clasped her face in his hands and smiled. "Wait right here."

He bent over and picked up a nearby shell. Smiling, he got down on one knee and looked up at her. "Now, with this shell as a symbol of the ring we'll choose together, will you marry me, Catherine Tibbs?"

Tears blinded her vision as she accepted the pink and white scallop shell that he handed her. "Yes, Jackson Hubbard, with this symbol and with my whole heart, I will marry you! I love you and want to share the future with you as your wife."

Jackson rose to his feet and embraced her, rocking her

back and forth in his arms. "I love you, Cate. I always will."

"Congratulations!" cried a woman waving to them as she walked along the beach near where they were standing.

"She said yes!" Jackson called to the woman, his voice ringing with excitement.

The woman gave them a thumbs-up signal. "May you always stay this happy!"

"Thank you!" Cate called to her, wishing their life together would be as magical as this moment.

Jackson took hold of her hand. "C'mon! I've got to call my parents. They'll be thrilled."

"They're such good people," Cate said, smiling at the thought of their reactions. "I can't wait to become an official part of the family."

"They already feel you are," Jackson said, "but you know Mom, the more, the merrier. She'll hope for us to start a family right away."

"I hope so too. When I get home, I'll make an appointment with my doctor."

Jackson smiled and shook his head with disbelief. "I can't believe we're finally doing it."

A nervous giggle escaped Cate. What to others might seem so ordinary as being married and starting a family, this was, for her, a huge emotional commitment, something she'd been afraid of doing for a long time.

CHAPTER FOURTEEN

CATE

Jackson called his parents and gave them the news, placing them on speaker phone so Cate could hear their congratulations.

"And Cate," said his mother, "I hope you'll allow me to help with the wedding or anything else you might need. Your own mother may be gone, but I'm here for you." Her voice grew wobbly. "You're like my own daughter."

Jackson's mother, Laurie, was such a good role model for her. She loved her children openly and yet commanded respect from them as she willingly accepted others into the fold. Tears sprang to Cate's eyes. When she and Jackson had children, she'd rely on Laurie and Jackson's father, Tom, for all the guidance they could offer.

"When's the wedding?" Tom asked.

Cate and Jackson looked at each other and shrugged.

"We haven't gotten that far yet," Jackson said.

"We want it to be small, intimate," said Cate. When Jackson's sister, Janis, had married, over 200 guests had attended. Cate didn't want that kind of ceremony at all.

"Well, first things first," said Laurie. "I'd like to throw you an engagement party for family and friends here in North Carolina. We'll talk about it later."

Jackson glanced at Cate, waiting for a response.

"Okay," Cate was unsure how she felt about the sudden plans. His family was used to loud gatherings assembled for any occasion.

Sensing how she felt, Jackson said, "We'll let you know, Mom. This is all new to us."

Cate smiled her appreciation at him. "We have a lot to think of right now. But, thanks."

"All right, but it's a great cause for celebration," said Laurie. "We've been wondering when the two of you were ever going to tie the knot."

"I know, I know," Jackson said, chuckling. "Look, we've got to go. We've got a big evening planned."

Cate shot him a look of surprise. She whispered. "We do?"

He wiggled his eyebrows. "Oh, yeah. We definitely do."

She laughed softly, and when it came time for her to say goodbye, she said, "Thanks for your warm welcome. Talk to you later."

As soon as they clicked off the call, Jackson wrapped his arms around her. "See? That wasn't so bad. Sounds like Mom isn't going to be too insistent on our matching Janis' and Jen's wedding parties and plans. I'll run interference for you."

"Thanks," Cate said with heartfelt gratitude. She didn't have many friends, but those she had were loyal, and she didn't want to end up having plans made that might be difficult for them to take part in.

"I think I'll wait to make my calls," Cate said. "Brooke and Amber are just getting back home, and I want to savor this moment alone with you. Tomorrow, there's a special place I want to show you. We can celebrate in style there."

"Sounds great." Jackson put his arm around her and grinned. "About that big evening I've got planned."

She laughed at his teasing. "All in good time, sweetheart. You must be feeling a whole lot better."

"You make me feel that way."

Smiling, they gazed into each other's eyes.

###

Later, after Jackson had proved to her how much better he felt, Cate stretched in bed and checked the bedside clock. "How about my fixing you the omelet that sounded good to you earlier?" she asked, getting to her feet.

"Great. I'm hungry after all." He rose and stood before her, patting his stomach.

She studied him, taking in the planes of his body, the hair on his chest that traveled in a line to his midsection and beyond. He took good care of himself, and it showed. Best of all was the tender way he was looking at her. They'd had fiery chemistry from the beginning but shared a deeper connection that only years together can bring. She wondered why it had taken her so long to commit to him. He was, as she'd inadvertently blurted out to her friends, such a wonderful man.

He walked over to her and drew her into his arms. Standing there, fitting her body to his, skin against skin, she marveled that life had given her such a wonderful opportunity to find acceptance and love —both physical and spiritual. She reminded herself as she'd done many times lately, that sharing love with Jackson would enable her to transfer that to their children. She knew from talking to a therapist her mother's desertion and her aunt's behavior were not normal.

She pulled away from Jackson and looked up at him. "Thank you."

"For what?"

Her eyes misted over. "For everything."

He squeezed her. "You have no idea how much I love you."

She smiled at him as contentment rolled through her, a wave of happiness that swept away hurt from the past. She put on a robe over her naked body and headed to the kitchen, suddenly hungry.

###

The next morning Cate left Jackson sleeping in bed, quietly dressed, and tiptoed out of the house. The sun was rising, sending streaks of pink into the gray sky, like fingers reaching for the day.

She wanted time alone to revel in the choice she'd made and to enjoy the prospect of a bright future with the man she loved. She wrapped her sweater tightly around her against the onshore breeze. The day would warm, but at the moment, she enjoyed the brush of coolness against her cheeks. The lazy part of her, the one that had wanted to stay in bed, was happy now that she had risen. Alone on the beach in front of the house, she stood and watched joggers and shell-seekers in the distance, their movements in concert with the waves hitting the shore and pulling away again.

At times like this, she couldn't help but wonder at the magic of nature, the continuous actions of natural life—things such as the patterns crabs made in the sand as they scurried along the beach's surface, the tiny footprints of shore birds running beside the frothy edge of the water, or the cry of the birds circling in the air above her, their wings spread wide against the sky.

Her thoughts turned to babies. They too were a wonder of nature.

She began walking, slowly at first, and then she started running for the pure joy of it. She was embracing life in a whole new way, and it felt good.

When she turned to go back to the cottage, she saw Jackson sprinting toward her, and her heart sang with happiness. He was the one who made her feel safe, made her feel loved.

As she reached him, Jackson swung her up in his arms and danced around awkwardly on the sand. "How's my bride?"

"So very happy," she said, hoping they wouldn't wait long for the ceremony.

"Beautiful morning. Maybe we should do a little exploring for the ring I want to give you. What do you think?"

"That sounds good. We can investigate a place for our honeymoon. I want to show you the Salty Key Inn. Gavin's restaurant there is a perfect place for a wedding reception."

He cocked an eyebrow at her. "Seems like you've been thinking of this for a while."

She laughed. "Brooke, Amber, and I had dinner there to celebrate our birthdays, and it was delicious."

"How are they? We haven't had a chance to talk about your weekend," Jackson asked as they started walking back to the cottage.

She stopped and turned to face him. "I'm worried about them." She explained what each of her friends was facing. "We've promised to keep in closer touch. I want them in the wedding, which means we need to wait until June for the end of the school year and to give Amber time to recover from the birth of her baby."

"That's a great time for a wedding. I'll have the whole summer off from school to celebrate. I might even get your cabin done."

"Uh, I told Amber she could come and stay there if she needed an escape from New York."

His eyebrows shot up. "Hmmm. Guess I'll have to get to work on it sooner rather than later. I know how important she and Brooke are to you."

She patted his cheek lovingly. "You're the best. You know?"

"That's what everyone tells me," he joked.

She took hold of his hand and kissed it. "Those clever, clever hands."

"Now you're talking," he replied, winking at her, letting her know he wasn't thinking of the cabin at all.

###

Her heart pulsed with excitement as Cate sat in the kitchen of Seashell Cottage and punched in the speed-dial number to call Brooke. Though it was still morning, she'd waited as long as she could, aware of the time change. It rang and rang. Finally, Brooke's voice came on in a short, clipped message: "Brooke Weston is not taking phone calls at this time."

Cate's stomach twisted inside her. Something must be wrong. She quickly tried to call Amber and was forced to leave a message.

"What's wrong?" Jackson asked, walking into the kitchen.

Cate told him about the response to her call. "I'm concerned about her."

He lifted her chin and gave her a steady look. "I understand, but let's not allow this to ruin our day. Okay?"

Cate nodded her agreement. "Yes. This is our special time. I don't want to do anything to spoil it."

"Good," he responded. "I've done a little research and found a great place that sells unique wedding rings. I've seen something I like, and I want to show it to you."

"Online?"

"No, it's at a store down the coast a way. I suggest we go there and then have lunch somewhere nearby."

"That sounds lovely. Give me a chance to shower and get dressed for the day." She rose on her toes and kissed him. "Make yourself comfortable. I won't be too long."

"Take all the time you want. I'll be sitting on the porch with a book."

Grateful for his understanding, she gave him a little salute and went into their bedroom.

Twenty minutes later, she emerged, ready to face the excitement of the day. For a long time, she'd thought their commitment to each other was enough, but making it official changed everything for her.

Jackson whistled when he saw her dressed in a short skirt, flowing top, and sandals that added an inch or two to her height.

"Looking good," he said, giving her a kiss on the lips. "Let's go!"

She drove them to the car rental agency in St. Petersburg so Jackson could be added to the rental contract.

Later, with him at the wheel, Cate was free to look around and absorb the sights around them. She liked it this way. Often, just seeing something sparked an idea for one of her stories.

They drove onto I-275 and crossed the Sunshine Skyway over the entrance to Tampa Bay heading south toward Bonita Springs and Naples.

Cate sat back enjoying the ride and the moment. With the convertible top down, she lifted her face to the sun and sighed, unable to remember the last time she'd given herself such a relaxing break from her normal routine.

Jackson reached over and gave her hand a squeeze. "Happy?"

She nodded and beamed at him, though the word happy didn't begin to express the joy she felt.

The storefront of The Treasure Chest was in a strip mall designed to look like a fishing village. Charming, the mall contained eight other retail outlets. But it was The Treasure Chest that caught and held Cate's attention. The front window display was full of beautiful jewelry in gold and silver.

"Don't worry about the nautical theme of the place, I've seen some of their items online, and you're going to love their things," said Jackson, taking her elbow and escorting her inside.

The shine of diamonds, colorful gems, gold, and silver sparkling in glass cases strategically placed around the room made it seem to Cate as if they had come upon a real treasure chest.

A tanned woman with long, dark hair and green eyes, wearing a simple turquoise sheath and lots of beautiful jewelry approached them with a smile. “Welcome to The Treasure Chest. I’m Nan Wilkins. You’ll find many unique pieces here, and if you want anything designed for you, my husband will be glad to talk to you about it.”

Jackson held out his hand. “Jackson Hubbard. And this is Catherine Tibbs. I saw an engagement ring online that I’m interested in.” He smiled at Cate. “Of course, you’ll have the final decision.”

Nan studied them a moment. “Let me guess. Was it the pink one?”

“Yep,” Jackson said, leaving Cate to wonder what he had in mind. He seemed so sure.

“Follow me.” Nan led them to the long counter in the middle of the room and went behind it. Opening the case, she lifted out a ring and held it out to them. “One of my favorite pieces.” She placed the ring atop a black velvet square to offset it.

Cate and Jackson leaned over for a better look.

“The stunning center pink diamond is a find, something my husband came upon unexpectedly through one of our suppliers,” explained Nan. “The fan of small white diamonds above it is designed to look like a scallop shell. That’s why we call the piece ‘the seaside promise.’ You can replace the pink diamond with a white one or any other gem, but, for me, it would ruin the ring to do so.”

Jackson clasped Cate’s hand and gave her a steady look. “What do you think?”

"I love it," Cate said without any hesitation. "It's as if it was made for us, with the shell design and the colors. But it looks very expensive."

"Try it on," urged Jackson, grinning at her.

Nan offered Jackson the ring, and he slid it on her finger.

Seeing it on her hand, wowed by the sight and beauty of it, Cate's vision grew misty. "It's gorgeous."

"It looks as if it was made for you—large enough to be noticeable on your hand, but not too flashy," Nan said to Cate, nodding her approval. "You've made an exceptional choice. Let me check the sizing. I noticed the ring is a little big. We can take care of that in a matter of an hour or so."

"Okay. That's it. Sold," said Jackson.

Moments later, as they left the store, Cate felt in a daze. She would have liked anything Jackson chose, but the story behind this one made it perfect for her, for them.

"Jackson, the ring is beautiful. Thank you so much. Are you sure you want to spend that kind of money on it?"

He smiled and gave her hand a squeeze. "I've been saving up for something like this for a long time. Ever since I knew you were the one." He bent down and kissed her, pulling away only when the sound of an approaching car stopped him.

Cate sighed happily and walked to their car. If the joy she felt could make a dancer out of her, she'd be the best ballerina the world had ever seen.

They decided to go closer to the water to find a place for lunch.

Loco Coco, perched on the shore of Fish Trap Bay, was typical of some other restaurants in the area, with wooden decks sitting over the water and docks at which boats of customers bobbed in the water. Inside the building, fishing nets, anchors, and other symbols of fishing decorated the wood-paneled walls.

They bypassed the bar, walked out to one of the decks, and waited to be seated. Though the air was cool, the sun was pleasant.

A waitress led them to a table nestled close to the building, protecting them from the breeze. "I'll be back to take your order," the waitress said, handing them each a menu. "Can I get you any drinks in the meantime?"

"Beer or wine?" Jackson asked Cate.

"Sure," Cate responded. "I'll have a glass of chardonnay." Her first full day of her engagement was amazing already and she didn't want the celebration to end.

Jackson looked over the drinks list, ordered her a California chardonnay she liked, and asked for a beer for himself.

After the waitress left, Jackson took hold of her hand. "You've made me a happy man, Cate."

"It feels so good to have made this commitment," said Cate. She was about to say more when her cell rang. She checked caller ID. *Amber*.

"Hi, there!" Cate chirped.

"Hi, yourself!" Amber responded. "Did you guys finally get engaged?"

"Yes," gushed Cate. "It was so sweet. I'll tell you all about it later. Jackson and I are having lunch at Bonita Beach while we're waiting for my engagement ring to be sized. It's breathtakingly beautiful."

"Send a picture. I want proof of this engagement of yours," teased Amber. "Congratulations and give my love to Jackson."

"Thanks. You got my message about Brooke?"

"Yes. I tried to call her myself and got the same message. Then I tried to text her, but no response there either. We have to hope nothing horrible is going on with her. I'll keep trying."

"What about you?" Cate asked. "How was your first day back at work? Did you see or talk to Jesse?"

"No. He's away on a filming trip for three weeks. It's not anything I want to talk to him about over the phone."

"Understandably," Cate agreed. "How about Belinda?"

"Same as usual. She's so difficult I sometimes wonder how I've ever managed to stick with the job. She wasn't in the office on Tuesday but she left me a note. You know what it said? 'Amber, I can't allow you to take this much time off again. I needed you here. Hope you didn't have too much fun over the weekend eating and drinking.' Can you beat that?"

"Remember, you've got my place if you need a hideout. Jackson said he'd hurry and finish the interior of the cabin."

"What a doll. Thanks so much. Oops! Gotta go! The dragon approaches."

The call ended.

"Things not going well?" Jackson asked.

"Amber couldn't reach Brooke either, and her boyfriend is away for three weeks, which means she hasn't told him about the baby. So, things aren't looking good at the moment except for me and the delicious day I'm sharing with you." She kept her voice light, but she was uneasy about Brooke.

The waitress came to take their order.

"I can't decide between the Grouper Sandwich or the Lazy Lobster Roll," Cate said.

"The Grouper Sandwich is a specialty," the waitress said. "You can't go wrong with it."

"I'll take it," said Cate, grateful for the advice.

"Make that two," Jackson said, handing the waitress his menu. After she left, he sat back in his chair and studied their surroundings. "I've been watching the birds. See the pelican sitting on the bollards at the end of the dock? Such an interesting creature. Did you know some pelicans can hold up to three gallons in their pouches? And though they are heavy birds, the air sacs in their bones help them to fly?"

Cate smiled. "Any more facts, teacher?"

"One. I love you, Cate." His blue eyes twinkled and then filled with affection.

"Love you, too."

In silence they watched the pelican take flight, leaving space for a seagull to land.

The salty air with a tinge of the smell of gasoline from the boats tied at the docks filled Cate's nostrils. She drew a deep breath, storing the sensations in her mind for later use in her writing. Who's to say another world of her creation couldn't have a scene similar to this?

After having lunch, they strolled leisurely around the area, gazing at the different boats.

Jackson's cell pinged with a message. He checked it. "Great! The ring is ready. Let's go."

When they returned to The Treasure Chest, Nan was waiting for them, a man in a wheelchair beside her.

Nan greeted them with a smile. "Hello! This is my husband, Darryl Wilkins, the designer of most of our jewelry." Though his legs were incapacitated, his upper body was broad and seemed solid. Dark-rimmed glasses accentuated his bright blue eyes, which were lit by a smile that crossed his strong facial features.

"I can't thank you enough for designing such a beautiful ring for us," said Cate. She told them the story of how Jackson had proposed with a scallop shell and how much the ring meant to her because of it.

"Ah, that makes me happy," said Darryl. "I love seeing my

customers so pleased. It gives me inspiration. I have to ask, are either of you in the art world? It takes a creative person to appreciate something like this."

"Cate writes novels," Jackson said. "And I teach school."

"And he's a wonderful woodworker and carpenter," Cate quickly added.

"Good. You two are a good match for the ring and for each other," Darryl said. "Nice to meet you both. Now, I'd better get back to work."

He expertly wheeled himself away.

Watching him go, Cate was struck by the idea that creativity in some form existed in all of us. She'd remember that in her writing.

CHAPTER FIFTEEN

BROOKE

Brooke arrived home with determination to get the issue between Paul and her resolved at once. After she greeted and kissed the girls hello, Brooke turned to her husband. Observing the dark patches under his eyes, the way new lines indented his forehead and the look of worry in his eyes, her stomach filled with acid.

Holding back a gasp at how ill he looked, she forced words out calmly. "Hello, Paul."

His smile wavered. "It's good to have you back. The girls and I missed you."

"Did you?" she said softly as the girls sprinted out of the front hall and up the stairs to their room. "What's going on? You look awful."

Hands knotted at his sides, Paul stood before her, back straight. He took a deep breath and closed his eyes. When he opened them, they were awash with tears.

"I'm sorry ..." he began.

She held up a hand to stop him. "Is this about an affair?"

His eyes widened. "An affair? Is that what you think has been going on? Oh my God ..." He rushed forward and pulled her into his arms. "Brooke, I love you. Why would you think something like that?"

Surprised, she stared up at him, speechless for a moment. Then anger filled her. "If it's not an affair, what in hell is going on? You've been sneaking around, unwilling to let me know where you're going, what you're doing. You've often come home late! You haven't been attentive. What else could I think?" She pulled away from his embrace and placed her hands on her hips. "You'd better tell me what's going on right now. I'm done with all this mystery. I've been sick with worry and ready to divorce you."

Paul seemed to collapse in front of her, like a balloon letting out air.

"What is it, dammit?" she demanded.

He took hold of her arm and led her to one of the couches in the living room. "Better sit down."

Her legs collapsed, giving her no choice but to sit. She stared up at him and watched his face grow pale. "I've been accused of sexual assault."

"What?" she screeched. "You?"

"Afraid so. I've been meeting with lawyers and my business partners, trying to stem the damage, but it's going to hit the news in the next couple of days."

"I don't believe it," said Brooke. "It can't be true."

Paul sat down on the couch and faced her. "It isn't true. I promise."

"Then, why?"

"It's the patient from the incident in the past. She's now claiming that it wasn't just a kiss, but my forcing her to do all kinds of things." Paul looked as if he might throw up.

Brooke felt that way too. She reached for his hand. "I know you, Paul. You wouldn't do something like that."

Tears escaped his eyes. "I didn't, and I wouldn't."

"Then why is she doing this?" Brooke asked, and suddenly knew. "It's money, isn't it? She knows I'm rich."

"Yes. It seems she's down on her luck. Her husband divorced her, and she's out of a job. My lawyer says it's a classic case of someone trying to take advantage of an unfortunate incident to get money. She wanted me to pay her several hundred thousand dollars to keep it quiet, to save my medical practice. When I wouldn't agree to do that, she went to a lawyer. It's turned into a 'she said, he said,' kind of thing. The worst thing is some newspaper reporter got hold of the story and is threatening to go live with it."

"Oh my God! What do your partners say about all this?"

Paul's lips thinned with anger. "They've asked me to step aside for the moment, feeling it will hurt business. As bad as things have been, that's the hardest blow to me."

"Oh, Paul. I'm so, so sorry. I know how decent you are, how hard you've worked for your practice and your good name."

Paul lowered his head. His shoulders shook.

Brooke wrapped her arms around him and pulled him close, sickened by all she'd heard.

"What's going to happen to us?" Brooke asked quietly.

He looked up and gave her such a look of devastation, her heart sank. "My lawyer thinks this can all be settled out of court, but we will face a storm of protest from women's groups demanding justice."

"Even though you didn't do it?"

He swallowed hard and nodded. "We're trying to get her to recant. She's had some mental problems recently. Nevertheless, my reputation will be stained and my practice here blemished. Bob and Phil have asked me to take a leave of absence from the group practice."

Brooke shot to her feet, too upset to stay seated. "Do they remember how generous you were to them when you three first opened the practice. Without our loans they might not have been able to be in practice here."

"I know. I've gone over and over it in my mind."

"It's not fair!" cried Brooke.

"I know, but life isn't fair. Give me time, and I'll work something out," said Paul.

Brooke sat down beside him again and hugged him hard. "We'll get through this together."

Brooke's heart beat steadily as determination filled her. It was time for her to show her true self. Not the little girl she'd once been, but the woman she'd become with the help of The Beach Babes and the loving support of her husband.

CHAPTER SIXTEEN

CATE

Cate sat at the desk in her bedroom at Seashell Cottage while Jackson was out by the pool enjoying the sun. An identifying song on her cell phone lilted in the air. Cate snatched it up. "Brooke! Are you all right? I've been trying to reach you."

"You and Amber both. And no, I'm not all right."

Cate heard the tremor in Brooke's voice. "What's going on?"

"It's Paul. He's being sued for sexual assault."

Every nerve ending in Cate's body came alive. "Wha-a-at? I can't believe it. He'd never do something like that."

"No, he wouldn't," Brooke said. "But that woman with whom he shared that infamous kiss is claiming he took advantage of her emotional state and did much more. He's devastated."

"Oh, my God!"

"Apparently she threatened to go public if he didn't pay her to be quiet. That's what's been going on all the time I thought he was having an affair. He promised me he didn't do it. She doesn't know that I've known all about the time alone with her in his office. If you remember, it happened because she went into a tailspin after having a miscarriage. He tried to comfort her and it led to something else, a hug and a kiss."

The sound of Brooke's quiet sobbing broke Cate's heart. "Do you want me to come there to be with you?"

"No, not yet. Paul and I are working together to try and

straighten things out. You can imagine what it's done to his practice. His partners have forced him to stay away from the office for a while. He's trying to keep busy, but it's driving him crazy. You know how slow the wheels of justice turn."

"I'm so, so sorry about all of it, Brooke. I've known Paul for a long time, and he's a good person. Certainly, all his patients are behind him."

"Oh, yes. He has plenty of people who are willing to testify for him. His lawyer says it won't go to trial. The awful thing is this should not have gotten this far. But if Paul agreed to pay to make her go away, it would only cause more problems."

"Yes, that would be a disaster. Is there anything I can do?"

"You know that cabin you were talking about? Maybe the girls and I will take a break and come visit you. P.J. is doing okay at college, but rumors have started here. Both Paul and I talked to the girls, and they understand as much as they can."

"You can come anytime."

"Thanks. How are you?" Brooke asked.

"You'll be pleased to know Jackson and I are officially engaged. There's a cute story involved with the proposal and my ring."

"Ring? Oh! Send me a picture. I'd love to see it," said Brooke, her voice high with excitement. "I'm so happy for you both."

Cate heard noise in the background and then Brooke said, "Gotta go. Some news trucks are outside. Don't call me. I'll call you when I can. And will you tell Amber what's going on? See you. I ..." The call abruptly ended.

In the quiet that followed, Cate sat a moment, trying to take in everything Brooke had told her. It was awful for both Paul and her.

She got to her feet to go to Jackson, but stopped when she heard a ping on her phone indicating an email. She quickly checked her computer and saw that it was a message from her publisher. She opened it and stared with dismay at the cover for her new book. It wasn't anything like she'd imagined. It was, in fact, all wrong.

She quickly called her agent.

"Hi, Cate! What's up?" Abby answered in an upbeat tone.

"Have you seen the cover for the new book?" Cate asked. "It's terrible. Simply awful. Too dark, too unimaginative. You've got to tell them it won't work. I want something more in line with the other books. This one doesn't even look like part of the series."

"Oh? That bad? Don't worry. Send me what you've got, and I'll talk to them. Your editor was due back from maternity leave. If she's not there, I know one of the people in the publicity department who can take a look at it with me. Don't worry. How's that vacation going?"

The anxiety that had ripped at Cate's stomach disappeared. She held out her hand as if Abby could see it. "That hunk you usually tease me about is now my fiancé. We are officially engaged."

"Wonderful," Abby exclaimed. "It's about time. I'm so happy for you."

"Yes, me too."

"Hopefully, you'll put off a wedding until after the first draft of the book you're working on is completed."

Cate groaned. "I knew you'd say something like that. At the moment we're thinking of a mid-June wedding. Please keep that in mind."

Laughing softly, Abby said, "Will do. Now go and enjoy that man of yours."

"I intend to." Still smiling, Cate hung up the phone.

She changed into her bikini and headed out to the pool. The sun in the sky warmed the air, making it a good afternoon to laze in the pool. Back home, New York was experiencing a gray, rainy day that made her time in Florida seem even better.

Jackson was sitting on the steps of the pool when she emerged from the house. He saw her, and let out a long whistle. “Babe, you look hot!”

She felt her cheeks grow warm. “You look pretty fantastic yourself,” she said, easing down in the water beside him, gasping at the chill of it.

He pulled her to him. “Let me warm you up. Once you get used to the temperature, it’s great.”

She nestled up against him for a moment and then took off, moving through the water at a steady pace. Brooke’s father had insisted that all three girls become good swimmers so he would feel okay about leaving them alone at the summer house for varying periods of time. Though Brooke and Amber hadn’t enjoyed it as much as she, Cate loved the movement of her limbs slicing through water.

When she went to make a turn at the shallow end of the pool, Jackson caught her in his arms. “Come here.” He brushed the hair away from her face, cupped her face in his strong hands, and kissed her. Against the coolness of the water on her face, his lips felt deliciously warm.

When he pulled away, he grinned. “Want to play?”

She eyed him warily. “Play what?”

“The sailor and his mermaid?”

She laughed. “Where in the world did you get that idea?”

“I get around. I teach biology, remember?”

“Now I know you’re joking. But ...”

“But?”

“Sure, why not? This vacation is turning into the best ever.”

He hugged her. “That’s my girl ... er, mermaid.”

Cate shook her head. Jackson was usually fun, but there

was a new depth about their relationship in him that she liked. She realized she'd been missing a lot by holding back.

It wasn't until they were sitting on the porch sipping wine that Cate told him about her conversation with Brooke and Paul's being accused of sexual assault by one of his past patients.

"Whew! With him being an Ob-Gyn that's a huge problem," Jackson said.

"Yes. Brooke and no one else can believe it, but the woman accusing him is the one he had a brief incident with, and that makes it difficult. She wanted money to keep quiet, and when he wouldn't pay her, she got a lawyer and now has gone public with her claims. Poor Brooke is a mess. She and the girls may come for a visit. While I was talking to her a news truck appeared."

"From the few times I've been with him, Paul Weston does not seem the kind of man to do something like it."

"No, and he and Brooke have been very happy until recently when this whole problem emerged."

"Poor guy. Maybe it won't be as bad as you think."

Cate shook her head sadly. "Paul's partners are asking him to stay low and out of sight for a while."

"Do you think that's a good idea?" Jackson asked.

"I'm not sure. I think Paul is trying to protect them and his family."

Jackson sighed. "Guess I'd better finish your hideaway in a hurry. Looks like we might be using it."

"Brooke asked me to call Amber. I'm going to try her now." Cate punched in the number for Amber and was forced to leave a message to call her back.

Still thinking about Brooke, Cate said, "The thing that

makes this so sad is if this woman either is found to be guilty of extortion or settles out of court like they think she will, then she's done a disservice to all the women who truly have been sexually assaulted or abused."

"I agree. Women, men too, need a clear voice, not one muddied up by someone lying about it," Jackson said.

"I've also been concerned about Amber. I knew she had trouble at home growing up. Her mother entertained different men frequently. This past weekend, Amber told us she'd once been sexually assaulted by one of them. She didn't dare tell anyone because she thought she might be placed in a foster home. How bad is that?"

Jackson let out a sigh. "I see kids from troubled backgrounds in my classes and try to help them if I can. But in today's world you have to be careful about how you ask questions and what you say. But every time I see or hear anything that I think I should look into further, I can't hold back."

"You're a good teacher and a good guy, Jackson. Your students are lucky to have you."

"Thanks. There are times I wonder if I've done the right thing by going into teaching, but then I connect with one of my students, and it all seems worthwhile."

He stood and held out his hand. "How about a walk?"

Cate got to her feet and took hold of his hand. She'd miss times like this when they returned home. If things went the way she hoped, they'd come to Florida in June for their wedding and honeymoon. Jackson had loved the idea of a beach wedding here at Seashell Cottage and thought Gavin's and the Salty Key Inn were the perfect places for a wedding dinner and for his family to stay while they, themselves, rented Seashell Cottage. As soon as they firmed up a wedding date, they'd make the reservations. She glanced down at the ring on her finger. It shimmered with hope for a future filled with dreams come true. She wished the same for her friends.

On the flight home, Cate studied the clouds outside the plane wondering what having a child would do to her publishing career. Maybe while she was stuck at home with a little one, it would be a good time to start a new series, something a little lighter. She was in the middle of her initial draft of the fifth book in the Galeon War series and knew she'd get restless if she wasn't working on something. Recently, she'd begun dreaming about new characters, people in a contemporary setting on earth. She'd talk to Abby about it.

Cate's thoughts flitted to her best friends and the dilemma each faced. Back in high school, they'd bonded over typical teen issues troubling them. Now that she knew what had actually happened to Amber in her own home, she understood better why the girls in high school called her "The Ice Princess" and the boys said she was a "Cock Tease." Both hurtful. Amber had had reason to withdraw from friendships with girls who sometimes turned mean, and though she naturally had a way of moving that showed off her body, Amber never initiated a relationship with boys. No wonder Amber, Brooke, and she had remained so tight through the years. They'd each had reasons to hold onto the trust they'd built between them.

Cate glanced at Jackson sitting next to her on the plane reading a magazine. The first thing she'd do after she got home was to make an appointment with her doctor to have her IUD removed. Some people thought forty was too late to start a family, but Cate was in good health, and she would continue to take care of herself.

They landed at Kennedy Airport in New York as scheduled

a little after noon. As she and Jackson fought the crowd heading to the baggage claim area, Cate felt the muscles in her neck tighten. Vacation was over.

CHAPTER SEVENTEEN

AMBER

Early Wednesday morning, Amber walked into her office feeling as unsettled as she had last week. She took off her coat and hung it up in the executive coat closet Belinda reluctantly allowed her to use. After closing the door, she took a moment to study her surroundings. The sleek glass and metal furniture suited the stark white walls covered here and there by large, poster-sized color photographs of various models in a variety of settings. Belinda Galvin may be known in circles as being the biggest bitch in the business, but she was successful. It was this need of hers —to succeed without the help of a man—that Amber admired. Probably because of her mother's need for any man to justify herself. He didn't need to be understanding or kind or have a steady income. He just needed to show the slightest interest in her mother to reel her in.

After Amber made sure that the tea Belinda liked was out and ready to use, along with the special English bone china tea cup and saucer Belinda insisted upon using, she turned on the lights in her boss's office and hurried to her own to collect and print out messages for her. If they weren't waiting on Belinda's desk, stacked neatly, it started the day off wrong, and even the best of days with Belinda would be anyone else's nightmare.

Amber had learned to live with Belinda's condescending ways as a matter of survival. She hadn't gone to college like her two best friends but had, instead, come to New York to begin her career. Instead of full-time modeling, as she'd hoped, she'd ended up working for a number of people and Belinda, learning the business side of things. Surprisingly, Amber liked being in charge, dealing with numbers, and handling clients, and discovered she was good at it.

When she was given the part-time contract with the perfume company through Jesse, Amber was grateful for the money but knew she couldn't do that for long. Now that she was soon to be forty, she was sure it was almost a given that the contract wouldn't be renewed.

She was sitting at her desk when Belinda strolled into the office, wearing sunglasses and a white-fox wrap around her shoulders that gave her the appearance of a movie star. Drama suited Belinda. She strove for it in both appearance and action, assuming a model's gait as she made her way toward Amber.

"Well! You're back, I see. No more long weekends for you. I needed you. Stand up."

Curious, Amber rose to her feet.

"Just as I thought. You must have eaten yourself silly. Looks like you gained a couple of pounds. I can't have a ... a *fat* person working for me. Watch out, Amber."

Amber swallowed the retort in her mouth. Someday she'd tell Belinda where she could stuff that fur wrap of hers. And when she left, she'd take a lot more than severance pay with her. She'd take a wealth of knowledge that would help her in the future. If not in New York, then anywhere she wanted.

As Belinda swept by her, Amber shrugged off her dislike of the woman who ruled her workdays. She'd learned to put it aside and move forward, enjoying the aspects of her job that Belinda didn't ruin for her. Amber had a core of people who worked in the business who respected her and how she made things easier for them. It was just one reason she'd been hired for the job with the perfume commercials. Amber smiled at the memory of Jesse standing firm on his desire to have Amber involved, warning Belinda he wouldn't do it without her.

Working for Belinda might be hard, but it had been worthwhile. Especially because of her relationship with Jesse.

CHAPTER EIGHTEEN

CATE

When Cate walked into the house, Buddy barked and then yowled to see her. Cate swept him up in her arms and nestled him close to her chest. He licked her face and wagged his tail so hard he wiggled back and forth, making it almost impossible to keep hold of him.

"Wonder how he's going to handle a baby in the house," Jackson said, chuckling. "You'll have to give him a lot of attention."

"Don't worry, I will," Cate replied. "He's my baby too." She set him down and went into her office. On the plane, she'd come up with a few story ideas and wanted to get them down on paper.

The message light on her office phone was blinking. She punched in the button and listened:

"Hi, Cate. This is Abby. Good news and bad news. First, the good news is that I was able to reach someone in the marketing department at the publishers, and they will work with us on a change to the book cover. Bad news is that they will fight you on the color. And the very bad news is that your editor has decided not to return after having her baby. So, my dear, you are what is called an "orphan" in the business. I talked to the editor you've been assigned to, and she's not enthusiastic about your work. In fact, she says the book you're working on will be published only because it's been contracted with you. Sorry, Cate. We'll figure something out."

Cate sank onto her desk chair, feeling as if she'd been

slapped across the face. *The editor didn't like her work?* She probably had an author of her own who did similar work and was going to promote *her* instead of working with Cate. She'd heard someone talk about that before. What an ugly business!

Jackson poked his head inside her office. "I've put your suitcase in the bedroom. And now I'm going to check on the cabin. I'll make a list of things required to finish it, and we can talk about it." He frowned. "Everything okay?"

"No," Cate answered, shaking her head. "You know the idea I had about changing genres? I'm probably going to be forced to go ahead with it. I've been 'orphaned.'"

"What in hell does that mean?"

"My editor left the publishing house. I might as well be on my own. Abby and I will work out details, but I'm going to try something new."

"I'm sorry, Cate. But, then, you haven't been as excited about writing the series as in the past. Maybe it's a good thing this has happened."

"I know," she admitted, unwilling to tell him how bruised her ego was. But she couldn't let her feelings of insecurity get the best of her. Not when so many other things were about to happen to her.

Jackson left, and Cate looked down at the notes she'd made. They had nothing to do with the Galeon War series. Fierce determination filled her. This kind of work is what she should be doing. Her mind was urging her to write it, just as it had once called to her to write about Serena and Rondol.

Cate left the office to unpack. She was a planner, someone who liked to know what challenges she faced. This time, she had no idea what the future held for her. She simply knew it was going to be different, and she was more than a little afraid.

Later, she left the bedroom and went to find Jackson. She'd seen an article about she-sheds on line and fell in love with the idea of a space to call her own. A place to escape to. A place where her imagination could take flight with words, and there'd be no interruptions to bring her back to the present with a jarring thump. The cabin was perfect for her.

She approached the building that looked more like a tiny country house than a shed. Gray-painted clapboards covered the sides of it, white flower boxes hung beneath the two windows on either side of the deep-purple door. It wasn't until one stepped inside that a visitor realized the depth of the building, which accommodated a tiny kitchen, a small office, a living area that would hold a pull-out couch, and, in the back, a bedroom and bath.

Tape measure in hand, Jackson looked over at her and smiled. "Just about finished here."

"I think we'd better hold off on shelves in my office for the time being. We might have to use the room for Brooke's girls to sleep in. We may end up with more people than I thought. Amber will want to make sure I'll still have space for her."

"No problem. Less work for me," said Jackson.

"Thanks. Amber's sensitive about things like that."

"I get it," said Jackson. He came over to her and pulled her into an embrace. "I get this, too." His lips met hers.

She melted into him, taking a moment to simply enjoy being with him.

Later, when she returned to the house, she went into her office and called her doctor. It was time to move forward.

A week later, sitting in the waiting area for her doctor's appointment, Cate studied the other women in the waiting area. Some had rounded stomachs in varying stages of pregnancy. Others looked anxious or bored depending upon their circumstances, Cate supposed. She, herself, was both excited and nervous.

"Catherine?" said the nurse, signaling her to come.

Cate drew a deep breath and followed the nurse to the doctor's office. Marc Tomason, a kind, gray-haired man, had been her doctor from the time she'd first moved to Ellenton. She'd always liked him.

She entered his office, and while the nurse closed the door, she sat in one of the chairs in front of his desk.

Dr. Tomason smiled at her. "I see from your records we recently saw you, so I'm wondering why you're here. Are you feeling okay?"

"I'm a little scared, but happy," she admitted. "My boyfriend and I have decided to marry and start a family. I need to have the IUD removed."

"Ah, such happy news. That won't be a problem. We can take care of that today." He studied her a moment. "I'm pleased for you, Cate. I see no reason you shouldn't proceed. You're a healthy woman."

"Some people say it's too late to have a child," said Cate.

Dr. Tomason smiled. "We'll let nature answer that question. Why don't you get ready, and we'll take care of step number one. The rest will follow in due time."

Excitement filled Cate as she left his private office and entered the examination room the nurse indicated for her.

A short while later, Cate emerged, fully dressed. Removing her IUD turned out to be easier than she'd expected, though she'd experienced some discomfort and might for a day or two. But it would all be worth it. She and Jackson had already decided not to wait to try for a baby.

When Jackson came home from work, he handed her a bouquet of fall flowers. He grinned playfully. "We ready to start now?"

She laughed. "Well, we may have dinner first, but why not? Dr. Tomason says I'm healthy and ready to go."

He laughed at her response. "What's for dinner? You told me you were doing something special."

"I'm fixing you my lemon and chicken casserole."

"Nice. One of my favorites. You didn't do a lot of writing today?"

She shook her head. "No, the incentive has evaporated with the news that this is the last book in the series. I have to rethink my plot a bit."

"Don't let it get you down," Jackson said, giving her a hug. "You're happier when you're working on something."

"I know. Honestly, it's been an up and down day."

"Let's make it a good day. Want to take a walk before dinner?"

Buddy barked and wagged his tail with expectation.

Cate and Jackson looked at each other and laughed.

"Guess we have to now," said Cate, feeling better.

Outside, the last of the colorful leaves were clinging to the branches on the trees as if they were afraid to let go. This time of year made Cate want to bustle around inside the house, stockpiling supplies and making things comfortable for the months ahead, like a squirrel gathering nuts for the winter.

Jackson held her hand as they walked through the neighborhood.

"Cate! Wait up!" cried a woman running to catch up to them.

Cate smiled at Julie Howard. She and her husband Rick were good friends. "Sorry, I missed your call this morning. What's up?"

Cate proudly held out her left hand. "We did it! Jackson and I are engaged."

"Oh, hon! I'm so happy for you," cried Julie, giving her a big hug. She pulled away and hugged Jackson. "You too, Jackson. You two are great together. Let's celebrate!"

"Why don't you come for dinner? I've made a casserole big enough for all of us," Cate suggested.

"And I'll make one of my salads," added Jackson.

"Deal," said Julie. "We'll bring the wine for the guys. Rick should be home any minute." She bent down to pat Buddy on the head and then straightened. "I'm excited for you both. It's been a long time coming."

"Tell me about it," Jackson grumbled, and they all laughed.

Later, after a wonderful evening, as Cate closed the door behind Julie and Rick, she felt a deep sense of gratitude for their friendship. They were genuinely pleased for Jackson and her, and, more importantly, Julie had promised to be a support to her over the coming months. Julie was seven months pregnant and hoped their children would one day be friends.

As the days moved forward, Cate discovered a new reverence for the lovemaking she and Jackson shared. Their love was about to produce a child. She could hardly wait to see their baby, and imagined a variety of faces and features.

Though she was both disappointed and exhilarated by the fact the book she was working on would bring a close to her series, she worked steadily on it. After listening to Julie talk about the preparations for her baby, she realized she'd need time to get ready for the changes she was sure were coming.

The week before Thanksgiving, Cate received a phone call from Amber early one morning. "Can you meet me for lunch,

Cate? I need to talk to you."

"Sure. Is everything all right?" Cate's stomach knotted. Amber sounded miserable.

"No, it's not good, but I can't talk here in the office."

"Okay. Tell me when and where, and I'll be there. I'll take the train into the city."

They agreed to meet at one o'clock at a small French restaurant away from Amber's office. Cate mentally changed her plans and headed into the shower. She'd wanted to ask Amber about Jesse, but knew it would be unfair when Amber couldn't speak freely.

After a quick shower, she called Abby and arranged to see her before meeting with Amber. Might as well make a day of it, she decided, wondering if she could convince Abby to represent an author who wrote contemporary women's fiction under the name of Cate Hubbard instead of Catherine Tibbs. If so, Cate had a lot of work to do to create a whole new profile. She was growing to like the idea of becoming a different writer.

Before leaving the house, she left a note for Jackson and dropped Buddy off to Doggy Camp.

Later, sitting on the train, Cate thought about Amber. When they'd first met, Amber was a twelve-year-old full of sass and a confidence Cate couldn't imagine. It took a while before Amber showed her true self to Brooke and her—a wounded person who didn't trust others. Her mother, of course, was responsible. She hadn't married Amber's father and couldn't stop searching for the "right man," someone who'd solve her financial problems and make her happy. Entertaining various men consumed her. Affection between Amber and her mother ended when the men she entertained became interested in Amber. Then, her mother became competitive and mean.

Cate stirred restlessly in her seat. She hadn't known Amber had been raped, but looking back, she recalled how Amber's dislike of her mother had intensified in high school. At the time, she'd attributed it to Amber realizing how unhealthy her mother was. But now she knew it was so much more.

The woman sitting next to her got up to exit the train. With a jolt, Cate realized they'd arrived at Grand Central Terminal. She got to her feet, left the train, walked through the terminal, and entered the bustle of the city.

Abby's small office building, two blocks away on Madison Avenue, was an easy walk. Cate reveled in the activity all around her. She loved seeing it for a brief time, but was happy to go back home to relative peace and quiet.

As she rode the elevator to Abby's fourth-floor office, Cate rehearsed in her mind what she wanted to say to her. Abby was a tough negotiator, someone highly respected in the field, but she had no tolerance for people who were not willing to fight for what they wanted. Cate had to convince her that even with the twist in her personal life, she intended to continue her career either along a new path or with a different editor.

Cate entered the office and told the receptionist, someone new, who she was and that she had an appointment with Abby. With three others working in the office, it was a busy place.

Abby appeared, looking frazzled. A tall, thin, striking woman with gray hair worn short, Abby's had a brusque manner that was sometimes intimidating to Cate.

"Good to see you, Cate. Let's talk. I have an important call coming through from Hollywood in twenty minutes."

Cate followed Abby down a short corridor to her office, which wasn't the least bit fancy. It had a fairly small window looking out onto the street, but that was about as glamorous as it got. Bookshelves lined one entire wall of the office and were overloaded with books of clients. Cate checked to find hers as she took a seat in the chair Abby indicated in front of her desk.

Abby clasped her hands in front of her and studied Cate. "I hope you're not here to bail because the editor doesn't like your work. The publishing business is tough as you well know, and pushing an editor to like your book never works. Believe me, I've tried."

"I've decided to take a different route," Cate said, feeling better about her decision. She pulled several sheets of paper from her oversized purse. "I've brought you a rough idea of a book I've been thinking about writing. It's a new genre for me, but I think I might like to make a change."

"Instead of my reading this, why don't you tell me about it?" Abby leaned back in her chair and gave her an encouraging smile.

Cate drew a deep breath. "It's about three women who meet at a spa and discover they've dated the same man at different periods in their lives. Each has a different regret for letting him go. When he dies, they come together to fight for their rightful inheritances."

Abby gave her a thoughtful look. "Sounds intriguing. Write a true synopsis and I'll nose around the industry to see if there's any interest. Have you started the book?"

"No, I've just worked on some ideas."

"Good. Keep going. Now tell me about your plans for the future." Abby smiled. "I'm happy that you and Jackson are engaged. He's a nice guy."

Cate grinned at the memory. "He asked me to marry him with a seashell as a proxy for a ring."

Abby chuckled. "What?"

Cate held out her left hand. "Let me tell you the story."

Abby listened to her, made some notes on a piece of paper

and said, "Your description is wonderful. If you can do that with your new books, I think the genre might work for you. You understand how to make our contemporary world come alive. Work on the plotting."

Cate let out a breath she hadn't realized she'd been holding. No matter what happened, she couldn't ever give up writing. It was part of who she was.

They chatted about possible publishing companies and editors, Abby's daughter, a junior in high school who was looking at various colleges, and then Cate's time with Abby was up.

Cate left the office and decided to go on to the restaurant. She didn't mind getting there early. While she was waiting for Amber to appear, she'd make a few notes on her meeting with Abby.

CHAPTER NINETEEN

AMBER

Le Jardin was a neighborhood café that locals loved and tourists wished they'd known about when they read reviews of it. Unpretentious, it sat on a corner and oozed French charm along with mouthwatering aromas.

As Amber waited for Cate to show up, she perused the menu, changing her mind as quickly as she read. All of the offerings looked fabulous. Her mouth was still watering when Cate walked into the restaurant.

She set down her menu and tried not to cry as she watched Cate make her way to her table. She was grateful Cate had so quickly agreed to meet her. But then, who else could she trust to help her deal with the latest news?

"You're here early! What's wrong?" Cate asked, clasping Amber's hand as she lowered herself into a chair opposite her.

Amber's eyes filled. She closed them, drew a deep breath, and with a trembling voice whispered, "I arrived at the office early this morning to check Belinda's messages. Jesse had left one telling her that he'd be late on a project he was working on for her because he'd unexpectedly met his ex-wife, Simone, in Paris a couple of weeks ago, and they decided to get m ... m ... married again. He said they want to give it another try."

"That jerk! He was dating you!" Cate couldn't hide the disgust in her voice.

Amber shook her head sadly. "That's just it. He told me he wasn't interested in any long-term relationship, that he was still suffering from his divorce of six years ago. He's a decent guy who doesn't deserve to have any problems with me or the baby."

"Whoa!" said Cate. "Like it or not, he deserves to know that you are pregnant and he's the father. If he's the decent guy you say he is, he'll want to do the right thing for you."

"I don't want him to be part of my life or the baby's if he feels obligated." Though she dabbed at her eyes with a tissue, Amber felt the warm tears that escaped down her cheek.

Cate handed her fresh tissues. "Take a deep breath."

Amber patted her face. "Thank God I got a corner table. I don't want anyone to see me like this. What am I going to do?" She patted her stomach. "I'm already beginning to show."

Cate hesitated, then spoke. "The way I see it, you have no choice but to meet with Jesse and tell him the truth. In today's world, all kinds of unusual family dynamics exist. It might mean Jesse and his new—old— wife would want to be part of the baby's life. One thing is for sure. Belinda isn't going to like any of this for many reasons."

"I know. Belinda thought she and Jesse had something real, but he told me he was honest with her, and he knew from the beginning it wasn't going to work, which is why he quickly ended it."

"And what about you?" Cate asked.

"He wanted to see where it might lead, but there was no real commitment beyond that between the two of us," Amber replied, feeling miserable. "He was very careful about using condoms. My getting pregnant was just one of those mistakes you hear about. You know how cautious I am about getting too close to anyone, but I thought I loved him." Her lips quivered.

"And now?" Cate's voice was gentle.

Amber sighed. "I can't marry him. Maybe it's all for the best."

"You're going ahead with the pregnancy. Right?" Cate's

gaze remained on her.

Amber felt her eyes widen. "Of course! There's no way I would ever do anything to end it."

Cate smiled. "Good. Perhaps our children can play together one day."

Amber gripped Cate's hand. "Oh my God! Are you pregnant?"

"Not yet," Cate said. "But I hope to be soon."

Amber studied the ring on Cate's finger. "It's beautiful, and like you said, it's a wonderful symbol for the two of you." Her vision blurred. "Sorry, I'm so emotional."

"I have to believe that things will work out for you, Amber," said Cate, looking up as a waiter approached their table.

"Are you ladies ready to order, or should I give you more time?" he asked, carefully avoiding looking at Amber's tear-streaked face.

"A few minutes more," said Cate. She lifted her menu and spoke quietly to Amber. "This lunch is on me."

"I'm going to order a veggie omelet. I might even order dessert," said Amber. "To hell with what Belinda thinks."

"That's more like the Amber I know," said Cate, smiling at her. "Let that defiance get you through the next several months."

After the waiter left their table with their orders, Amber said, "What's the latest on Brooke?"

"I saw a small notice in the *L.A. Times*. It seems that Paul's accuser has retracted her statement. His lawyers discovered how she'd tried to blackmail another man, and rather than go to court and lose, she agreed to drop the case. Brooke told me it was all about money. Regardless of the outcome in his favor, the damage has been done to Paul."

"Poor Brooke. She must be dying inside with

mortification," said Amber. "How about you? Everything all right? At least your job and your life are secure."

"Maybe not," said Cate. "I've been what they call 'orphaned' in the industry, and my new editor doesn't like my work. The book I'm working on now will be the last in the series. But I'm talking to Abby about writing in a new genre."

"I don't know what I'm going to do if Belinda fires me," said Amber. "I'll wait as long as I can before telling her I'm pregnant."

"You're her assistant who's stayed the longest with her. Maybe she'll realize she needs you."

"Not likely," Amber scoffed. "That woman doesn't like to be beholden to anyone else. In her mind, she does everything herself, even though I follow up on most of the details for her. Without me, she'd look pretty bad. Not that she'd ever admit it. She thinks I, like everyone else around her, am easily replaced."

"But she pays you a lot of money. That must prove something to her and to you."

"If not me, someone else." Amber gazed into the distance.

"Maybe you'd be happier working for another agency, something less stressful."

"I've thought of it," Amber admitted. "But I doubt I'd earn as much as I do now."

"There are trade-offs," said Cate. "Money isn't everything."

"I know," Amber said, but Cate didn't understand with her new condo payments and some of the unexpected expenses of owning it, she was worried about money.

"What are you doing for Thanksgiving?" Cate asked. "Jackson and I are staying home. Want to join us?"

Amber grinned. "That would be wonderful! I need to get away from the city. Belinda is going to Vermont, and I'll be able to escape for a few days."

"Great! We'd love to have you," Cate said.

Relief flooded Amber. Being together for Thanksgiving would be a perfect way to prepare for the months ahead.

CHAPTER TWENTY

CATE

When Cate arrived back at her house in Ellenton, she called for Jackson and Buddy, but neither answered her. She stuck her head out the back door. When she heard the whine of a power saw, she walked toward the cabin.

Jackson was inside with Buddy. He looked up and smiled at her before he finished making his cut.

"Hey, Cate. I got your message and thought I'd better get to work on the finishing touches. Once the trim is put up, caulked, and painted, it won't take long to get the carpet laid and appliances put in. Then it'll be up to you to decorate."

"I've already ordered a lot of décor items, but I still need to decide on a few things. Even so, I think we'll put Amber in the guest suite of the house."

"I'll keep working here. Dinner is on you tonight," he said.

"How about pizza? I've got some research to do for Abby."

He chuckled. "Fine by me. I know you don't like to cook."

She walked over to him and threw her arms around his neck. "But you do! Did anyone ever tell you that you're the most wonderful man in the world?" Closing her eyes, she reached up to kiss him.

His arms tightened around her. His lips met hers sending sensations rolling through her.

She gave in to the need that ran through her and responded with equal intensity. It had always been this way between them.

Buddy barked and jumped against Cate's leg. Chuckling, she ended the kiss with Jackson. "Someone's jealous."

Jackson's gaze met hers. "Why wouldn't he be? He knows how hot you are, how you make me feel."

"Oh? And how is that?" she asked, playing along.

"Like I've found the right woman," he replied. He gave her a quick kiss on the lips. "Guess I'd better get back to work. We can finish this conversation up tonight."

Cate picked up Buddy, cuddled him for a moment, and left the cabin, thinking how lucky she was. Conversations in bed with Jackson were usually physical.

Cate was sitting in her office making notes on various publishing companies and editors when her cell phone rang. *Brooke.*

"Hi," Cate warbled, excited to hear from her friend. "So nice that you called. Amber and I were talking about you earlier today."

"I hope it was something good. How are the two of you?

"I'll fill you in on Amber, but first, how are you? I saw the article in the newspaper stating that Paul's accuser has retracted her statement."

"Yes, we knew it was about money, but it didn't make it any easier to have her accusation dragged into the public. She's a sick person who's all but destroyed our family."

"I'm so, so sorry," said Cate, aware her words were not enough to express her pain for one of her dearest friends. "What are you going to do about it?"

"That's why I'm calling. Paul is interviewing for a teaching position at the department of Obstetrics and Gynecology at Weill Cornell Medicine and New York Presbyterian Hospital."

"Wow! That's a big change for all of you," said Cate, unable to hide her surprise.

"Yes, but after being disappointed here in L.A. by people and professionals we thought were friends, Paul and I have decided it's time for a change," Brooke said with a bitterness to her voice that Cate recognized as hurt. "A friend of Paul's, an older man who teaches there, has been after Paul to join the professional staff for some time. It seems like a good idea to do it now, rather than later."

"I can understand why. Anything I can do to help you?"

"As a matter of fact, you can. How would you feel about having my family for Thanksgiving? Paul, P.J., the girls, and I will be in New York for the long weekend while Paul meets with his mentor and I begin looking for a house. Paul has already been told he has the job."

"Thanksgiving will be fantastic with all of you here. Amber's going to be here too, which will make it perfect."

"Wonderful! How is she? I was planning to call her after I talked to you."

"You won't believe what has happened! She's a wreck." Cate proceeded to fill in Brooke with all the details of their conversation at lunch. "Amber is not blaming Jesse and says he's a decent guy. Since his divorce six years ago, he's been careful about making any commitment to her or anyone else. Apparently, he was crushed by the divorce and still loved his wife."

"Poor Amber. He's the first guy she's ever been so serious about. It's too bad it's worked out this way."

"I think it may end better than we all think," said Cate. "The structure of family is fluid in today's world."

"I hope so. How are you doing, Cate? I loved the photo of the ring you sent. I can't wait to hear the story behind it."

"Thanks. I'm officially trying to get pregnant. One cycle has come and gone, but after having the IUD in for so long, I know it sometimes takes 3-4 months to get pregnant."

"Or longer at our age," said Brooke. "Don't be discouraged early on. I remember what it was like trying to get pregnant before the twins came along."

"One baby is enough for Jackson and me. At least to begin with," said Cate, horrified by the idea of having twins. It was going to take all her energy and commitment to do a good job of mothering just one.

"Thanks for letting me invite my family to your house for Thanksgiving," said Brooke. "I've got to go. I'm meeting with a real estate agent soon, so I'd better get off the phone."

"Wow! You're moving pretty fast on the change."

"Not fast enough," said Brooke. "I'm done with the humiliation, sly looks, and worry about what people are saying about us."

"I don't blame you. Where are you looking to buy?"

"Someplace near you. West Walles looks nice, and there are good schools there."

"It's very nice," agreed Cate. It was much too expensive for her, but Brooke had family money and could well afford a home in the exclusive nearby town.

"We'll see," said Brooke. "I've started research on line. There are a few places that might be of interest."

"Wonderful!" said Cate. "Then the three of us Beach Babes can get together much more often."

"Yes, that's definitely in my plans. After realizing how many people I knew were so quick to turn on me and my family, I want to be with people I can trust. Let me know what I can do to help you for Thanksgiving. I know Jackson enjoys cooking for a crowd, but I want to help in some way."

"Bring the wine," Cate suggested. She knew Brooke would go overboard unless given a specific task.

"Great! I will. We'll be staying in the city, but we can come to Ellenton anytime you want us."

"Why don't you come in the morning? We won't eat dinner until 4 or so. And if you and the family want to spend the night with us and not worry about getting back to the city, we've got room for all of you."

"Is the cabin done?"

"No, but it will be. I start painting the inside tomorrow."

As soon as Cate hung up, she made notes on the manuscript so she'd remember what thoughts she had for the next few chapters. Then, she rose and went out to the cabin to talk to Jackson to see what she could do to help him. It seemed the house would be full for the holiday.

The minute Amber drove into the driveway, Cate knew something was up. Even though Amber was a fast driver, she was speeding much too fast, as if she couldn't reach safety fast enough.

Cate left the front of the house where she'd been waiting, playing with Buddy, and went over to the asphalt apron at the side of the two-car garage.

Amber stepped out of the car and stood for a moment, her face to the sky.

Cate hurried over to her. "You look great!" Not only was she beautiful, there was a new sense of peace about her.

Amber smiled at her. "I saw Jesse last night. He's not mad. In fact, he's going to do everything he can to be part of this baby's life. I'll know more after he talks to Simone, but even if she is reluctant to be involved, he promised to help financially. In fact, he's already set up a sizeable bank account for me to cover any expenses. Even though I hate to take money from anyone, I'm accepting it to please him."

"Wow! That's great!" said Cate. Her own father had

disappeared before Cate was born. She still didn't know who he was, and though her curiosity sometimes flared, she had no intention of trying to find out who it might be.

"Like I've said, he's a decent guy."

"So, how is Belinda going to handle this? The word 'decent' doesn't come to my mind."

"She's going to be pissed for so many reasons," said Amber, "but right now, I'm going to enjoy Thanksgiving with you. I'm not going to let her ruin it for me." She gave Cate a quick hug. "Thanks for letting me come here."

"Jackson and I are very excited to have a full house. Brooke and her family will come here tomorrow morning, and from my last conversation with her, it sounds as if the whole family will spend a couple of nights with us, so we three Beach Babes can have time together."

"Great. I'm so happy they're going to move close."

"Me, too. Now, come inside and we'll get you settled. We're giving the cabin to Brooke and her family so they can have a little more privacy."

"Wow! You must have made it roomier," said Amber.

Cate laughed. "Not so big, just well laid-out. Jackson took one wall out and added another. Believe me, it's going to be a bit crowded, but Brooke understands. We have sleeping space for each of them."

When they entered the house, Jackson emerged from the kitchen, wearing a chef's apron. "Hi, Amber. Good to see you."

Friends that they were, they easily embraced.

"What are you cooking?" Amber said.

"I'm brining the turkey and doing a little prep work for tomorrow. After you get settled, I'll show you my latest masterpiece."

"The cabin? I'd love to see it. It's amazing what you two have done to what was once an old farmhouse and now you're working on the old cabin on the property."

"It's taken seven years to get things the way we wanted, but it's well worth all the work," said Cate, smiling at Jackson.

"And now things are about finished," Jackson said.

"The two of you are an inspiration to me," said Amber. "Someday, maybe I'll be as lucky."

"I hope so too," said Cate, thinking it took more than luck to make a relationship work. The early years had been about discovery of one another's foibles and then building trust and openness between them.

Cate led Amber upstairs to the guest suite.

While Amber unpacked, Cate sank down on the bed. "Was it hard talking to Jesse?"

Tears filled Amber's eyes. "I was so scared. You know my history with men, and I thought he might be angry. He told me that being with me was special, that he didn't want me to think otherwise."

"Yes, but ..."

"He said he knew there would be repercussions for me in the industry because of Belinda, and he would do his best to help me there too. He's been so generous." Amber sighed. "The problem is I might need to make a change in my professional life, and I don't know what I want to do."

"Maybe you and Brooke could find something to do together. Something to help other women," said Cate, her thoughts racing. "Brooke will be at loose ends for a while, getting settled in a new place. The girls have been accepted at a private day school, which will leave Brooke alone at loose ends with P.J. away at college and Paul busy with his new job."

Amber frowned at her. "Do you think Brooke and I would be able to work together? She can get pretty intense."

"You have a good business sense and Brooke has the artistic flair. Start thinking of ideas and see where it goes,"

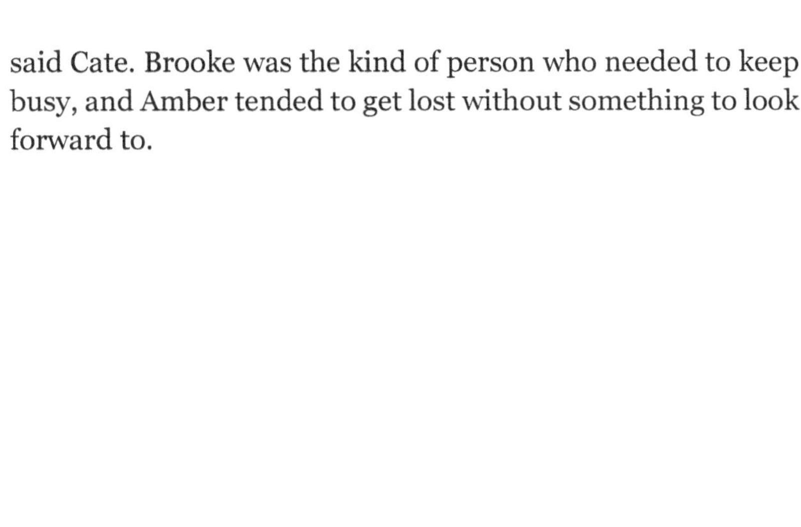

said Cate. Brooke was the kind of person who needed to keep busy, and Amber tended to get lost without something to look forward to.

CHAPTER TWENTY-ONE

CATE

The skies on Thanksgiving Day were as bright and full of promise as Cate felt. She and Jackson liked to entertain, and this was the perfect time to do it. Jackson reveled in his role as chef, and Cate enjoyed showing off the house that she'd worked so hard to own. Jackson had made it his home as well and had worked side by side with her and sometimes alone on making the renovations to it. Sitting on two acres of land, and with three bedrooms and two and a half baths, the farmhouse-style home had been in disrepair when Cate bought it from a widow who'd let it go. But the bones of the house were good, and from the beginning, Cate could imagine how it would look with a lot of loving care.

Now, Cate studied the dining room table she'd covered in white linen and set for eight people with antique, cut-glass water goblets and second-hand silver she'd picked up here and there. She'd known nice things from her aunt's working at Mr. Pennyman's mansion, but had nothing like it of her own from the unhappy life she'd shared with her.

"Gorgeous," said Amber, coming into the room. "Yesterday, I ordered flowers from the cute little place downtown. They just delivered them." She handed Cate a basket filled with gold and red roses, lilies, greens, and colorful fall leaves.

"It's beautiful! Thank you so much, Amber!" Cate set the basket down on the table and gave her a quick hug.

"I know how much you like all the nice things you didn't

have growing up," said Amber. She studied the space around them. "You've made everything beautiful."

Cate heard a car pulling in and grinned at Amber. "I think Brooke and her family are here."

Together, they hurried to the front door and went outside to greet them.

Cate stood by with Amber and watched Brooke's kids emerge from the van Brooke and Paul had rented. Her heart filled with affection.

P.J., at nineteen, was a tall, young man with dark hair and green eyes, who had the classic features of his maternal grandfather, a man Cate had loved like a father. He even moved like Brooke's father—with a slow and easy grace.

Brynn and Bradley followed him out of the van. With their curly red hair and easy smiles, they were lovely ten-year-olds who, though they looked a lot like their mother, were thinner and more confident than Brooke had ever been at that age. Still sweet in nature, they rushed forward into Cate and Amber's open arms.

Brooke approached Cate and Amber, beaming her excitement. "The gang's all here." She turned as Paul walked toward them.

Not a particularly handsome man, Dr. Paul Weston exuded kindness and interest in others that people found compelling. Blue eyes shining, he smiled at Cate and brushed back a thinning lock of light-brown hair. "Thanks for having us, Cate. Nothing like having Thanksgiving with close friends." He turned to Amber. "Congratulations!"

Brynn studied Amber. "Is it true? You're going to have a baby?"

"Yes, that's right," said Amber, giving her stomach a gentle rub Cate found touching.

"Mom says you're going to be a good mother," said Bradley.

"I think so too, Auntie Amber."

Amber's face flushed with emotion. "I hope so," she managed to say.

"And Mom says Auntie Cate is going to have a baby too," said Brynn as Jackson approached the group with a smile.

"Is that so?" he said to her, accepting a hug from Bradley, quickly followed by Brynn.

Watching them, Cate sighed. Jackson was going to make such a good father. Kids of all ages loved him. P.J. was shaking hands with him now.

Cate turned to Paul. "I'm so sorry you had to go through all the recent legal mess."

His brows drew together in a V of disapproval. "It was unnecessary and painful. I'm grateful Brooke stood by me like she has. I wouldn't ever want to hurt her or the kids. My lawyer kept telling me the truth would win, but it can sometimes take a long time for justice to be met."

Jackson approached and clapped Paul on the back. "Good to see you, Doc. Glad you could come. I intend to put those medical hands to good use carving the turkey."

Paul laughed. "You, the chef, trusting me? I'm honored."

Cate left them to join Brooke and Amber. It pleased her that Jackson and Paul got along.

"Oh, hey, Cate," said Brooke. "I was just telling Amber I think I've found a house in the Carrington development in West Walles. We put in an offer and will wait to see."

"Mom, can we get a dog like Buddy?" One of the girls asked, hugging Buddy's front end while her sister hugged the back half. Buddy's lips were pulled back into a doggy smile between licks of his tongue.

"Put the dog down and we can talk about it," Brooke told them. "The house we like has a nice, big, fenced-in area."

Cate oversaw the way the girls gently placed Buddy on the

ground, careful to see that they didn't hurt his back, and laughed when he barked for more attention. He was such a glutton.

P.J. walked up to Cate and stood nearby. Cate gave him a big hug. "How's my godson? And how are you liking college? It looks as if you could use one of Uncle Jackson's meals."

He laughed as he returned her hug. "Sounds good. And, yeah, college is great. I have two cool roommates. And the girls are cute."

"And the parties?" Cate asked, cocking an eyebrow at him.

"Don't tell Mom, but they're cool too." He cast a glance at Brooke. "Mom thinks I'm too young for all that, but what she doesn't know won't hurt her."

"Well, as your godmother I'm warning you to be careful. Alcohol and drugs can be anyone's downfall. I'm sure you know a lot more about it than I do."

His expression sobered. "It can be pretty bad."

"What are you two talking about?" asked Brooke joining them.

"College. It sounds like P.J. is doing well," said Cate. "How is it going with him so far away?"

"It's hard for me but it's all part of him growing up. Right?"

Cate nodded along with P.J. but couldn't help wondering how it would feel to have a child leave home and go off on his own.

"Okay, everyone! Come on inside. Treats await," announced Jackson.

Though dinner wasn't until four, Jackson had prepared a tray of nibbles for those who needed a little something to get them through the wait.

Cate took Amber's elbow and Brooke's arm, and together the three of them followed the others into the house.

While the men fussed and talked easily to one another in

the kitchen, and the kids played computer games in the den, Cate led Brooke and Amber to the sitting area in the master bedroom suite. She loved this spot, which overlooked the back yard and the pine trees protecting its privacy.

As Amber told Brooke about Jesse's response to her pregnancy, her voice grew wobbly. "I'm not sure how I feel about everything, but I'm going to make it work somehow."

"I'm impressed," said Brooke. "You kept telling us what a good man he was, and now, I believe it."

"I still don't know what will happen at work. If word ever gets out about us, it could be bad."

"I told Amber she should think of something different she'd like to do if she's forced out of the fashion business," said Cate. "In fact, I think you two could come up with something together. You're going to be bored after you get settled in a new place, Brooke."

Brooke and Amber studied one another.

"Do you think it could work?" Brooke asked in a hopeful voice. "I've been worried about how I'm going to fill my time."

"As I told Amber, she has good business sense, and you have a lot of artistic flair. I'm sure we can come up with a plan for the two of you to do something together," said Cate.

"What about you?" said Brooke. "It could be The Beach Babes all over again."

Cate smiled. "If writing books in a new genre doesn't do well, I'll be there. In the meantime, I'll help any way I can."

"Good," said Amber. "We'll each be thinking of different ideas." She lifted her cup of tea in a salute. "Here's to The Beach Babes!"

Cate and Brooke lifted their mugs of coffee.

"Onward and upward," cried Brooke.

They clicked mugs and cup and sat back. Together, the three of them would succeed, Cate thought with confidence.

She studied her friends, content that after a couple of harrowing months, things were going well for them.

After grace had been said, Jackson carried the platter holding the turkey into the dining room so everyone at the table could see the beautifully cooked bird. Paul rose and joined him in the kitchen to carve the bird. Cate had already done her part. Cranberry sauce, rolls and butter, water, and wine were on the table. While Paul carved, Jackson placed the stuffing, mashed potatoes, sweet potato casserole, and French green beans in the center of the table so that everyone could serve themselves.

Looking at the abundance of food, seeing her friends' happy faces, tears misted Cate's vision. What might be usual for someone else was rare and much appreciated by her. As a girl, she'd been invited to share Thanksgiving with Brooke's family, but it couldn't compare to having others in her own house. Hearing the chatter of the girls, she smiled. It was interesting to hear them talk. It was as if they knew what the other was going to say before the words were actually spoken.

The meal was as delicious as promised. Cate ate the last of her slice of pumpkin pie and promised herself to not eat quite as much next time. But she knew it pleased Jackson to see all of them enjoy his cooking.

"Who wants to go for a walk?" she said, rising.

"I do," said Brooke. "But not until I help you clean up."

"Deal," said Cate. "There are plenty of leftovers for sandwiches later on, if you choose. And plenty for tomorrow too."

"I'll help with the dishes, and then I'm going to take it easy. I need to settle my stomach," said Amber, getting to her feet with a little groan. "It's been wonderful here away from the city. I feel as if every bone in my body has turned to liquid."

Cate studied her. Amber might not be experiencing the morning sickness that some suffered, but she seemed tired all the time, and not that she'd mention it, Amber didn't have that healthy glow some women got when they were pregnant.

CHAPTER TWENTY-TWO

BROOKE

The next morning, Brooke tiptoed into the kitchen. It was early, but, as a favor to Cate, she'd agreed to make sure coffee and a few breakfast items were set out on the counter for everyone. Later, Jackson would cook a hot meal.

She startled when she saw Cate at the kitchen table, sipping coffee. "Good morning! Did you have a good sleep? I thought you'd still be in bed."

Cate smiled. "I decided to get up. My mind was spinning from all the talk we shared yesterday."

"I know what you mean. I couldn't stop thinking about the house we like. Do you mind if I turn on the news?" Brooke asked. "I didn't want to wake Paul and the girls."

"Not at all," said Cate. "Just keep it down so we don't wake Amber and Jackson upstairs. P.J. is still sleeping in the den."

Brooke turned on the television in the kitchen, keeping the volume low. "Hard to believe Christmas is coming until you see all the ads," she murmured. "Hopefully, we'll be celebrating the holidays here in New York."

"That would be nice," said Cate, smiling at her.

Brooke glanced at the television and froze. "Oh, my God!"

"What's the matter?" Cate asked, turning away from the coffee machine.

Brooke's hand shook as she pointed to the television. "Look!" The screen showed a small plane that had crashed. But it was an announcement scrolling at the bottom of the screen that had caught her attention.

"Oh, no! Turn up the volume!" said Cate, her face turning white.

"The Art and Fashion Industries are mourning the deaths of Jesse Carpenter, his wife, Simone, and their two children, Andrew and Christiana. Jesse was flying his own Cessna to Vermont for a family Thanksgiving getaway and lost control of the plane outside of Burlington. Onlookers described the plane as literally taking a nose dive, smashing nose first into a field not far from the airport. The control tower had received a report of trouble aboard the plane and stood by for a difficult landing, but the plane didn't make it that far."

Blood pounded in Brooke's ears, making her unsteady on her feet. She gripped the back of one of the kitchen table chairs for support. "Oh my God! What are we going to tell Amber?"

Cate's expression was stricken. She gazed at Brooke with tear-filled eyes. "Oh, no! It can't be true. How awful."

Brooke plopped down in a chair and held her face in her hands, attempting to catch her breath. "You know Amber. She'll think it's all her fault for being with him. We have to help her understand that it was an accident."

"Right. Her mother made it seem as if anything bad that happened to her was Amber's fault. I'd forgotten how twisted that woman was, how badly it affected Amber."

They stopped talking and turned to listen as an interview was done with the fire chief on the scene. In the background, yellow tape encircled the remains of the plane.

"We've recovered the four bodies from the plane. The FAA is sending someone to inspect and try to determine the cause of the crash."

The commentator came back on the screen. "Jesse Carpenter's work was lauded for both practical and artistic reasons. He was known to fly to Europe on a moment's notice to do a fashion shoot or to photograph a dignitary. Not long ago, his photographs were featured at one of the top galleries in New York City, and he recently published a book of them that was well received."

Brooke swayed on her feet as she and Cate exchanged looks of horror.

Amber walked into the kitchen stretching her arms. "I can't believe I slept for ten hours. It feels so good." She stopped and studied them. "What's the matter? What's wrong?"

Brooke hurried over to her and put an arm around her. "Here, hon. Come with me. Have a seat."

"Why are they showing photographs of Jesse's work?" Her voice rose. "Oh my God! What happened?" Tears welled in her eyes. "Did something happen to him?"

Cate hurried over and took hold of one of Amber's hands as she sat down. "I'm so sorry, Amber. There's been an accident. A terrible, terrible accident."

"He's dead?" cried Amber. "Oh no! Not Jesse!"

"I'm so sorry, Amber. He and his family were in the plane," said Brooke quietly. "It happened yesterday."

"No-o-o!" cried Amber. "It can't be." She gaped at the television, then broke out in heartrending sobs.

Brooke rubbed Amber's shaking shoulders. "I'm so, so sorry."

Cate squeezed Amber in a fierce hug. "We're here for you, honey."

Amber lowered her face into her hands. "Oh God! Oh God!"

Brooke searched for comforting words but could find none. "They don't know what caused the accident. They said Jesse was a good pilot."

"Yes, yes. I've flown with him in his plane," said Amber, her voice catching. "Jesse gone? No! No!" She looked up at them. "I think I'm going to be sick." The pain on her face stabbed

Brooke's heart.

Cate hurried over to the sink, wet a paper towel with cold water, and pressed it against Amber's forehead.

"I have to lie down," Amber said.

"Come, we'll help you back to your room," said Brooke gently, her own eyes filling.

Cate took one arm, Brooke the other, and they led Amber back upstairs to her room.

"Let me fix the bed for you," said Brooke, straightening the bed and turning back the cover. "There."

They helped Amber into the queen-sized bed and then sat on each side of her. Amber rolled onto her side and cried into her pillow.

After she'd calmed, Brooke said, "No matter what happens next, we'll be here for you."

"Always," added Cate.

Amber rolled over and looked up at them with a guilt-stricken expression. "Do you think he was punished for being with me? Or it's my fault that he died?"

Brooke took hold of Amber's hand. "No, Amber. It doesn't work that way. I know your mother made you believe such things happen, but this was an accident—a horrible accident that had nothing to do with you."

"Amber, you can't go down that road," said Cate, admonishing her in a gentle tone.

"His entire family gone? How awful!" Amber's lips trembled. "When I talked to him, he was excited about having all of them together for the holiday. I can't believe this has happened."

Brooke handed her the glass of water sitting on the bedside table. "Here, hon."

Amber sat up and took a sip. "I'll always remember how Jesse was about the baby. He transferred money into a special account for me." Fresh tears spilled from her eyes. "How sweet is that?"

"You've said he was a great guy," Cate said softly. "That proves it to me."

"Now, it will never happen. And that's the way it will be. I don't want anyone else to know the baby is his. What a scandal that would cause. I won't let that happen."

"You might want to change your mind later," Brooke said to her. After being in a legal battle with Paul's accuser, she knew how important it was to be honest.

"No, I won't change my mind!" snapped Amber.

"Whoa!" Brooke said. "I'm sorry. I didn't mean to upset you."

"Of course not," Cate said, easing the tension between the two of them.

"But I do want to go to the funeral," said Amber. "I owe it to him to do that."

"I'm sure they will make an announcement about that when the time comes," said Brooke. "Who do you think will make those arrangements?"

"Probably Jesse's assistant, Gayle Nickerson. I don't know of any other family member, and she'd know most of his friends and business acquaintances. She's been with him forever." Amber leaned back against her pillow. "If you two don't mind, I'd like to be alone for a while. Thank you so much for your help. I love you both."

"Sure, sweetie," said Brooke, getting to her feet. "Just give us a call if we can do anything for you, anything at all."

"Why don't I let you rest for a while," said Cate, "and then I'll bring you a cup of tea and a slice of toast. You can decide what you want to do from there. Sound good?"

Tearing up again, Amber nodded.

Outside the bedroom, Cate and Brooke exchanged worried

looks.

"There are going to be some rough days ahead," said Brooke, following Cate downstairs. "I'll help all I can, but I need to get back to California. If our offer on the house is accepted, we'll be moving in four weeks."

At the bottom of the stairs, Cate placed a hand on Brooke's shoulder. "Don't worry. I'll be here. And Amber can stay for as long as she wants."

"Thanks," said Brooke, giving her a quick hug. "You're our anchor, Cate."

Cate smiled. "The two of you are my anchors. Without our friendship, I'd be sailing in a sea of trouble. Remember, you both encouraged me to try writing."

"And it was you who urged me to marry Paul, that he was a good man. I'm so glad you did. After all we've gone through, our marriage is stronger than ever." Brooke felt her cheeks grow hot. "The kids and I love him so much."

Jackson came down the stairs. "What's up? Is something wrong? I heard Amber crying."

Cate pulled him into the kitchen. The television was still on, but had returned to regular programming. "There's been an awful accident. Jesse Carpenter, the father of Amber's baby, and his entire family were killed in a plane crash yesterday."

"Wow! That's awful!" He turned as the news of the plane crash appeared on screen again.

Paul joined them. "I heard about the crash. How's Amber?"

"Not well," said Brooke. "She's very upset. If she doesn't seem better later, we might need you to check on her. We don't want anything to happen to the baby."

"Be sure she has plenty of water," he said, "and give her bland food until her system settles."

"Where are the girls?" Brooke asked him.

“Watching television and eating the cereal that Cate and Jackson nicely provided.” He lifted a finger in warning. “Beware. They love the cabin and want one just like it.” His cell rang. “It’s the real estate agent.” He stepped outside to take the call.

“Let’s hope this works out,” said Brooke. “Amber is going to need a lot of support in the coming months, and I want to be here to help her.”

CHAPTER TWENTY-THREE

CATE

The day that had begun so horribly was tempered by the excitement of Paul and Brooke's offer being accepted. The kids were ecstatic about being close to Cate and Jackson, and with the promise of a small cabin for themselves, the girls decided living in New York was going to be even better than being in California.

While Paul and Brooke spent the morning with the real estate agent, Cate stayed close to the house as Paul had suggested. It worried her that he was so concerned about Amber, but then she was too. Amber refused to get out of bed. And the last time, Cate had checked on her, Amber admitted she was having cramps.

Paul and Brooke returned with the news that the real estate agent had agreed to leave the keys to the house that afternoon so they could do a walk-through, take measurements, and make notes of any changes they wanted to make.

"She gave me a list of home improvement contractors she recommends," said Brooke. "Better yet, she called a painter she uses and got him to agree to work on the interior of the house for us next week. I have to choose colors before I return to California."

"What about the owners? Until the closing happens, the house is technically theirs," said Jackson.

"No problem," said Paul. "Both agents are pushing for closing next week. We're renting the house from the owners to allow us to go in and begin some of the work. For the time being, all we're doing is painting interior walls, and they've agreed to that."

"You guys are moving fast, but then, if you want to be here for the holidays, you have to," said Cate.

"I want you and Amber to see the house," Brooke said to her. "Will you go with me? You're so clever with ideas of color and design, I need your opinion on a few things before the painter comes in to redo some of the walls."

Flattered, Cate readily agreed. After restoring the farmhouse for many years, she'd learned a lot about what worked and what didn't.

They went to find Amber.

She was sitting in bed staring dully at the television there. She looked up and gave them a weak smile. "Heard you got the house. Congratulations, Brooke. I'm happy for you."

"Do you feel up to going to see it? I'm giving Cate a tour of it and would love to have you join us."

Amber shook her head. "Thanks, but no thanks. I'm staying right here." Tears filled her eyes. "I started bleeding."

"Oh, no!" said Cate. "Are you having a miscarriage?"

"I don't know. I was waiting for Paul to come back. I need to ask him a few questions."

"I'll go get him," said Brooke. "But, Cate, you're going to have to stay right here. He'll insist on having someone else in the room and it can't be me."

"I understand," Cate said.

Stomach whirling, she went to the little side chair in a corner of the room and sat.

Paul entered the room with a look of concern and walked over to Amber. "How are you feeling?" he asked gently.

"I don't know," she answered. "I've been bleeding. I tried to hold my legs together to stop it, but I'm pretty sure it hasn't stopped." She looked up at him and tearfully asked. "Am I losing the baby?"

"Not necessarily. Tell me more about what's going on, giving me the details."

Wanting to give them privacy, Cate tuned out as Amber and Paul talked quietly, and then was jarred out of her stillness by Paul calling to her.

"Cate? Will you accompany Amber to the bathroom? I want you to steady her."

She jumped to her feet. "Sure."

Cate held onto Amber's arm as they made their way into the bathroom. Once Amber was seated, Cate moved away but not before realizing the pregnancy was over. Tears blurred her vision. "I'm sorry, Amber. I'm so sorry."

Amber lowered her face in her hands and sobbed. "I've made such a mess of everything. Thank God no one else knows. I'll have to keep it my secret."

Cate hugged her. The hurt of some secrets didn't ever go away.

After they returned from the hospital, they settled Amber in front of the television in the guest room, Cate stood with Brooke at her bedside.

Staring glumly at them, Amber said, "You two can't stay here and fuss over me any longer. Go! You've got your new house to look at, Brooke. Remember all the details to tell me, Cate."

"I will, hon. I'll take plenty of pictures too."

"You sure you're all right here?" asked Brooke. "I can stay if you want."

Amber waved her away. "Go. I'll be fine. There's nothing you can do for me. I'm going to take a nap."

But both Cate and Brooke knew she wasn't fine at all. The

pain in her eyes said it all.

Brooke directed Cate to Carrington, a high-end development in West Walles, New York, next to Ellenton.

Pulling up in front of a two-story, brick house with one-story, white-clapboard wings on either side, Cate studied the sprawling house with an artistic eye. The two-story white pillars that flanked the front entry suited the almost-Southern style of the house and balanced the wings.

She got out of the car and stood a moment to gaze at the landscaping. The leaves had fallen, leaving tree branches bare, but she could see how they and a variety of bushes added to the elegance of the house. In the spring, it would look amazing. Dogwood and flowering fruit trees were interspersed with several evergreen trees.

"Wait until you see the inside," gushed Brooke. "You're going to love it. It needs a little freshening, but that's all. I don't think the owners spent much time here at all."

As Cate stepped inside the house, she was met with a view from the entry hall to the living room and beyond it through sliding-glass doors to the outside, where she observed an in-ground swimming pool covered for the winter months.

"Lovely," Cate murmured, eagerly following Brooke for a look outside.

Afterwards, Brooke led her through the rest of the downstairs, past a sizeable dining room that opened into a modern, upscale kitchen Cate knew Jackson would love to have for his own. A huge master suite dominated the wing on that side of the house. The other wing housed a library/den, a small workout room, a home theater, where the previous family must have viewed movies, and a full bath that led to the outside pool area.

"Come on upstairs. There are five bedrooms and three baths there. I figured I'd better have a room for my mother." Brooke made a face. "She's already informed me she needs to be able to see her granddaughters whenever she wants."

"Sounds like her," Cate said. "She's going to be impressed. The house is gorgeous."

"We're getting it for a good price because the owners are anxious to sell. They've already moved to Florida." A flush of happiness spread across Brooke's face. She had a lot of money at her disposal but was careful with it.

"Okay, let's go through the rooms one by one, and we'll talk about colors and whatever else you want," said Cate. "It's something I love to do."

"Thanks. I can't wait to hear your opinions."

Jackson approached them. "Paul and I are going to cruise around the area to get a better sense of what he might need to know. We'll take the girls with us. I know you're going to be a while longer."

"Thanks," Cate said, glancing at her watch. "We'll check on Amber, but when you get home, please make sure she's okay."

"All right. Will do," he said, giving her a small wave before he left them.

Cate followed Brooke from one room to another, discussing colors and what furniture Brooke would bring with her. They decided on the palest of grays for the living room and dining room. In the master bedroom, Brooke wanted a lemony yellow to match what she had in California. The audio/visual room would be done in a dark-gray similar to what was there already.

Upstairs, selections for the bedrooms went quickly. The connecting rooms for the girls would be painted in a matching shade of purple, P.J.'s room a warm beige, the guest room a soft peach, and for her mother's suite they chose a deep rose.

"Thanks, Cate," said Brooke as they headed back to the car. "Now, let's see to Amber."

"I'm going to encourage her to stay with me for a while." Cate couldn't imagine the physical and emotional pain Amber was experiencing.

Brooke shook her head sadly. "I wish I could stay too, but I trust you to watch out for her."

"I will," Cate said, hurting for Amber. It would not be good for her to be alone.

Back at the house, all was quiet. The men were outside on the patio having a beer when Cate found them.

"Hi! Where are Amber and the kids?" she asked them.

"The kids are in the cabin, and Amber is napping upstairs," said Jackson. "Come sit outside with us."

"Let me check on the kids first," said Brooke. "Then I want to hear about the things you showed Paul."

"I'll check on Amber," Cate said, and hurried upstairs.

Opening the door to Amber's room as quietly as she could, Cate stuck her head inside.

Amber gazed up at her. "Come on in. I can't sleep."

Cate went into the room and sat on the edge of the bed. "How are you doing? Is there anything I can do to help you?"

Amber shook her head. "I just need to get through the next several weeks."

"After Brooke and her family leave, why don't you consider staying here for at least the next week? I can help you make an appointment with my doctor to check you out. Even after that, you could move into the cabin. It might be easier to come home to us than to an empty condo in the weeks ahead."

Tears welled in Amber's eyes. "Thanks. I'll stay for the next week and then I'll need to go on as usual so no one suspects what part Jesse played in my life. Because of Belinda, we were discreet about meeting outside of work. But if she ever finds out, she'll fire me for sure."

"Okay, but sometimes the things we try to hide are the very things that need to be out in the open. But, in this case, I agree with you. The fewer people who know about you and Jesse, the better."

She sat up and dabbed at her eyes with a tissue. "How's Brooke's new house? Fantastic, I imagine."

"It's a wonderful house. I'm thrilled she'll be close to us. When I arranged the weekend in Florida, I had no idea with all the changes in our lives, The Beach Babes would be back in action."

Amber smiled at Cate's attempt at humor. "Well, I guess this Beach Babe better join you. I can't change what has happened by lying here."

"The weather is so nice that we're sitting out on the patio. Join us when you're ready." Cate hugged her and got to her feet, glad to see that Amber was doing better.

When Amber joined them, the men stood and waited while she sat down between Cate and Brooke.

"They've just announced that Jesse's funeral and that of the family will be private, but friends and family are invited to a memorial gathering at his penthouse next Friday. Gayle Nickerson, Jesse's assistant, is making the arrangements," said Brooke. "Do you know her?"

"Oh, yes," Amber said. "We worked together on the perfume ads. I want to go to the memorial gathering." She turned to Cate. "Will you go with me?" Amber's eyes turned liquid.

"Of course," Cate answered, patting Amber's shoulder. "I'll

stay right by your side."

"I'd come with you, if I could," Brooke assured Amber. "As it is, I'm going to fly home tomorrow after Cate and I pick out the paint swatches for the painter. Paul and the kids will fly home Monday as scheduled."

"I'm happy you'll be so much closer," Amber said.

"Cate told me you're invited to stay here for as long as you wish."

"I've agreed to stay for the next week. Next Friday, I'll go to my condo to prepare for the following week of work. Belinda should be back by then." Amber sighed. "Thank God she decided to go away for a long holiday."

"As I said earlier, if you find you need company after you're back in your condo, you're welcome to come back here," added Cate.

"And we'll have plenty of room at our house," said Brooke. "I can't wait for you to see it."

"Thanks. All of you may be sick of me in the days ahead."

"No way," said Cate.

Brooke bobbed her head. "That's right."

They looked up as Brynn and Bradley raced over to them.

Brynn handed a sheet of paper to Amber. "This is for you."

"We made it especially for you," Bradley said, standing before Amber, moving restlessly.

Amber studied it and smiled at the girls. "Thank you. That's so sweet."

"You're welcome," said Brynn.

"We love you, Auntie Amber," Bradley added.

They took off for the cabin, running side by side in perfect step.

Amber held up the paper on which a giant red heart had been drawn. "It says, 'We're sorry you're sad, Auntie Amber. This heart is to carry with you so you won't feel so bad. Love,

Bradley, Brynn, P.J., Mom, Dad, Auntie Cate, and Uncle Jackson.'"

In the silence that followed, more than one eye watered. Cate gazed at her dearest friends. This, she thought, is my family. She glanced at Jackson, wondering whether they'd be able to add to it.

CHAPTER TWENTY-FOUR

AMBER

After Brooke and her family left, the house seemed quiet. Amber did her best to help Cate clean up. The cabin had proved to be a perfect place to host guests. The kids had loved it, and the space had provided both them and their parents privacy.

In the days that followed, while Jackson was at school and Cate worked in her office, Amber napped and took short walks in the neighborhood, building her strength and trying to come to terms with what had happened.

Cate took her to her doctor to be checked out, and both were pleased to learn that Amber was in good shape, not requiring any surgery.

"He told me I could have other children," Amber said in the car ride back to Cate's house. "Can you imagine?"

Cate shrugged. "I know it doesn't seem possible now, but maybe in the future ..."

"Don't even go there," Amber said, fighting tears. It would take a lot for her to build trust with another man. And children? That was another matter entirely.

On Friday, Amber drove Cate into the city to attend the celebration of life for Jesse and his family. They parked her car at her condo, and took a taxi to Jesse's home.

Cate gave her hand an encouraging squeeze as they walked inside a building not far from the Museum of Modern Art.

"I'll get through this," Amber said softly, though she was struggling with memories of being with Jesse and the guilt she couldn't quite drive away.

Standing in the elevator rising to the top floor and Jesse's penthouse, Amber wondered who would be attending the affair. She liked the idea of a celebration, not a grim affair for a man who'd seemed so alive with his art.

Next to her, Cate remained somber. Amber appreciated how hard Cate had worked all week to try and keep her spirits up.

The other people in the elevator eyed them curiously, no doubt wondering what they had to do with Jesse and his family. Amber did her best to ignore them, as Cate seemed to be doing.

When the elevator doors opened, Amber followed Cate into a vestibule outside of wide double doors that had been propped open.

They walked past a bench and large, potted plants on either side of the doors into a large living room filled with people standing around with drinks in their hands, talking to one another.

Maids passed trays of appetizers among them.

"It's a real party," Cate murmured to Amber.

She gave Cate a little smile. "He would love it. Such an open, generous man. No wonder he had so many friends."

Amber looked over to find Belinda Galvin marching toward them with a scowl. Her body tensed.

Cate reached for Amber's elbow to steady her.

"Hello, Amber. What in the world are you doing here?" Belinda said to her. "This celebration is only for family and Jesse's dear friends. I don't believe you would be invited."

Amber studied the woman known for terrorizing staff and co-workers. Tall and bone thin, Belinda wore her silver-gray hair pulled away from her face and tied behind her head, giving her a severe look. Her face, carefully shaped by plastic surgery, was more handsome than beautiful. But it was Belinda's eyes that caught her attention. They were a steel-gray and held no warmth. Amber doubted they ever had.

"Jesse and I worked well together," said Amber in a cold tone that belied any sign of fear. "I've come to pay my respects just as Gayle Nickerson asked."

Belinda placed her hands on her hips and studied Amber. "Why would Jesse's assistant ask you to be here?"

"Probably because she knew Jesse and I were actually friends," Amber said. She felt the anger that ripped through her.

Cate glanced at Amber and then said to Belinda, "What are *you* doing here? You're simply someone he sometimes worked for. Right?"

Belinda straightened, becoming even taller, more formidable. Her eyes bore into Cate's. "*Who* are *you*?"

Amber silently applauded as she observed Cate straightening, remaining calm in the face of such haughtiness. Before she could answer, a woman rushed up to her. "Catherine Tibbs? I loved your last book, and I can't wait to read the next one."

Amber smiled gratefully at the person who'd interrupted what might have become an ugly confrontation. "Excuse me, Cate. I'm going to find Gayle."

Cate nodded and then ignoring Belinda, turned back to her admirer.

Left on her own, Belinda walked away.

Amber made her way past people she recognized as being well-known in the arts world and noted a photograph of Jesse with his wife and children prominently displayed on a side table. Such a shame, Amber thought, fighting the nausea that had plagued her all week long at the horror of it. A whole family gone.

A tall, handsome, gray-haired gentleman smiled at her, his blue eyes lighting. "Amber?"

Amber paused. "Yes?"

"Hello, I'm Wynton Burr, a friend of Jesse's."

"Oh, yes. Nice to see you again."

They were still making small talk when Cate approached them.

Amber made the introductions and then Wynton left them to greet someone else.

"Wow! He's impressive," said Cate.

"He's a lawyer who commissioned Jesse to do a portrait of his daughter. I met him at a party I once attended."

"Are you ready to go home?" Cate asked.

"Yes, suddenly I'm exhausted. It will be good to have the weekend ahead of me to get accustomed to my city life again." She glanced around the room. "Gayle's busy speaking to others. I'll call her later. Let's ease our way out of here so we don't run into Belinda."

"She's such a nasty woman. I don't know how you can stand to work for her."

"It may not be for too long," Amber said, patting her stomach. "She's still under the illusion that she and Jesse had something special, when I know very well that they didn't."

They managed to reach the entrance before Belinda caught sight of them. "Don't forget to come in early on Monday, Amber. You're going to be busy." She turned to a couple at her side and said in a loud enough voice for several people to hear, "Amber's my assistant. That's why she's been allowed to attend."

"I'm your assistant and a friend of Jesse's," said Amber with cold, crisp words, frustration welling inside her, making her dangerously close to crying.

Cate took hold of Amber's arm and led her away.

In the privacy of the elevator, Amber glanced at her reflection in the mirrored side panel, studied the frightening image of the anger on her face, and crumpled.

CHAPTER TWENTY-FIVE

CATE

On the train ride back to Ellenton, Cate stared out the window at the passing scenery, lost in thought. The way she saw it, Amber was caught in a horrible circumstance. Though she loved being in the city and in the fashion industry, Amber wouldn't be able to stay at her job with that vicious boss of hers if it were ever found out about her relationship with Jesse. Amber had previously told her how competitive everyone was. Thank goodness, Amber had never been caught up in any drug scenes, like some in the business.

Cate remembered her first experience with marijuana. One Saturday night, Amber had called Cate and Brooke and asked them to meet her at the house. She and her mother had just had a fight over one of her mother's boyfriends staying over. Now, with her mother out for the evening, Amber was more than ready to do anything to get back at her.

It was a grim group that night. Cate was appalled by the mess and the air of negativity inside the house and couldn't wait to leave.

Brooke was depressed. A rash of pimples had broken out on her face. She tearfully announced she was ready to give up the fight of trying to look pretty to please her mother. It was an ongoing battle, one that she couldn't win. They all knew it.

After several sessions of marijuana, Amber had brought out gin and vodka, her mother's choices of booze. A bad decision. Amber became violent, smashing plates and glasses in the kitchen sink, railing against her life. Brooke had sobbed uncontrollably before grabbing a knife and threatening to kill herself. Cate became sick as a dog, throwing up and retching for hours.

It had been a wake-up call for Cate. She had no problem following her mother's rules about either drugs or alcohol. Even in college, she'd been teased for being such a "goody two-shoes." While it bothered her to be called names, Cate wasn't about to have more than a casual drink or two. Even now, she was careful.

The train pulled into the station. Pushing the past away, Cate got out and headed to the parking lot. She'd parked her SUV there before climbing into Amber's car to go into the city.

On her way home, she stopped at Brooke's new house to check on the painter. She'd been doing so every day as Brooke requested. She knew from past experience with the renovations on her own house that it was best to show up unexpectedly.

She walked inside the house and stood a moment in the foyer, gazing up at the winding stairway. It seemed so right that Brooke would be living in such an elegant home.

Cate went into the master bedroom and was pleased to see the work was almost done. The yellow paint on the walls was perfect, giving the room a pleasant glow that would make wintry days seem brighter. Cate took photos of the room to send to Brooke. Paul would see it himself this evening when he came to stay at Cate's house for the next few nights. He wanted to be close by to make sure other, smaller projects were done on the house before flying out to California to help with that end of the move. The way things were going, The Beach Babes would celebrate Christmas together. Cate could hardly wait.

At home, Cate decided not to wait a moment longer to

decorate. She went into the attic and found the box of Christmas ornaments she brought out every year. She was in the kitchen sifting through the decorations when Jackson arrived home.

"Hi, sweetie? How are you?"

"Okay, I guess." Jackson set down a stack of papers and a notebook on the kitchen table. "My mother called and asked if we'd come to North Carolina for the holidays. I told her no, but she's dying to talk to you about wedding plans and the engagement party she wants to throw for us." He gave her a worried look. "I told her we'd go there for Valentine's Day so she could throw the party for us then. Okay?"

Cate paused. "Sure. We'll make it work. But, Jackson, I don't want a big wedding. If we don't stand firm on that, it's going to be a disaster."

"That's what I told her. My parents love you and want the best for you. They think because you don't have family of your own, they should make it nice for you."

"I don't want any conflict with them. They've always treated me well." She shook her head. "It's so ironic—the difference between my family and yours."

Jackson grinned and tugged her into his arms. "And how about me? Where do I fit into the picture?"

She chuckled. "Well ... Prince Charming comes to mind."

"That's my girl," Jackson said before lowering his lips to hers. In his embrace, Cate let her worries go. His parents weren't being unreasonable, just enthusiastic.

Just as Buddy began to bark for attention, Cate's cell phone rang. *Brooke.*

"Hey there! Did you get the pictures I texted you?" Cate asked, still heated from Jackson's kiss.

"Yes. They're lovely. Thanks. I appreciate all you're doing for me. I'm trying to reach Paul. Is he there?"

Cate's stomach twisted. There was something about the tone of Brooke's voice that spelled trouble. "I don't expect him until later. Why? What's up?"

"We got an offer on the house," Brooke replied.

"But?"

"But it's very low. Word has spread that we're desperate to escape the truth about Paul and will sell at any price." There was a moment of silence and then Brooke added, "Why are people so vicious? Isn't it enough that Paul's reputation has been ruined by lies?"

"I'm so sorry to hear this. Is there anything your real estate agent can do about this?"

"She's having an open house tomorrow. Even though I'm in the middle of sorting and packing, she says it's important. She told me she'll clear things up with other agents and buyers then. Speaking of that, I'd better go. Who knew we'd accumulate so much stuff?"

"It's a big house," Cate reminded her.

"I swear it seems to grow as I sleep," said Brooke. "Can't wait until the moving people come. They'll do the heavy packing. Until then, I'm uncovering all kinds of treasures from the last fifteen years."

"Could be fun," said Cate, half-teasing.

"I have to admit, seeing the baby equipment stored away had me briefly thinking of trying for another baby."

"Wouldn't it be fun if we were pregnant at the same time?" Cate said.

Brooke laughed. "That's the last thing I need right now. I'll spoil any baby of yours instead. No news yet?"

"Not yet. I'm keeping my fingers crossed," said Cate, rubbing her stomach.

CHAPTER TWENTY-SIX

BROOKE

Brooke hung up the phone, still thinking about her remark to Cate. Did she want another baby? She looked at the mess around her and shook her head. What she really wanted was a life of her own. Not as Paul's wife, or the twins' mother, or the mother of a young man in his first year of college. She needed to be Brooke Ridley Weston, artist, or Brooke Ridley Weston, entrepreneur. She was a creative person who'd lost herself. Amber had referred to it as being sucked dry by her family but Brooke didn't feel that way. She loved her family. But maybe it was time to love herself a little more.

On cue, her mother called. "Hi, Brooke. Today at lunch with friends, I heard the most horrible thing."

Brooke sighed. She knew a zinger was coming. "And what that might be, Mother?"

"I heard that you and Paul are all but dumping your house in an effort to get away. You know better than that, Brooke. The house is in a prime area and is worth a lot of money."

"Mother, you can't believe everything you hear. You're going to have to trust Paul and me on this. Besides, what we do is not your business."

"Well! I guess I caught you at a bad time. Don't get overtired, darling. When you get stressed, you tend to eat."

Brooke clicked off the call and sat with her head in her hands. To her mother's friends, Diana Ridley was kind and thoughtful. But whenever she dealt with Brooke, her mother couldn't control an undercurrent of thoughtlessness that hurt.

The twins entered the house, their chattering voices a welcome difference. Brooke got to her feet to greet them. Being home for them was a decision that both she and Paul had agreed to, but with the move to New York, they'd be gone even longer each day and she'd be left with nothing to do without her usual volunteer and civic activities in California. Another reason to change her life.

"What's up, girls?" Brooke asked cheerfully and then noticed their drawn faces.

"Kids are saying bad things about Dad," said Brynn.

"You, too," Bradly added. "They're saying we're running away because Dad did something awful."

"I'm sorry to hear that," Brooke said, working to control the frustration that wanted to leak out of her in a burst of anger. She put her arms around the girls. "Those are rumors. Sometimes you have to let those things go. Rumors are not true but are often spread out of boredom by ignorant people who don't know the facts. We're not running away, but rather moving to be with Dad at his new job. That's a big difference and one you don't need to be ashamed of."

"That's what I told Kendall, but she said her mother was talking to a friend, and she heard it." Brynn's eyes filled with tears. "I hate her."

Brooke cupped Brynn's cheek and studied her. "I don't want you to hate anyone. Her mother obviously doesn't know all the facts."

"But, Mom, Kendall doesn't care. She's telling everyone to stay away from us." Brynn's chin trembled.

Swallowing hard, Brooke looked at her daughters and wished she could wash the pain away from their sweet faces. "You have only one more week of school here in California, and then we'll be on our way. Kendall wasn't a close friend. If you're lucky, your true friends will stand by you. Like Auntie Amber and Auntie Cate have done for me."

"I love them, Mom. They're the best aunties in the world," Brynn said with passion.

"Me, too," said Bradley. "What's for snack time? We're hungry."

Brooke let out a sigh of relief. Her girls would be all right. They'd stick by each other.

As she went about preparing a snack for them, Brooke fought the temptation to call Kendall's mother, then realized it would only make matters worse.

By the time Paul phoned, she'd moved on to other issues related to their move. The real estate agent was holding an open house in the morning for other agents in the area, enticing them to attend by offering a catered lunch.

CHAPTER TWENTY-SEVEN

AMBER

As Amber dressed for her first day back at work in over a week, she told herself to let go of her anger. She couldn't afford to mess up her life any more than it already was. The fact that Belinda was able to push all her emotional buttons was worrisome. She had to keep her job for the time being. She'd already looked at other opportunities in the fashion business, and she hadn't found anything of interest in either opportunity or pay.

As she'd been trained to do, Amber did a final inspection of herself in the mirror to make sure her appearance was as perfect as possible. She'd once loved the idea of being dressed in the latest, most becoming styles acquired through her connections. Now, she longed to go back to bed and forget all the things that had happened. In the corner of her mind was the question—what if Jesse and the baby had lived?

Amber straightened the collar of her sapphire-blue silk shirt and slid on the jacket of the black wool suit she'd chosen to wear, hoping the sadness that still caught her breath every now and then would remain hidden. Taking a deep breath, she entered the bustle of activity on the streets of the city.

Twenty minutes later, she opened the door to the offices of The Galvin Agency and stepped into the quiet of the early morning hours. In thirty minutes, the place would come alive with noise and activity. Right now, the office was hers.

She hurried to her desk to check for messages for herself and Belinda, took care of them, and went into Belinda's private office to start setting up the tea service for her. It had to be done a certain way, of course. Just one of the things that could make the difference between a rough start or one even worse.

Satisfied that the task was done properly, Amber went back to her private office just outside of Belinda's.

Jodie Pearson, the receptionist, appeared, and the day began.

Amber was on the phone when Belinda entered the office. Signaling Amber to join her, she marched past Amber's desk and into her office, shutting the door behind her with a resounding bang.

Amber's stomach clenched at the thought of the day ahead. She finished her phone call and, sighing heavily, rose to tend to Belinda.

She knocked on the door and opened it.

Belinda was standing by the tea service, filling a fragile tea cup. "I couldn't wait for you to fix it for me. It's one of those mornings you wish you'd never awakened."

Amber's mouth turned dry as she stood by, waiting for Belinda to offer her a seat.

Belinda waved her to one of the upholstered chairs in front of her desk and sat behind it.

"I've been thinking about this all weekend and need to warn you that I came this close to firing you." Belinda held up a manicured hand, first finger to thumb, red polish on her nails gleaming dangerously.

Amber remained quiet. No way was she going to ask why. *Let the bitch tell me.*

Belinda's cold eyes assessed her. "You had no business being at the reception for Jesse on Friday. You work for me; you are not friends with my clients. Understand?"

Amber forced herself to remain quiet.

"If you cannot keep your place, you'll have to leave the business," Belinda continued, waving her away. "You may go now."

Amber rose to leave.

"By the way, Amber, you're looking heavy in that outfit. I'd be careful if I were you. Clothes like that are available to you through me. Remember that."

"Is that all?" Amber asked, pausing on her way out.

"Isn't that enough?" Belinda shook her head. "Yes, indeed, you're becoming fat."

The temper that Amber had fought all weekend rushed to the surface too wild to control. "And you're looking ... gaunt."

Belinda's eyes widened with surprise, then narrowed.

Amber braced herself to be fired.

Suddenly, Belinda laughed. "Ah, yes! My minion. Okay, go now, before I lose my temper."

Amber hurried out of the office grateful she'd caught Belinda off guard. Later, Belinda might get back at her, but then she probably thought being gaunt was just fine.

CHAPTER TWENTY-EIGHT

CATE

Sensing something was wrong, Cate opened her eyes and stared at the early dawn light seeping into her bedroom through the half-open blinds. The quiet outside lured Cate to the window. She peered out to the white-covered lawn and the pine trees whose boughs were iced with snow. She paused, wondering what had awakened her and felt a pain ripple across her abdomen.

She gripped the window sill and blinked back tears. *Her period.*

Moving quietly so as not to awaken Jackson, she crossed the carpet to the bathroom and closed the door behind her.

When she checked, she saw the evidence and sighed. Even though she knew it might take a few months for her uterus to adjust to having had the IUD removed, she'd foolishly hoped to get pregnant right away.

She took care of the problem and crawled back into bed with Jackson.

He turned to her and asked sleepily, "Everything all right?"

"I got my period. No baby."

He pulled her close. "It's early yet. Don't be discouraged."

She nestled up against him, finding comfort in his arms. In the morning, things would seem better. But at the moment, she couldn't help thinking of Brooke and all the times she'd tried for a baby after P.J.'s birth. It had been a terrible time for her. And Amber had gotten pregnant when she didn't want to and had gone on to lose the baby. Cate prayed she wouldn't have to go through that awful experience.

Later, when Jackson's alarm went off, Cate slid out of bed and wrapped her warm, fuzzy robe around her and slid into her Ugg boots. "Come on, Buddy. Time to get up."

From beneath his blanket on top of the bed, he peered at her and burrowed into the quilt, dismissing her.

Chuckling, she drew him out and held him in her arms. Winter mornings like this usually made Buddy grumpy. She couldn't blame him. With his little, short legs, winter snows froze his underbelly. Not pleasant.

She carried him downstairs and put him outside on the back deck. He looked up at her with such a disgruntled expression, she laughed. "Hurry! Do your business and we'll go right back inside the house."

As Buddy trotted away, Cate studied the scene around her. Normally, she didn't like snow, but on this morning the sun was rising in a pink sky, changing the pristine white snow around her into something that looked like pink icing coating the trees and bushes nearby. Captivated by the beauty, she clasped her hands. Descriptive words flowed in her mind and she tucked them away for future use in a book.

Buddy's bark caught her attention, and the magic disappeared.

Inside, Cate turned on the coffee maker and set the table. Jackson's usual breakfast consisted of a glass of juice, a bowl of granola with fruit, a cup of coffee, and little conversation. Evenings and daytime chats made up for that lack. Paul had told her not to fuss, but she cut up extra fruit and set out yogurt in case he wanted some.

When the coffee was ready, Cate poured herself a cup and sat at the kitchen table. Today she had to get back to work on her book. She'd wasted too much time between Thanksgiving and all the trauma afterward with Amber and helping Brooke out with the house.

"Morning," said Jackson, sitting down at the kitchen table. He studied her for a moment. "How are you feeling? I don't want you to get discouraged. We've only begun."

She smiled at his attempt to cheer her. "I realize we should just continue as we are without even thinking about it or we'll start a roller coaster ride like Brooke and Paul experienced."

His expression serious now, he nodded. "Agreed."

Paul joined them. "Good morning. Thanks for having me stay the night. Brooke and I appreciate it."

"No problem," said Cate sincerely. "You're family. Sure you don't want to spend another night?"

He shook his head. "No, I promised Brooke I'd go home. Things are tense there with neighbors and friends of the girls." He sighed. "It's sometimes hard for me to believe all that's happened."

"I'm sorry you've all had to go through this. But it's almost over. In another week, you'll be on your way here to stay."

"It can't happen soon enough," said Paul.

"Help yourself to breakfast. If you need anything else, just ask," said Cate. "I hope you gentlemen don't mind, but I'm going into the office. Have a good day."

Buddy followed her and settled on his soft blanket beneath her desk, tugging at the corner of it until he'd covered himself.

Jackson knocked and entered. "See you tonight. Call me if you need me to bring home anything. I'm dropping Paul off at the train station." He kissed her, and left.

She got up to say goodbye to Paul. He was putting his coat on as she approached. "Safe travels," she said before giving him a quick peck on the cheek. "See you soon."

"Thanks again. I'm sure Brooke will be in touch to let you

know how things are going."

"I'm sure she will," Cate said. They looked at one another and chuckled. Brooke might be three thousand miles away, but she was definitely in charge of the new house.

Sometime that afternoon, restless, Cate got up and went into the kitchen to fix herself a cup of hot tea. Writing had become frustrating, mostly because of the sense of failure she felt personally. She went from thinking getting pregnant would happen so fast she wouldn't be able to finish the book to thinking it wouldn't happen. No matter how much she tried to be patient, she worried. She sighed, wondering if this was how it was going to be for the foreseeable future as her emotions took her on a roller-coaster ride.

Waiting for the water to boil for her tea, Cate studied the photograph Brooke had sent after their trip to Florida. In the picture, they'd tried to recreate the original Beach Babes shot of them at thirteen. The three of them sat on the sand, smiling at the kind stranger who'd agreed to snap the photograph. *Not bad for close to forty*, she thought, looking at her two friends. Studying them, no one would guess all the troubles they were experiencing. As for herself, she no longer had that self-contained shyness but looked genuinely happy with a bright-eyed smile. That, she knew, was, in part, because of the decision she and Jackson had made.

CHAPTER TWENTY-NINE

AMBER

Amber was in the middle of checking over a weekly schedule of models' activities when a delivery man approached her desk. He held up a large, flat, square package wrapped in brown paper. "Receptionist told me I'd find you back here. This is a special delivery for you from Gayle Nickerson. She said for me to hand it to you personally."

"For me? Thanks." Amber accepted the package from him and laid it across her desk. "Hold on. Let me give you a tip."

He held up his hand. "No, that's already been taken care of." He turned to go.

"Wait! Any idea what it is?"

He shook his head. "I was just told it was something special, to handle it with care, and to deliver it to you personally."

As he walked away, Amber tore the paper off and stared at the smiling image of herself, inside a silver-tone, metal frame. Goosepimples raced up and down her spine. She remembered the exact moment Jesse took that photograph. They'd been shooting the perfume commercial in the islands, and she'd taken a break from the sun beneath a palm tree. Clad in a light, filmy, white sundress, she looked up at him as he called her name. They'd made love the night before, and she knew then what she felt for him was deeper than she'd felt for a man before. She trusted him enough to acknowledge her feelings to herself.

"What's this?" asked Belinda, coming out of her office.

"It's a photograph from the last perfume shoot," Amber said, studying the picture, hoping no one else could see what she'd been unable to hide.

Belinda stood quietly, focusing on the photograph. The harsh lines of her face froze. "My God! You and Jesse? How could you?"

"What do you mean?" Amber said, forcing herself to speak calmly though her heart had begun to pound so hard she felt dizzy.

"Any fool can see the way you're looking at him, the sensitive way he caught you, the look he must be giving you." Her normally pale face flushed bright pink. "You betrayed me. You knew how I felt about him, Amber! You bitch! You're fired! Get your things, including this godawful photograph, out of here!"

Her need to protect herself reared inside her. "On what grounds are you firing me? Jealousy?"

The flash of Belinda's hand was the only warning that Amber needed to move.

She grabbed Belinda's wrist to prevent the blow. "Oh, no, you don't. You're not hitting me. Understand?" Staring at the woman who'd made her life miserable for so long, anger such as Amber hadn't allowed herself for years, spilled out of her. "You are a detestable person who wouldn't ever deserve anyone as kind, as sweet as Jesse. It's no wonder he broke things off with you."

Belinda's eyes widened. She tugged her wrist free. "Get out of here," she screamed, causing people to rush into the office and gather around them.

Seeing them, Belinda said, "What do you people want? This is none of your business."

Forcing herself not to run, Amber picked up the framed photograph, grabbed her purse, and on shaking knees walked away with as much dignity as she could muster. She needed to put space between Belinda and her before she gave in to temptation and ripped the hair out of Belinda's head.

Back in her condo, Amber studied the photograph. At the memory of that time in the islands, tears filled her eyes. Making love with Jesse had been such an awakening for her. She studied Jesse's signature and noticed the letter "L" he'd written discreetly above his name. The tears that had blurred her vision spilled down her cheeks. He had loved her, though not in the way she'd hoped.

The doorbell rang. Pulling herself together, she went to the door and after checking the peephole, opened it. Jodie Pearson, the receptionist from the office, stood there with a large cardboard box in her hands. Amber shook her head. Belinda had wasted no time clearing her desk.

"Come on in." She helped Jodie with the box and together, they set it down on the entrance floor.

"I'm sorry about what happened," said Jodie. "Belinda is still in a rage. Everyone, including me, is staying out of her way. She had me gather all your personal items. I think they're all here."

"There wasn't much. Another of Belinda's rules. She was pretty used to firing people before I came."

"I don't know what's going to happen at the office. You practically ran the show while she took all the credit. What are you going to do now?"

Amber's smile was genuine. "I'm going to take some time off and spend the holiday with friends."

"Sounds good," said Jodie. "I wish you all the luck in the world. If I could, I'd leave too, but the job pays well. So, I guess I'll stick it out, though the next few weeks will probably be a bit ugly. I've never seen Belinda so upset."

"Would you like to stay for a cup of coffee or a glass of wine?" Amber asked, relieved she wouldn't have to deal with Belinda's anger.

Jodie's face brightened. "Thanks, but I'd better be on my way. I have to report back to the office."

"Okay. Take care, Jodie. If I ever need a receptionist, I'll call you."

Jodie gave her a thumbs up. "I'd be there in a heartbeat. You're the best."

Smiling, Amber showed Jodie out and stood in the doorway wondering what would happen next.

Alone, Amber sifted through the belongings Jodie had packed up for her. As she'd said to Jodie, she'd kept few items of any personal nature in the office. She'd had the awful feeling that Belinda would check them out. The one picture she'd allowed on her desk was of The Beach Babes back when they were thirteen. It had been returned, along with lipstick, hand lotion, and sunscreen. Belinda could keep the plant she'd been given for her birthday, along with the silk flower arrangement she'd bought on her own. She didn't want them here in the condo. They'd remind her too much of her negative experiences at the office.

She wasn't the least bit concerned about any information stored on her computer at work. Aware of the kind of person Belinda was, she'd kept her private business on her personal computer.

Amber felt a wave of sadness. Three years of hard work and difficult times had been reduced to a cardboard box holding a few items and the memories she' had. Needing a comforting word, she picked up her phone and called Cate.

At Cate's bright "Hi, beautiful!" gratitude filled Amber. Her friends were so important to her, more like the family she'd never had. "What's going on?"

Amber gave Cate the details of her morning.

"Sounds like a typical Belinda move to fire you like that. Especially because of the picture. That photograph must be something."

"Yes," Amber said simply, taking a moment to rein in her emotions. "He loved me, as much as he could," she finally said. "It's so clear."

"I'm pleased that you know that now, though it must make things both easier and harder on you."

Amber thought of the times she'd shared with Jesse and the loss of their baby and remained quiet.

"Would you like to leave the city now and come up for a visit?" Cate gently asked.

"Thanks, but I think I'll stay here for a day or two. Hide out. Then I'd love to come earlier than we'd planned for the holidays. I'll help Brooke with her move. That should keep me busy."

"And you can help me decorate the house for her as a surprise," said Cate. "In the meantime, Amber, this might be a blessing in disguise. You've been at that woman's mercy for years. Maybe it's your time to fly, do something on your own. Like we tell Brooke about her painting, take time to enjoy your life to the fullest. Can't wait to see you so I can give you a big, big hug. Love you."

"Love you, too," said Amber, clicking off the call. She'd needed that kind of pep talk. It had already set her mind spinning.

As she studied the box, a new determination filled Amber. She knew enough about the business to be able to set up her own. Why not? While Belinda claimed all the credit for her success, Amber had done a huge part of the work. She'd listened, she'd learned, and she'd been the conduit through which people reached Belinda. All good experience.

If she remembered correctly, Belinda had not made her sign a non-competition agreement because at the time she was hired, Belinda hadn't believed Amber would be able to stick with the job. She'd hired her anyway because Amber had persisted. Belinda had been that vain, that sure.

If she decided to go into business it would be a very different operation from Belinda's. Amber's lips curved. Maybe being fired was just what she needed. She'd have to wait and see.

CHAPTER THIRTY

CATE

After Cate disconnected the call with Amber, she sat for a moment thinking of her friend. As happened so often, life was bittersweet. She was sorry Amber had lost her job but pleased that Jesse had not only set up an account for her but had planned a special gift for her before he died. After losing the baby and while coping with that loss, Amber needed the reassurance that their union had been more than a fling. She knew Amber well enough to understand her natural resilience would carry her through, but she deserved more. Good God, she'd even suffered sexual abuse and kept silent about it for years, acting as if it hadn't happened. Of the three of them, Amber appeared the toughest, but she actually was the most vulnerable.

Cate was pleased Amber would help her decorate Brooke's house for the holidays. It would be good to spend some time together. Brooke, Paul, and the girls would fly in on December 19th, and, P.J., Brooke's mother, and the moving van were scheduled to arrive a day later. Having a Christmas tree and a few other decorations already set up in the house would add to their excitement and eliminate that concern while trying to unpack and get settled. Some new furniture had already been delivered.

She sat back in her desk chair pondering what to write next. As she struggled through the last book of the Galeon Wars series, her mind kept flitting to the contemporary romance that was building inside her thoughts. Could she do it?

Become the author of a whole different kind of book?

Buddy barked and ran to greet Jackson. The winter break had just started, and he'd have two whole weeks off from school. Both of them were delighted he wouldn't have to rise so early on these cold mornings.

"Hi, Hon! How's the writing going?"

Cate sighed. "It's not. Ever since I've been told this will be the last book in the series, my mind has stalled. Nothing like being rejected before you even get it finished."

Jackson leaned down and kissed her forehead. "You're a good writer. Even if this new editor isn't enthusiastic, your fans are. Remember that."

"Thanks," Cate said. "I guess I hate the idea of not writing about Serena and Rondol again. They've become friends of mine over the years, you know?"

He emitted a chuckle. "Mine too."

She laughed. How many times had she discussed the earlier books with him? He was a good listener. That was a big reason why his students loved him in and outside the classroom.

"I'm thinking of a miso-and-ginger-glazed roast chicken for dinner tonight."

"Sounds wonderful. Before you go, let me tell you about Amber." She gave him the details of Amber's firing, and said, "Looks like she'll arrive in a couple of days. She'll help me decorate Brooke's house and stay here through the holidays. Is that okay with you?"

"Yes. I'm glad she's not staying in your cabin, because I plan to finish up your office there. A Christmas present for you."

"Thanks. Maybe the new space will clear my mind."

He chuckled. "That mind of yours will keep on spinning no matter what. You have more imagination than most people."

She smiled, wishing she could figure out the rest of the plot for her book. That's the trouble with being a "pantser," surprises awaited—some good, some not.

Amber arrived a few days later with a couple of suitcases and a bag of gifts. It filled Cate's heart to see her. She couldn't remember the last time the three Beach Babes had spent Christmas together

Cate's life filled with activity and laughter as she and Amber baked and got ready for the holidays.

On the day before Brooke was due to fly in to New York, Cate and Amber took the decorating treasures they'd bought for Brooke to her house. Outside, they hung a large, fresh, green wreath adorned with a big, bright-red bow on the front door. On each side of the door, they placed a potted spruce tree whose branches sported red-plaid ribbons tied to each end.

On the bar top in the kitchen, they set out six dinner and six luncheon plates in Spode's Christmas Tree design. They pulled green-linen napkins through special holiday napkin holders and placed them next to the plates. Nearby, a box of sturdy, plastic "silverware" sat ready to use, along with a couple of packages of Spode paper plates and bowls. Cate knew Brooke liked this kind of touch. She'd also like the tin of homemade Christmas cookies.

In the guest bath, Cate set out two hand towels embroidered with a Christmas motif. On the sink's counter, Amber placed a large, battery-powered, holiday candle whose glittery red coating brightened the room and added a festive touch. Better yet was the smell of pine that permeated the room from an incense container.

"Let's go get the groceries, and we'll be set," said Amber.

"I've put the wine in the wine rack and the special cheese tray in the refrigerator. But now we need ordinary groceries—milk, eggs, butter, bread, and all that."

"Sounds good," Cate replied, casting a satisfied glance around the room. It wasn't much, but enough to show they cared about helping Brooke and her family off to a good start for the holidays.

Later, after delivering groceries and filling the refrigerator with the things they thought Brooke might need, Cate and Amber returned to Cate's house.

"If you don't mind, I'm going to take a nap," Amber said to Cate.

"That sounds good. I might lie down myself." Since deciding to start a family, Cate was taking extra care of herself including napping every once in a while, something she normally didn't do. But she knew the days ahead would be busy.

CHAPTER THIRTY-ONE

BROOKE

Brooke stared with a new sense of disassociation at the empty rooms of the California house she'd called home. It had been a good house, but it had lost the allure of a home when neighbors and others who didn't know her or Paul that well thought it had housed a sex offender. If they only knew him, they'd realize that wasn't, couldn't be the case at all. As she observed him load the girls in the car they'd hired to take them to the airport, her heart ached for him. He carried himself differently now, as if the burden of the false accusations had bowed his shoulders. Her fingers itched to draw him. She locked the front door of the house for the last time and joined Paul and the girls in the car.

As planned, Cate and Amber greeted them in the baggage claim area at Kennedy Airport. Observing the smiles on their faces, Brooke filled with gratitude. New York was already feeling right.

"Welcome to your new home," said Cate, echoing Brooke's thoughts.

"So glad you're here," said Amber, giving her a hug.

"How are you doing?" Brooke asked her. "Are you still thinking losing your job might be a good thing?"

Amber drew a deep breath and let it out. "I think so. It's hard to break old patterns, but after you get settled and we all get through the holidays, I want to have a meeting of The

Beach Babes."

Brooke grinned. "Sounds like a plan."

While Paul and a Skycap retrieved their luggage from the conveyer belt, Brooke kept an eye on Brynn and Bradley. After experiencing bullying at school, they were as excited by the move as she. Cate, bless her heart, was patiently listening to the two of them talk to her at the same time.

Later, with Paul and the girls and their luggage settled in Cate's SUV and Brooke seated in Amber's car, they traveled out of the city to West Walles. On the way, Brooke knew that with her best friends sharing it, this phase of her life would be different, better. This one, she hoped, would be everything they all wanted.

When Amber finally turned the car into the driveway of her new house, Brooke gazed at it with fresh eyes. It was lovely, a place she intended to fill with love and support for her family. And on the occasions of her mother's visits, she would try extra hard to maintain peace between them.

Noticing the wreath on the front door and the pots beside it, she turned to Amber with a smile. "Oh, my! You and Cate have dressed the house for Christmas. Thank you!"

"It was such fun. We wanted to surprise you."

Paul walked over to Amber's car to help Brooke. A sweet gesture, she thought, climbing out and standing beside him.

"Here's to happiness in our new home," he said to her.

"Happiness and love," Brooke amended, pleased to see his smile widened across his face.

"Can we go inside now?" said Brynn. She shivered in the cold wind.

Beside her, Bradley hugged her arms around herself. "It's cold!"

"Sure, let's go," said Brooke, leading the charge to the front door.

They all stood by as Paul made a little ceremony of unlocking the door and flinging it open with a smile. “Welcome to our new home!”

After the luggage was unloaded from Cate’s SUV, Cate and Amber stood by.

“We’ll say goodbye to give you and your family some privacy,” said Amber. She kissed Brooke’s cheek. “Enjoy.”

“Thanks, Amber.” She turned to Cate. “And thank you.” They hugged. “I appreciate all you’ve done to help get the house ready. I’ll plan something special for the two of you after the New Year.”

“It’s not necessary,” said Cate. “We’re happy you’re here. Are you sure you don’t want to spend the night at my house?”

“Thanks, anyway, but we’re going to be fine here. The girls are camping out in their bedrooms, and the new bed for Paul and me is all set up, thanks to you.”

“Okay, then. I’ll see you later when you come for dinner. Jackson is making his famous spaghetti sauce. He knows how much your family loves it.”

“Bless you,” said Brooke. She saw them out the door and hurried upstairs to check on the girls. In one of their rooms, they were chattering as they gazed out the window to the back.

“What’s up?” she asked, pleased about their excitement.

“There’s plenty of room for a dog,” said Brynn.

“You said we could have one if we ever had a big, fenced-in yard. This one is enormous!” Bradley said, her eyes gleaming.

“Let’s get settled in the house first and then we’ll see.”

Bradley and Brynn gave one another a high-five and turned to Brooke. “Granny said she’d buy us one for Christmas.”

Brooke bit her lip to keep from saying something she’d regret. It was just like her mother to pull a stunt like this. “Like I said, we’ll see. How do you like your rooms?” The connecting rooms had been painted purple as they’d asked.

"They're cool, Mom," said Brynn, eager to please as usual.

"I'm going to make mine different with a pink bedspread, not a green one like Brynn wants," said Bradley, the more independent twin.

"Perfect," Brooke said. "You may each choose what you want for decorations."

Brynn smiled at her. "I'm glad we left our old house."

"Me too," said Bradley. "This house is going to be happy. I just know it."

Brooke wrapped her arms around her daughters, pleased with their response. They'd had a rougher time at school than she'd thought.

Later, after inspecting the house and organizing as much as she could, and after verifying that the movers were in town and would arrive at the house early the next morning, Brooke and her family left for Cate's house in the car Paul had had shipped from California.

On the way to Cate's house, Brooke realized she and Cate hadn't lived this close together since high school. It felt good. And with Amber in the city within an hour of them, it felt even better. It was bound to be an interesting time.

CHAPTER THIRTY-TWO

AMBER

Outside of Brooke's house, Amber turned to Cate. "I'll see you a little later. I'm meeting Wynton Barr, the lawyer friend of Jesse's. He's agreed to talk to me about what legal actions might be involved in planning for the future."

Cate smiled. "I saw the way he was looking at you at the reception for Jesse. No wonder he agreed to take time out of his schedule to meet with you."

Amber shrugged. "What can I say? He's a very nice guy."

"Well, good luck. I hope he can find a way for you to be free to do what you want on your own. I know how important that is to you."

"Thanks, hon! See you later. Don't worry, I'll be in time for dinner."

Amber climbed into her car and sat for a moment. The importance of this meeting didn't escape her. After the shock of almost being assaulted and being fired had worn off, a new resolve settled inside her. One person shouldn't have the right to determine the future of another. She'd fight for her independence, Belinda be damned.

Feeling more confident, Amber drove to a tony suburb a few miles away. Wynton owned a large home there. Although he maintained his office in the city, he'd explained that he sometimes met clients at his home for more privacy.

Because of his excellent reputation and well-known list of clients, Amber expected his house to be imposing. It was, instead, a tasteful, brick Tudor-style home sitting atop a knoll of beautifully landscaped land.

She parked the car in the wide driveway beside the house and made her way to the front door. Glancing at the leaded-glass windows facing the front of the house, she wondered what awaited her inside.

A woman wearing a white apron over a gray uniform opened the door with a smile.

"Miss Anderson?"

"Yes."

"Please come in. Mr. Barr is expecting you." She ushered Amber into a marble-tiled entrance and took Amber's coat.

Wynton emerged from the back of the house. "Hello, Amber. Come with me. My office is just down the hall." He turned to the woman. "Thank you, Emelda, for coming in today. Have a nice holiday. I'll see you after Christmas."

Beaming at him, she nodded. "Thank you for everything. My family thanks you too."

Fascinated with the conversation, Amber observed Wynton's cheeks grow pink when Emelda threw her arms around him and hugged him hard. Still smiling, she turned to Amber. "This is a good man."

Wynton chuckled and shook his head. "Emelda has been with the family forever. A good woman, for sure." He waved Amber forward.

Amber trailed behind him taking in every detail of artwork and décor. She stopped in front of a large, framed photograph of a beautiful young woman mounted on the wall. It was stunning. "Is this the portrait you commissioned Jesse to do for you?"

Wynton stopped and stared at it, his features softening with tenderness. "Yes, that's Samantha, my daughter."

"She's lovely," Amber said.

"She is that, but Jesse was very talented. He had a way of bringing out someone's inner feelings so a viewer could observe both the image and the emotions behind it."

Amber thought of her own portrait.

"Does your daughter live here?" Amber asked, anxious to make a comparison between the photograph and the person.

"No, she's away at college, but she's due to arrive here soon. We're leaving for our ski cabin in Vermont early tomorrow morning and I'm officially on vacation. She and I will celebrate the holidays there."

"No other family?" Amber asked, surprised.

His eyes filled with sadness. "My wife died of cancer three years ago."

"I'm so sorry. This must be a difficult time of year for you."

"Yes, my wife loved the holidays. How about you? Will you be with family?"

Amber's eyes stung. She blinked rapidly, wondering if this show of emotion was the result of her hormones still waging war after losing the baby. "I'll be with my two best friends and their families. We've been besties since we were young girls. They mean the world to me."

"Good. In my business dealing with all kinds of problems, you learn that friends can be much kinder, more loyal, and more loving than some family members. I'm glad you have them."

He turned, continued walking down the hallway, and entered an office that overlooked a sweeping lawn and an ice-covered pond, nicely lit by outdoor floodlights.

"Gorgeous," said Amber, taking a moment to contemplate the view before sitting in the chair he offered to her in front of his desk.

After taking a seat behind his desk, he steepled his fingers and studied her. "Let's talk about why you're here. You mentioned being fired. Tell me exactly what happened."

Amber stirred restlessly in her chair. "To begin with, I need you to know that I dated Jesse Carpenter for a couple of months before he reunited with his wife. I'd known him for years, but until then we'd simply been friends who sometimes worked together."

"As a matter of fact, I do know that."

Amber drew back with surprise. "You do? We tried to be discreet about it because of the work we sometimes did together."

"I had lunch with Jesse one day and he told me. He thought the world of you," Wynton said quietly.

Amber gripped her hands so tight her fingers turned white. Still, she was unable to hold back the tears that filled her eyes and spilled down her cheeks. "I'm so sorry," she began and then gave in to the grief that filled her.

Wynton got up and came over to her. "Here." He handed her a box of tissues. "Go ahead and let it out. It's nothing to be ashamed of. I've wanted to do a lot of that in my past."

Amber fought for control and managed to dab at her eyes as she forced herself to breathe in and out in calming breaths.

Wynton sat down in his desk chair and faced her. "You weren't like the others Jesse dated. I recognized that at the reception at his home honoring him."

"Others? Do you mean like Belinda Galvin?" Amber's voice hardened. "She's the reason I need your help. Jesse's assistant sent a photo portrait Jesse had taken of me to my office. Belinda saw it, realized Jesse and I had dated, attempted to slap me, and fired me on the spot."

"That's not a legal reason for firing anyone," Wynton said. "Go on."

Amber filled him in on the entire situation. "Rather than fight for a reason to stay at the Galvin Agency, I want to find a way for me to be free to set up my own modeling agency one day. Mine would be very different from hers, however."

"How so?" Wynton leaned forward and studied her with what could almost be called the beginning of a smile.

"I've worked for Belinda for over three years. During that time, I've gotten to know a lot about the business, many people in the industry, and those who've had conflicts with Belinda. I don't intend to compete with Belinda for new young models. I want to use older models and people who might not be considered beautiful by her standards. In other words, real people who have remarkable faces for their relatability, whose bodies aren't stick thin. There's a real desire among many people today to get away from unrealistic images. I think I can make a difference by taking advantage of those feelings."

"Who would you get for clients?"

Knowing she had his interest, Amber straightened. "As I said, I've been dealing with lots of companies, agents, and models for a long time, often trying to smooth ruffled feathers where Belinda was concerned. I'd start slowly and go from there."

"So, what is it you're asking of me?"

Amber drew a deep breath. "I know Belinda will fight me on anything I try to do. Once angered, she'll stop at nothing until she destroys her enemies. I need you to look over my contract to make sure legally I can do this, so if she tries to shut me down, I'll be all right. I didn't sign a formal non-compete clause if that helps."

He gazed at her thoughtfully. "That could be useful. But there might be other ways we can get around any legal action on her part. All of it legitimate. People like Belinda think they cannot be held accountable, but they're most often wrong."

"You'll do it? You'll help me?" Amber's voice lilted with relief.

His smile was genuine. "I'd love to take someone like Belinda Galvin down. Jesse filled me in on a few details about the difficulty of working with her."

"She has quite a reputation in the industry."

"And elsewhere," Wynton said. "I was witness to the way she treated you at the reception. Not only was it rude, it was cruel. No wonder Jesse didn't want to date her."

A knock on the door interrupted them.

Wynton checked his watch and then said, "Come on in."

A thin girl with dark hair opened the door and peered inside. "Sorry. I didn't mean to interrupt."

Wynton waved her inside. "Sam, meet Amber Anderson. Amber, this is my daughter, Samantha."

Amber and Sam smiled at one another. "Glad to meet you. I loved the photograph Jesse Carpenter took of you."

"He made me look a lot better than I actually am," said Sam easily, indicating her rather large nose with a tap of her finger.

"I think he had a lovely subject," said Amber, liking this young woman who seemed so comfortable in her own skin.

"I'll wait in the other room, Dad," said Sam, closing the door behind her.

Wynton glanced at Amber. "I think we've made a good beginning. As soon as we get back from Vermont, I'll give you a call. Perhaps, we can meet then to discuss various ideas."

"That sounds good," said Amber, pleased she'd be able to meet with him again. He hadn't laughed at her or told her a business like she envisioned wouldn't work. Instead, he acted as if it would be no problem at all.

"Let me get your coat for you," said Wynton, following her out into the hallway.

He checked the hall closet and pulled out Amber's camel-hair coat. "This is it. Right?"

Amber smiled her thanks as he helped her to slip it on.

She turned to say goodbye and stopped when she came face to face with him. For a moment, they gazed at each other, and then he said, "Merry Christmas. I'll see you soon."

Amber waved to him and Sam. "Happy Holidays."

She was aware that Wynton and his daughter Sam remained standing by the front door as she made her way down the steps to her car. Even though her back was turned to them, she felt their gazes on her. It felt good.

CHAPTER THIRTY-THREE

CATE

Cate was beginning to get worried about Amber being on time for cocktails and dinner when she noticed the headlights of Amber's car entering the driveway. As usual, Amber drove a little too fast, but then, Amber called Cate a pokey driver.

As Amber was getting out of the car, Brooke and her family drove up.

"Great timing," Cate called, approaching them with a smile. Jackson joined her and they ushered everyone inside.

"I get to sit by the fire," cried Bradley, taking off her coat, handing it to Cate, and hurrying toward its warmth. Brynn was right behind her.

"The girls aren't quite used to the cold," said Paul, giving them a tender look.

"But they love it," Brooke quickly added, and Cate realized how eager Brooke was to make Paul comfortable with the change.

"What does everyone want to drink?" Jackson asked.

He took orders, and he and Paul left the living room and went into the kitchen.

"How'd your meeting with the lawyer go?" Cate asked Amber as they took seats on the couch.

"Yeah, tell us about it," Brooke urged.

A pretty pink flush brightened Amber's cheeks. She sighed. "I think it's going to work out for me to have my own business one day if I choose to go ahead with it. Wynton Barr thinks he might be able to help. He and his daughter are going to Vermont for the holidays, but when he returns, we'll meet again."

"Good," said Brooke. "It would serve Belinda right to have you go into competition with her."

Amber shook her head. "If I decide to go ahead with it, I wouldn't exactly be competing with her. My business would focus on working with average people needed for ads, commercials, videos, and the like—models with whom Belinda wouldn't deign to work."

"Oh, I like that," said Cate. "I think a lot of people are tired of models who are unnaturally thin and enhanced by plastic surgery."

"Such a good message for young girls," added Brooke.

"There are other high-end models who've vowed not to work with Belinda again. And I know a couple of models who are in recovery from drug use. This might give them a second chance." Amber shrugged. "We'll see. But that's my plan for now."

Cate gave Amber an impulsive hug. "Did I ever tell you how much I love you? I'm so proud of how you're turning this disappointment around."

"Me too," said Brooke, rising from the chair in which she'd been sitting. She embraced Amber and sat down again. "Now tell us about this Wynton Barr. I've heard he's quite a guy. Single too."

Amber's smile caught Cate's attention. "He's a nice man, just like Jesse was. And he's smart. I have a feeling Belinda won't win any war she might want to wage with me. Wynton will look over my contract, of course, and search for any loopholes, but more than that he knows the cause of my firing. She'll blame it on something else, but the fact is she fired me for being with Jesse."

"Hey, why so serious in here?" said Jackson, carrying in a tray of drinks, followed by Paul carrying a large plate of appetizers.

"Just talking about Amber's new business idea," said Cate. "But now that you're here, let's celebrate Brooke's and Paul's move to New York."

Jackson handed out drinks to everyone, including glasses of apple juice for the girls.

"Here's to the Weston family! May your move here be everything you want it to be."

"The Weston family?" said Brynn. "That's us!"

The adults laughed and raised their glasses.

Later, after everyone had had their fill of Jackson's spaghetti, garlic bread, and fresh greens salad, Brooke rose. "I hate to be one of those people who eat and run, but tomorrow is a busy day, and the movers will be there early."

Cate rose. "We all need to get to bed early if we're going to be of any help to you."

Among hugs and kisses, the group dispersed.

While Amber helped Cate with the clean-up, they chatted about the change in Paul. He was usually a quiet man, but now he seemed almost broken.

"Brooke will help him," said Amber. "But we'll have to help Brooke."

"Yes," agreed Cate. Brooke would have enough to contend with—the move, getting the kids settled, and dealing with her mother.

The next morning Cate held onto her cup of decaf coffee and inhaled the scent of it. Since trying to get pregnant, she'd cut out caffeine. Still, that early cup of coffee was precious to her.

"You ready to go?" Amber asked her. Dressed in jeans and a Beach Babes sweatshirt Brooke had given them one year, she looked gorgeous. Better yet, she looked happy.

"Give me time for one more sip, then I'll be ready." Staring out at the clear morning sky, Cate was thankful the movers would be able to work without rain or snow to hinder them. She took a last sip of coffee, set her mug down, and went to get her coat. Helping Brooke would keep her mind off making love with Jackson last night. As usual, he'd been wonderful, but there was a new intensity to their lovemaking that was a bit awkward because both of them were thinking of the baby they hoped they were making.

Cate hurried to catch up to Amber, who was heading out the door.

Later, when they pulled up to Brooke's house, the van was already in place in front of it. When they saw the size of the truck, Cate and Amber exchanged wide-eyed glances.

"Oh, my God! This is going to take more than one day to unload," said Amber.

They got out of the car and walked inside the house where chaos reigned.

Brooke saw them and hurried over. "Thank goodness you're here. Cate, I need you to go upstairs and help Paul place furniture and boxes in the bedrooms. Amber, I need you to go to the kitchen and make sure boxes are stacked there as conveniently as possible. The moving company will unpack some of the boxes tomorrow. The rest, we'll try to do today. I've placed labels on the drawers and cupboards as to what goes where."

"Wow! You're really doing this right," said Amber. "I'm impressed."

Brooke cocked a questioning eyebrow at her and hurried away to talk to one of the movers.

Cate exchanged a soft laugh with Amber and said, "Guess we'd better do as she wants."

She raced up the stairs ahead of two men who were carrying a headboard behind her.

Late that afternoon, as they headed back to her house, Cate groaned softly and shifted her shoulders. "I'm going to warn Jackson that I'm never moving. Even with all the help Brooke had, it's not easy."

"And all that stuff? I swear I'm going to go through my closet and get rid of a lot of it," said Amber.

"You and she should open an upscale, gently-used-clothing store," Cate said and then stopped. "Wait! Maybe that's not a bad idea. What do you think?"

"If Brooke wants to do it, I'd be glad to give her some of my clothes, and I know a few others who might be willing to do the same. Let's talk to her about it after things settle down. She's a lot more organized than I thought."

Cate chuckled. "Did you see the look she gave you when you commented on it? It was a lot like one of her mother's."

Amber grinned. "Better not tell her that."

When they entered the house, wonderful aromas seeped from the kitchen to Cate's nose. She walked into the kitchen to find Jackson basting two chickens. "Smells delicious."

"Thanks. One is for Brooke's family; the other for us. When I get everything set to go, you and I can deliver food to them."

"Brooke will be thrilled. Her mother is arriving any moment, and she's in a tizzy with all that's going on."

"Her mother makes her nervous anyway," said Amber. "See you guys later. I'm going to lie down for a while."

After Amber left the room, Jackson put down the metal spoon he'd been holding and swept Cate into his arms.

"Maybe *we* should go lie down."

Grinning, she pushed him away. "After the holidays, we'll have all the privacy we want. Right now, I need a good hot soak in the tub."

They smiled at one another, and Cate realized that after a baby came, they wouldn't have the privacy they were used to. It was a sobering thought.

CHAPTER THIRTY-FOUR

BROOKE

Observing P.J. and her mother emerge from the car Paul had hired to bring them from the airport, Brooke experienced a mixture of emotions. She was happy to see her son, but she thought having her mother here for the holidays at the same time she was trying to get settled in a new house was more than she could handle. Paul had promised to step in if necessary, but as she considered the days ahead, her neck and shoulders tensed.

Brooke went to the door to greet them. Her heart lifted as P.J. cried, "Hi, Mom!" and gave her a hug she'd missed. Her mother stood outside surveying the landscape. With a satisfied smile, she then studied the façade of the house.

"Hello, Mother," said Brooke. Diana Ridley did not like being called 'Mom.' The girls called her 'Granny' one time and had been told that she was 'Grandmother' to them.

"Hello, darling," said her mother. "Looks like you did well at choosing a house. I can't wait to see my rooms."

"I hope you'll like them. Cate helped me select the color."

"Oh, good. Cate has good taste. She's done a lovely job with that little farmhouse of hers."

Brooke let the verbal slam go and turned as Paul joined them at the doorway.

"Hello, Mother Ridley. Glad you got here safe and sound. Come inside and hand me your coat, and then I'll take your suitcases upstairs for you."

"Thank you, dear," Diana said. "I think I'm going to like

living here. The location is perfect."

A warning tremor shook Brooke's body. "What do you mean?"

"I've decided to move to New York. What's the point of living in California if my grandchildren are here?"

Brooke swallowed hard. "I'm sure there are plenty of suitable condos in the area."

"I thought I'd stay with you while I make up my mind about where I want to live."

Brooke worked to contain her composure, but she was tired, and it was a real struggle. She did NOT want her mother living with her.

Paul noticed her reaction and quickly said, "I'm sure we can find a suitable place for you. Our real estate agent was terrific."

"Thank you, dear. But I'm not going to rush into anything. It's a big move."

P.J. came bounding down the stairs. "My room looks great. When are we going to eat?"

Brooke looked at her son and smiled. "Uncle Jackson is sending over dinner for us. In the meantime, you can have a snack."

"Where are my granddaughters?" Diana asked.

"Upstairs, organizing things in their rooms. I'll take you up to see them and show you the suite we've set aside for you," said Brooke. As she moved toward the stairway, her feet felt as if weighed down by stones.

"Grandmother! You're here!" cried Bradley, beaming at Diana. "Want to see my room?"

"In a bit, dear. I want to get settled in my room first, then I'll have you show me anything you want."

"Hi, Grandmother," Brynn said, sticking her head into the hallway and waving.

The enthusiastic smile that crossed her mother's face both pleased and irritated Brooke. She loved that her mother adored her children, though, and that was more important to her than any old resentment that reared its head once in a while.

"Your room is this way," Brooke said, leading her mother away from the girls. Cate had helped to make the bed and arrange the furniture. Aside from a few finishing touches, it was pretty much done. Brooke had made sure of it. She opened the door and stood aside.

"Oh, how ... different," her mother said. She paused, studying the room. "I mean, I like the colors. It's nice, Brooke. Thank you."

"Make yourself comfortable, Mother. There should be plenty of hangers and anything else you may need. I've set a pitcher of water and glasses on your bureau." She turned to go.

Her mother faced her. "Brooke, I mean it. Thank you."

Brooke bobbed her head. "The kids wouldn't want Christmas without you. It wouldn't be the same."

She and her mother exchanged quiet looks and then Brooke left the room, wishing she could be truly happy her mother was with them through the holidays and beyond.

CHAPTER THIRTY-FIVE

CATE

The holidays passed in a blur for Cate. She felt pushed and pulled in all kinds of directions, tending to Amber, helping Brooke, and escorting Brooke's mother around the area, talking to her about the nearby towns while Brooke used the time to get settled. Cate soon learned that Diana Ridley would not live in any area that wasn't known as highly coveted.

When Amber declared she was going back to the city to celebrate New Year's with some of her business associates, Cate agreed it was a good idea. As Amber explained it, by socializing with them in a casual way, she might discover whom she could count on in the future to help her with her own business, if that's what she decided she wanted to do.

Hearing the news that they'd be alone, Jackson was as pleased as Cate once again to have the privacy they'd lost.

"What do you want to do for New Year's Eve?" Jackson asked one morning as they sat alone in the kitchen, eating breakfast.

"Honestly? I want to stay home, have a simple meal, maybe pop some popcorn, and watch a movie with you."

"Sounds like a plan. I know your friends like my cooking, but I'm ready to slow down. Besides, it's a good time of month for us to be alone, right?"

Cate nodded, but it left her feeling diminished somehow. She hated that their lovemaking had become tied to a calendar. It was so unromantic.

He rose and hugged her to him, and she immediately felt better.

After Jackson left for school, Cate sat in her office wondering where to begin when her office phone rang. *Abby Francis, her agent.*

She picked up the call. "Happy New Year, Abby!"

"And to you," Abby said cheerfully. "How are you doing on the Galeon Wars book?"

Cate made a face. "Frankly, I'm stuck. I've been busy over the holidays with personal things and haven't had time to go back and review what I've written so I'm clear on where I should go from here."

"How would you feel about filling in the proposal for the contemporary you want to write? Do that and give me the first three chapters. I have something in mind, but I'm not ready to discuss it with you."

Cate's curiosity was piqued. "You want me to stop work on the Galeon book and focus on the proposal? That doesn't sound like you at all, Abby."

"It's not, but it may be worth it. Trust me."

A fluttering of excitement entered Cate. "When do you need it?"

"As soon as possible, but I want you to be thorough. Know your new world as well as you do Galeon. 'Gotta go. We'll talk later."

Cate clicked off the call. Abby had sounded very excited, not her usual calm self. Whether she went back to her old world or created a new contemporary one, it was time to get busy.

She pulled out her notes on a book she'd temporarily titled "Girls' Night Out." The story took place in New York City, an easy place for her to research. Although she had the setting, she needed to know much more about her three main characters—Allison, Babette, and Cissy.

Looking at the names, Cate shook her head. Had she really intended to write a book about her two best friends and herself? She crossed out the names of the characters and wrote down three others. Then she began to write a short story about each one—their history, their likes, dislikes, challenges, internal goals, external goals, quirks, anything else that made them real, letting her imagination fill in blank spaces.

By late morning, the first character was done; the second started. Unlike her character Serena, these modern women had flaws that even Cate hadn't seen at the beginning.

When Buddy barked to go outside, Cate was eager to join him. It was a clear, crisp morning. The fresh air would help clear her mind.

Outside, while she tossed a ball for Buddy her mind remained on her characters. Each was different from the other, but what kept them together as friends? She thought of Brooke and Amber. Her friendship with them was based, in large part, on trust to help one another, and to be kind.

As if her thoughts had conjured her, Brooke called on her cell.

"Hi, Brooke. How does your first morning alone feel?" Cate asked.

"Alone? Not quite," Brooke said. "My mother is out with the real estate agent, but she'll be back any moment. Can I come see you?"

Cate hesitated. She usually set aside her mornings for writing. "Sure," she answered. Later, she'd tactfully explain her schedule to Brooke. Otherwise, her mornings would be taken away from her. Even those who knew about her writing and the books she'd published had no idea how much work went into them each day and why she had to be persistent in keeping mornings to herself.

When Brooke arrived, Cate was glad she hadn't put her off. She needed to stop the spinning in her mind, changing one idea after another. It would be good to step away from the project.

"Thanks for letting me stop by. I know how busy you must be after having so little time to work over the holidays."

Cate hugged her. "Though I usually schedule mornings for writing, it's always good to see you."

"Thanks. I needed this break," said Brooke, accepting a cup of hot coffee from Cate. "If you keep mornings for writing, what are you going to do when you have a baby? How will you be able to keep to that schedule?"

Cate sighed and took a seat at the kitchen table opposite Brooke. "That's something I'll have to figure out. Abby called with some kind of secret proposal she wants me to put together, along with the first three chapters of a new book. A contemporary one, this time."

Brooke grinned. "Sounds interesting. I like Abby. She's been good for you."

"Yes, she has," Cate agreed. "Enough about me, what's going on in your world?"

"It's only been a few days since we've seen one another, but I feel as if it's been weeks. You're someone I can talk to about my frustrations with my mother. To anyone else, she sounds like a charming, likeable person. But you know how she subtly puts me down. Honestly, I feel as if instead of turning forty, I'm about to turn four."

Cate smiled and patted Brooke's hand. "I understand. I've known her for a long time."

Brooke let out a big sigh. "Thanks. That's all I needed to hear—your being aware of what I'm dealing with on a daily basis. Now, let me tell you about the girls' new school."

Cate listened as Brooke spoke about the facilities at the school and how two girls in their class had already spoken to the twins. "I'm hopeful this semester is going to be good for them, both academically and socially."

"Me, too," said Cate. She studied her friend. "What about you? What are you going to do with your time?"

"I might go back to painting," said Brooke. "But I'm not sure. I haven't settled in enough to do volunteer or community work just yet."

"Amber and I have a suggestion for you. Wait until this weekend when we meet Amber for lunch, and we'll talk about it then."

"What's going on?" Brooke said. "Can't we talk about it now?"

"Not yet, because it has something to do with the business that Amber might establish. And, Brooke, the more I think about it, there might be a place for your mother too."

Brooke's face brightened. "My mother? Well, then, we'll talk about it this weekend. Anything to keep her out of my hair."

Because they'd been friends for a long time, Cate understood the smile that spread across Brooke's face.

CHAPTER THIRTY-SIX

AMBER

When Amber answered the phone, she was surprised but pleased to see Wynton Barr's name on the screen of her cell. She picked up the call with a pleasant, "Hello."

"Amber, this is Wynton. I'm back from Vermont and wondered if we could meet. I've gone over your contract with the Galvin Agency, and I think you'll be interested in hearing what suggestions I can offer."

"Great. I'm back at my condo, so I can meet you here in the city anytime."

"How about lunch? My schedule is pretty full this afternoon, but I have time to see you during lunch break."

"That would be wonderful," Amber said, checking the time. She'd have to hurry to get dressed for the day, but she could do it. They agreed to meet at Jake's, a pub near his office, and then Amber hung up. She'd been lolling around her condo doing research on the internet and was still in her pajamas. Hurrying into the bathroom, she quickly took a shower. Instead of putting on a dress suitable for work, she donned a pair of black wool slacks, black boots, and a bright-blue sweater she knew matched her eyes. She kept her makeup limited to lip gloss, eye shadow, and mascara. Now that she didn't have to dress to Belinda's standards at the office, it felt good to go with a more natural look.

###

Jake's was full when she arrived. She checked her watch and looked around the crowded restaurant, searching for Wynton when a hostess approached her. "Amber Anderson? Wynton Barr asked me to escort you to his table. Follow me."

She led the way through the noise from the people gathered at the bar to a table at the back of the room.

Wynton was on the phone, but when he saw her, he waved, smiled, and stood, quickly disengaging from the call.

"Amber. Nice to see you again. I'm glad you were free to meet me."

She smiled. "These days, I'm very free. But I don't mind it. I've been on such a busy work schedule and under so much pressure for the last few years, I'm enjoying the time off."

He helped her into her chair and sat down facing her. "I can well imagine the kind of work life you led under Belinda Galvin. I'm impressed you lasted so long. In doing some research, I uncovered a lot of things about her. She's a nasty person to work for. I'm curious. Why did you stay so long?"

Amber sighed. "It may sound silly, but I wanted to learn all I could about the business, and then more and more people depended on me to make things right with Belinda. I became a buffer for them. A lot of the models who worked with her couldn't deal with her at all."

He gazed at her with such intensity Amber felt her cheeks grow hot. She shifted in her chair. "I had a tough life growing up. I guess that's why I was able to do it."

"Interesting. After reviewing your documents, I think you should be able to set up your own business without too much hassle from Belinda. She'll threaten to sue, like she's prone to do, but I don't think it will go anywhere. The thing is, she screwed up by not following through with you on a specific non-compete. The standard stuff isn't strong enough and is, instead, drawn up for models, not administrators."

Amber couldn't stop a smile from spreading across her face. "I'm not sure what I'm going to do or when, but knowing I'm free to do whatever I want is exhilarating." She didn't mention that the money Jesse had set aside for her was enough to keep her from panicking over a lack of a job for several months.

He chuckled softly. "I understand. But don't be fooled, Belinda won't go away without a fight. And I suggest you wait a good six months before contacting anyone else about a new business. Should it go to court, that will help your position."

"I went to a party over the New Year to catch up with old friends in the business, and I think I would have a lot of support for what I want to do."

The waitress arrived and they quickly ordered their food—chicken Caesar salads for each.

As they waited for their food to arrive, they continued to talk.

"How was Vermont?" Amber asked him.

"Going there for the holidays is a tradition I carry on for my daughter, Sam, but, truthfully, I'd rather stay home. With my wife gone, it's not the same for either one of us."

"I can understand how difficult that would be. You must have loved her very much."

"I did," said Wynton. "It's why I haven't dated too much."

"I admire that kind of devotion."

"How about you? How did you spend the holidays? With those friends of yours?"

Amber smiled. "Yes, with them and their families. I have no family to speak of." She paused. "Well, actually my mother is alive, but we've never been close."

"The tough childhood you spoke of?"

"Yes," said Amber, startled by the sting in her eyes. She didn't really know Wynton, but he had a way of reaching inside her that was unsettling … yet nice.

By the time they finished their meal, they were laughing over something that Brooke's girls had said about their brother.

Wynton paid the bill and walked Amber to the outside of the restaurant. "In the next day or two, I'll send along a report of my findings and you can take it from there." He shook her hand. "You're a nice person, Amber. Let me know how things go. I wish you all the luck in the world."

"Thank you. I appreciate your help," she said. "Please send me the bill."

He shook his head. "This is on me. But maybe you'll consent to go out to dinner with me sometime soon."

"I'd like that," she responded. "Thank you."

He gave her a brilliant smile, checked his watch, and turned to go.

Amber stood a moment, watching him weave his way through the throngs of people on the sidewalk, and then she, too, moved on, filled with a new sense of hope for the future.

On Saturday, Amber opened her door to Cate and Brooke and ushered them inside. Earlier in the week Brooke had called pleading to know what idea she and Cate had for her. Unwilling to get into it without Cate, Amber put her off. Since then, she'd developed a loose business plan for running a retail store of previously owned clothing. She and Cate had gone over it together and agreed it was perfect for Brooke. Amber would work with her until she felt it was safe to open her own business. Wynton had suggested waiting for a while.

Cate and Brooke removed their coats as they chatted about the unusually cold weather.

"Oh my God!" shrieked Brooke, staring at the framed

portrait of Amber hanging in the hallway. "This is Jesse's photograph of you? Amber, it's stunning!"

Cate studied it and turned to Amber. "Wow! He did such a fantastic job of showing the tenderness inside you. He must have truly cared about you. It shows so clearly."

Amber's sigh came from deep inside. "That's what Belinda saw. That's why I'm in such a mess and why I'm not going to get interested in anyone for some time. I'll be too busy in the future anyway."

"Talking about being busy, just what do you and Cate have planned for me?" Brooke said. "You promised you'd tell me today."

Amber exchanged glances with Cate. "Let's have coffee first, and we'll talk about it." She led them into the small space she jokingly called a kitchen. A small, round table and three chairs sat in a corner.

"How did the girls do their first week of school?" Amber asked Brooke as she went about fixing cups of coffee for them.

A wide smile spread across Brooke's face. "They loved it. I'm so relieved. Their last week in California was very difficult. I dreaded seeing them off to school each day. Here, it's worth it to get up at 6:30 to get them to school."

"Isn't there a bus service?" Cate asked.

"Yes, but we elected not to do that until we know the girls are fine."

Amber handed out cups of coffee and sat at the table. "So glad you could come and have fun with me today. It almost feels like old times—the three of us together."

Brooke chuckled. "With a lot of changes."

"But, hey, we're not so bad for our ages," said Cate. She leaned in. "But I have to confess, I pulled out a gray hair this morning. I had to. It was staring me in the face."

"Better that than a chin hair," said Brooke. "Ugh."

"Let's talk about something better," said Amber. "Brooke, you wanted to know about the idea Cate and I had for you. Here it is. An upscale store of previously used clothing for women and girls."

Brooke's eyes widened. "Why would I want to do that?"

"To get you involved in the community and keep you busy. This is a time of new beginnings for all of us," said Cate.

"Hold on! I'll be right back," said Amber. She left and returned with a manila folder.

"Here, Brooke. Here are some ideas about the business. I'll help you set it up and get it running. Wynton doesn't feel I should do anything about my own business for a while."

"I'll use some of my local contacts to find the perfect place for it," offered Cate. "Or maybe your real estate agent will help."

"I have several contacts in the fashion business who would gladly donate their clothes or consign them," Amber offered. "The thing is, it used to be so important to have a lot of clothes on hand, but except for the top social groups, it isn't important anymore. Many people are downsizing and simplifying."

"I see this as a way to help women in business—perhaps single moms who can't afford a lot of nice things for themselves," added Cate.

"And for their daughters too. Remember how I took used clothes and made them mine with a little care, a little added extra?" Amber hadn't had a lot of brand-new clothes.

"You have such a flair for doing things like that," Brooke said. "So, tell me more."

The three of them discussed the idea and then began to get serious. "First of all, we'd need a name. Cate, you're the wordsmith. Think of one," said Amber. She turned to Brooke. "Think of location and logistics. For instance, I'm pretty certain we'd want to start with limited hours. I was thinking

Thursday through Saturday."

Brooke smiled. "That could be doable."

"I've got it!" said Cate. "How about something like 'Renewable You?' or 'Fresh as a Daisy?' or simply 'Refresh.'"

Amber and Brooke exchanged glances and said "Refresh!" together.

"I love it," said Brooke. "That name could mean so many things. It would give us an opportunity to sell more than clothes if we wanted."

"Guess she's in," said Cate, grinning at Amber. "You realize what you just said, right, Brooke?"

"Yes. I've wanted to do something on my own for a long time. This would keep me busy, but not so occupied I couldn't paint too. Later on, after things get down to a routine."

Amber remained silent, but wondered if Brooke realized the work it would take to make even a small retail operation like this successful.

After talking a lot more about it, Brooke stood. "I don't know about you, but I'm hungry. Let's go out for lunch."

"I recently ate at Jake's. The food was delicious, and it's only a couple of blocks from here."

"Sounds good," said Cate. "I'm ready for a walk."

Amber was surprised to find the restaurant crowded on a Saturday, but then, as she'd told her friends, the food was good. They found their way to seats at the bar, and with the cooperation of a customer who willingly moved, sat together.

"I don't know about you," said Brooke, "but I think we should toast the beginning of Refresh."

"Just this once for me," said Cate. "I'm watching what I drink."

"Me, too," said Amber. She was happy to be less rigid about

her weight, but she couldn't be foolish.

After they ordered their drinks and their food, Amber sat back in her bar stool and studied the crowd, feeling more relaxed than she had in a long time. She was slowly learning to let go of the pressure of working with Belinda and meeting her constant demands.

"Hello! What are you doing here?" came a familiar voice behind her.

She swiveled around to find Wynton Barr smiling at her. Dressed in a pair of jeans and a black sweater that fit his body, he looked, well ... delicious. His smile created a bubble of happiness inside her.

"Hi. I could ask the same of you."

He laughed. "I had to catch up on some work at the office, and this is a great place for lunch."

"Yes, until we had lunch, I'd forgotten how good it is." She realized Brooke and Cate were staring at them. "Wynton, I'd like you to meet my friend Brooke Weston. You've already met Cate Tibbs."

His eyebrows rose. "Ah, the best friends I've heard about." Still smiling, he bobbed his head and shook hands with both women. "Nice to meet you, Brooke, and to see you once more, Cate. My pleasure." He turned to Amber. "Good to see you. Maybe we can do lunch or dinner to further discuss your plans?"

"Yes, that would be nice," Amber replied, realizing how much she wanted that to happen.

Wynton gave them a little bow and made his way toward the front door.

"Wow!" said Brooke. "He's downright handsome."

"And into you," said Cate. "I could tell."

Amber held up her hand to stop them. "Just friends. That's all."

"Hmm," said Brooke. "I know you don't want to talk about it after everything that's happened, but, Amber, he's a friend you'll definitely want to keep."

Amber grinned, unable to deny the feelings he brought out in her.

CHAPTER THIRTY-SEVEN

BROOKE

All the way home on the train, Brooke talked to Cate about the idea of Refresh.

"I'm thinking of it more as a service to others than a retail store. Amber mentioned her clothes growing up. They were so important to her. Think of how we can help business women, single moms, teenagers. And if the contacts Amber has through her work with Belinda come through, we'll have a whole range of top-end clothes to offer. I might be able to get clothes through the girls' school, which includes grades kindergarten through high school."

Cate smiled at her. "Nice, but you might have to limit it to women first, then teenagers. But I like the idea of its being more of a service than anything else."

Brooke felt the smile that crossed her face. "Me too. I've been very fortunate all my life."

Cate nudged her affectionately. "And you've always been generous because of it."

"Thanks. I try. I have to talk to Paul, of course, but I think he'll be pleased I've found something new to do. Heaven knows I won't be lounging around the pool in this weather!"

Cate laughed with her. "Not for a long time."

Brooke was still feeling upbeat as she entered the house. She hung up her coat, already able to envision the success of the store.

When she went into the kitchen, her mother was sitting at the table, a book in hand, a cup of tea nearby.

"Hello, Mother. How are you? Any success with the realtor?"

Her mother looked up at her and smiled. "As a matter of fact, I've found something I like a lot—a lovely, small home within easy walking distance. I think it will be perfect for me because I can be here at a moment's notice. Without any friends here, I'll have someplace to go to whenever I need to get out of the house."

Brooke's heart pounded with dismay. "I thought you'd want to be closer to the city to enjoy all the activities there."

Her mother looked down at her hands and then gazed up at Brooke with watery eyes. "I know we haven't had the best relationship, but I am your mother and would like to try to be a better companion to you."

Suspicion reared its head inside Brooke like a wary snake. "Why the change, Mother? What's wrong?"

"I just feel as if I'm getting old too quickly, and being with your girls reminds me of all I missed with you growing up."

Brooke sat opposite her, wondering what to say. Her mother was right. They'd never been close. And at this stage of life, she doubted they ever would. Not when she'd suffered verbal and emotional abuse from her mother in subtle ways through the years.

She remembered her father's efforts to bring them together and drew a deep breath. For his sake, she'd give it a try. "We can start by giving each other space, but at the same time, we'll set up a schedule for regular time together until you build your own circle of friends. Does that sound reasonable?"

Her mother frowned. "It's more like a business arrangement." Brooke remained quiet. It was the best she could do for now.

"Okay," sighed her mother. "I'll try not to intrude, but if we're going to try to become friends, we have to spend time together. Agreed?"

"Yes, of course. Now, tell me about this house. You seem pleased."

Her mother gave her a triumphant smile. "I'm told it's in the best section of West Walles, a little farther north of here."

Brooke forced herself to keep her smile. Her mother might talk about change but it wouldn't happen anytime soon, if ever.

"It's only four years old and in very good condition. The woman who lived there died suddenly, and her family is selling it. My real estate agent has already put in an offer even though it hasn't officially come on the market."

"She's good. Paul and I liked her."

"Yes, she understands what I like, what I need. At any rate, she thinks the family will accept my offer, and I'll be able to move in within a month."

"Nice," said Brooke, relieved it wouldn't be longer than that. "Would you like Paul and me to take a look at it?"

Her mother smiled. "Yes. That would be lovely. Maybe later when Paul gets back from wherever he is?"

"Sure. I'll ask him. I need to talk to him anyway. Amber and Cate have come up with an exciting business idea for me."

"Oh?" Her mother leaned forward.

"Yes. Amber would collaborate with me to set it up and get it going. It's a store for upscale, gently used clothing. We'd call it 'Refresh.' It would be a way to help businesswomen, single moms, and teen-age girls. Nice, huh?"

"You'd become a shopkeeper?" Her face held a look of horror.

Brooke emitted a whoosh of frustration. "Mom, puhleeze. You sound as if we're English royalty, too high-falutin' to do anything like this."

"It's just that your father worked so hard to take care of us, make sure we'd never have to work."

"In this day and age, even if some women don't need to work to put food on the table, they want to have meaningful lives, and do for others. It's a basic premise of living a good life."

Her mother set down her tea cup and glared at her. "Are you suggesting I'm not living a good life because I'm not a ... a ... shopkeeper?"

"Let's not go there, all right?" Brooke stood. "Can I get you hot water? More tea biscuits?"

"No, thanks, dear. I'm fine."

"Then, I think I'm going upstairs for a while to check my email before it's time for me to pick up the girls from their friend's house."

"I'm so glad they're settling in so quickly," said Diana.

"Me too," responded Brooke, pleased they could agree on something.

With Paul and the girls, Brooke trailed her mother and the real estate agent through the relatively small, but tasteful home her mother wanted to buy. It was lovely. Her mother might be difficult, but she had impeccable taste.

"What do you think?" the real estate agent asked Brooke.

"It's perfect. When will my mother hear about her offer?"

The agent checked her watch. "Hopefully in a couple of hours. I've advised Diana to make a more than fair offer to prevent the house from going on the market. Once that happens, bidding wars will escalate the price."

"Let's hope the family is reasonable," Brooke said. The house was farther away from her own than she'd been led to believe. And the thought of having her own space back was tantalizing.

That night, after the household was quiet, Brooke lay next to Paul in bed and told him about her idea for Refresh.

"Is it something you really want to do or are you doing this to please Amber and Cate?"

Brooke blinked in surprise. Could that be why she'd suddenly clung to the idea? She shook her head. "No, I've been struggling with how I want to fill my life with P.J. away at college and the girls becoming more and more independent. Cate and Amber know this and came up with the initial idea. But I've tweaked it a bit and am going to make it a charity instead of a for-profit business. And because the store will be open only three days a week, I'll have time for the family. I may even get back to my painting. Of course, Mother says I'd be a shopkeeper."

He rolled over and smiled at her. "My wife, the shopkeeper and the artist."

She laughed. "Can you believe my mother calling me a shopkeeper? I don't understand her. You'd think she came from a wealthy background instead of the blue-collar family she detests."

"I think her attitude covers up a lot of pain. In the past, she might have been ridiculed for her background. She's certainly maintained her distance from it. In all the years we've been together, I haven't ever heard her mention her family."

"You're right. Maybe I should cut her some slack."

"Maybe you should take advantage of her being here and put her to work at your store. Who better to offer high-end clothes to people who might not know their value?"

"Oh my God!" Brooke giggled and covered her mouth. "She

a shopkeeper? What a perfect solution for keeping her busy and out of my hair." She turned to Paul. "Do you have any idea how much I love you?"

"I think you'd better show me," said Paul with a sparkle in his eyes that had been missing.

As Brooke reached for him, she thought that turning forty wasn't going to be so bad after all.

CHAPTER THIRTY-EIGHT

CATE

As she did every day, Cate checked her email, her phone messages, and her sales figures. It had become a habit to do so from the time she was starting out in the book business. It grounded her and gave her incentive to keep going when she saw how many readers loved her books. Of course, not all reviews were five-star. But the good came with the bad. Private messages were the best. She thought of some of her faithful readers as real friends.

She'd spent the last couple of weeks alternating between ideas for her new book and trying to add to her Galeon Wars book. Now that she knew it would be the last one, the ending weighed on her mind. She wanted to get it right.

On this late January morning, Cate sat in the kitchen unable to get started on either the new book or the old. Her period had arrived along with cramps that destroyed any thoughts of being successful at making a baby. She thought of all the times she and Jackson had made love, trying for a baby, and couldn't stop the feeling of failure or the sting of tears.

With a sigh, Cate rose. She'd lock herself in her office—no phones, no email, no Facebook, No Instagram, Twitter, or any other social media so she could work on her books. Her agent and editor were waiting. No more excuses.

Buddy seemed to know how important this time was, and instead of demanding her to lift him into her lap—something that didn't quite work with his long body—he lay down on his soft blanket beneath the desk.

Cate took a deep breath and went back to the battle scene between Serena and her arch enemy, Santor, king of the Argoes. As the queen of the Galeons it was Serena's duty to fight until the end to protect her people from invaders like Santor. She'd left Serena facing Santor in a duel in front of the castle. His troops and hers stood ready to battle at the first sign of dominance, but until then it was up to the two leaders to fight it out.

Cate began typing:

Serena lifted the sword her father had passed down to her and swung it as high as she could. Santor was taller than she by a good eight inches. But what he had in height, she had in speed. The trick was to keep him moving in circles.

Swoosh! Her sword came down and struck ... air! She rocked back on her heels, tugging against the hand that held her dark hair in its grasp.

Furious that Santor was playing dirty, she whirled away from him and lifted her sword again. As she prepared to bring the sword down on his, she saw the way Santor was trying to trip her with his large feet and leaped out of the way.

"Ack! You're no fighter! You're a dancer!" cried Santor, charging her, his teeth bared.

"Watch out!" Rondol called to her. "He's trying to force you out of the circle."

One of the rules of the contest was that both contestants had to stay inside the circle that had been drawn into the dirt. Serena ducked as he lunged forward. Santor tripped over her and landed outside the circle.

Serena lowered her sword. "Enough, Santor. I win."

He turned and swiped at her with his weapon, making a cut across her forehead. "You may win this battle, but you'll always carry my scar," he sneered.

Serena lifted a hand to her face and felt the warmth of her blood. "You will never be allowed to return. You and your people leave now, or we'll not let them go."

At a cry from Santor, his troops began attacking the Galeons, which was against all the rules.

Serena entered the fray, trying not to pay attention to the pain in her forehead, the way the blood was dripping in her eyes. She felt a movement at her side and turned. A small dragon flew above her shoulder, protecting her arm holding the sword.

"Who are you? Where did you come from?" Serena asked, relieved to have the help. The duel with Santor had drained her energy, and she was having a hard time coping.

"I'm Condora," the little dragon said as the Galeons forced the Argoes into the air.

A cheer went up from the crowd as the last of the Argoes lifted into the sky and flew away.

Rondol came to Serena's side and wrapped an arm around her. He smiled at the dragon still fluttering nearby, a tiny stream of smoke pouring from her nose. "I see you have a new protector," he said to Serena.

"Yes," said Serena. "Her name is Condora."

"Who sent you?" Rondol asked, holding a cloth to Serena's wound.

"The Dragon Queen," said Condora, settling on Serena's shoulder.

"You're so young," said Serena, stroking the dragon's back.

Condora bobbed her head. "Yes, the Queen thought I should grow up with your baby."

"Baby?"

Condora lifted into the air and shook her head. "Sorry! I wasn't supposed to tell you that. It's a secret. One of many such of that kind."

"Do you mean one of many babies?" Serena said, blushing when she saw the look of pride on Rondol's handsome face.

Condora fluttered her wings frantically. "Oh no! I wasn't supposed to tell you that, either."

Serena reached up and drew the little dragon to her chest. Giving her a hug, she whispered, "That's the best surprise ever. Now that my people can live peacefully, I can raise the family I've always wanted. My children will, in time, help keep our kingdom strong."

"Yes," Condora said nodding in agreement. "That's what she told me."

Cate stopped typing as tears filled her eyes. She loved Serena, wished she could be like her. But now, she wondered if it would remain an impossible dream. Having committed to starting a family with Jackson, she wondered if it would ever happen. She hadn't believed children would be part of her future. Now, the future seemed empty without the promise of them. The thought made her cry.

By the time Jackson came home, Cate had wept and railed all she was going to do. She couldn't let her disappointment destroy her relationship with him. She'd read too many stories about similar circumstances doing that to other couples.

“Hey, sweetheart, how’re you doing?” He swept her into his arms. “I got your text message. I’m disappointed too. But it’ll work out. It’s still early in the game.”

She nestled against his warm sweater and felt a new wave of hope roll through her. They were two healthy people who’d keep trying to start a family.

He lifted her chin and kissed her.

She responded, as she always did to the surge of energy between them.

When he pulled away, he said softly, “Love you.”

“Me, too. Love you,” Cate responded, uttering the rhyme that brought smiles to both faces.

“I heard from my mom today. She can hardly wait for us to get to North Carolina. She said she’s kept the party pretty low key, as you wanted, but then she has a million friends, so I’m not sure what she is talking about in numbers. Anyway, it’s only for a weekend.”

“Okay, but, Jackson, I’ve been thinking instead of a church wedding, I want to be married on the beach at Seashell Cottage. We’ve discussed a June wedding. June 17th would be perfect. Let’s go ahead and make the reservations. That way, it will be what we want. What do you say?”

He grinned. “I say you’re pretty smart. By making those reservations, we’ll avoid all discussion of having something different. Those of my family who can attend can either rent a house of their own or stay at one of the nearby hotels.”

“Like the Salty Key Inn,” said Cate, becoming excited. “They’ll love it.”

“High five!” Jackson held up his hand and Cate slapped it gleefully. “Don’t worry,” he said. “I’ll take care of my family. What are you going to do about Amber and Brooke?”

“I’ve already figured it out. They can stay at the Seashell Cottage with us. Brooke’s mother can watch the girls at a different location. We'll go someplace else for our honeymoon."

"I've got something in mind," said Jackson, "but I'm not ready to discuss it."

"Oh?" She stared at him. Jackson loved surprises.

"Not telling," Jackson said, laughing and moving away from her.

CHAPTER THIRTY-NINE

AMBER

Amber stood in her bedroom and gazed down at the massive pile of clothing on her bed. After cleaning out her closet of classic clothes that she had no intention of wearing again, she felt as if she weighed pounds lighter. She'd discovered that each time she did something to free herself from her past work life, she grew more optimistic. For years, people had asked her how she could endure working for Belinda. She and her counselor had even talked about it. Now, it seemed foolish for her to have stayed so long.

When her cell rang, she checked the caller's name and eagerly answered. "Hey, Brooke! What's up?"

"I think I've found the right spot for Refresh in a little town near my house. I want you to take a look at it, and if you like it, I'll sign a lease on a month-to-month basis."

"Smart idea. Sure." She looked at the clothing on her bed and decided she could wait to fold and sort them. "I can come out this afternoon. Will that do?"

"Yes. Why don't you plan to spend the night? We can talk about a lot of the details and go over the suggestions you sent."

"Great. I'm ready for a break. I'm not used to not working."

"Don't worry. If we get this up and running, you won't be hanging around the city anymore. Any thoughts of moving out this way?"

"Actually, I have thought of it, but I don't want to do anything about it until I decide if I want to open my own business."

"Okay. Let me know when you're on your way, and I'll phone my real estate agent. She's as excited about the place as I am."

Amber clicked off the call and smiled. Brooke had become a different person since she started to work on the ideas for Refresh. That and the move had given her a new energy, a reason to use her organizational skills, and a means to be apart from her mother's disapproval. She and Cate had shared a good laugh over Diana's horror of Brooke being a "shopkeeper." That attitude was so typical of her.

As Amber pulled out her small overnight bag from the closet, her cell rang. Thinking it was Brooke, she picked it up and said, "What now?"

"Sorry. Did I catch you at a bad time?" said a deep voice that Amber instantly recognized. Her pulse raced. She'd been thinking about Wynton a lot.

"Hello, Wynton. I'm sorry. I obviously thought it was someone else. What can I help you with?"

"I'd like to take you to dinner tonight, if you are amenable to that."

"Oh ... I just made plans to leave the city and spend the night at my friend's house in West Walles," Amber said, unable to hide her disappointment.

"We could make it someplace close by. My house is not far from West Walles. I'm staying there tonight."

Amber's thoughts flitted to Brooke. "That might work. Let me check with her, and I'll call you right back." She clicked off the call, her emotions whirling. The connection she'd made with Wynton through their friendship with Jesse felt like a blessing. They were two of the best men she'd ever met, inspiring trust in her from the beginning.

She called Brooke and asked if she could beg off having dinner with her.

"Oh, yes! By all means, go out with Wynton. I saw the way you two smiled at each other."

"We're just friends," said Amber, not ready to address those feelings. "He still misses his wife, and I'm not over Jesse."

"Whatever you say," said Brooke. "I'll see you this afternoon. And if you want to spend the night, your room is ready."

"Thanks," said Amber. "That means a lot."

She ended the call and phoned Wynton. "If the invitation for dinner is still open, I accept."

He chuckled. "It is. Text me the address and I'll pick you up at eight. Sound okay?"

"It sounds lovely," she answered truthfully.

"See you then," he said and ended the call.

The lilt of happiness in his voice delighted her.

Amber was standing with Brooke outside the storefront waiting for the real estate agent when Cate showed up. "Am I too late?"

"No, we're waiting for the agent. She's on her way," Brooke said.

"Check out the front of the store. Isn't it darling?" said Amber. The tiny building on the main street of a nearby town looked more like a small gingerbread house than a store. The tan-painted clapboards were accented by purple trim.

"This used to be the shop of a seamstress, where I had some work done," said Cate. "I was sorry to see her go out of business, but now I'm glad you will be able to use this building. It's going to be perfect for what you want to do."

"When we're not actually open, we'll have plenty of room to process new clothing and get it ready to go on sale," said

Brooke. "There's a big work table in the back room and lots of places to hang clothes." She turned and waved at the driver of a silver Mercedes.

Amber watched as a middle-aged woman emerged from her car. She straightened a pale-blue suit jacket, smoothed down the coordinating plaid skirt, and headed toward them with an eager gait.

Brooke went to greet her and led her to Amber and Cate. "Cassandra, you've already met Cate at my house when we first bought it. She helped me with the paint colors. But you haven't met Amber Anderson. She's another of my dearest friends and is actually helping me with this project."

"How nice. Haven't I met you before? Seen you before?"

"Perhaps," Amber said, giving Cate and Brooke silent messages to say nothing about the perfume ads. She shook hands with her. From all she'd heard about her, Cassandra was a force in the real estate business in the area. If, in the future, she ever decided to move closer to Cate and Brooke, she'd keep her in mind.

"Let's take another look inside, shall we?" Cassandra said, fussing with the lock box on the door. "The only reason the owner would consider a month-to-month rental is that he wants to sell the property but hasn't had any reasonable offers. It is a bit out of the way for some businesses, but for what you want to do, Brooke, I believe it will suit you just fine."

Amber had drawn up a mental checklist of features she'd like to see in the property and mentally checked them off as they were given a tour inside. There was plenty of natural light through the front windows, good storage space, places for dressing rooms, a tidy bathroom, and, as Brooke had mentioned, convenient work space. Out in back of the building, two parking spaces were available.

"This seems perfect," said Amber. "I say go for it, Brooke."

Cassandra smiled. "I have the paperwork all set to go. It just needs your signature. But I suggest you look through the lease carefully. Remember, the owner has to give you only a thirty-day notice to vacate the premises. I took the liberty of adding a clause that says if he finds a legitimate buyer for the property, you have that same thirty-day period to match the offer or better it. I also added a budget for new carpeting."

Amber smiled. Cassandra was as good as she'd heard. She asked about any other things they should be aware of, and then, when all questions were answered, Brooke signed the agreement.

Cassandra handed Brooke a set of keys. "Congratulations, ladies. Refresh is about to be born."

A wave of excitement engulfed Amber. By helping Brooke, she was on to a new phase in her life. Something that had nothing to do with Belinda Galvin. And, boy! did it feel good!

After Cassandra left, Amber walked through the store again, making notes with Cate and Brooke about extra things Brooke would need.

"I'll offer the services of Jackson and myself to put a fresh coat of paint on the walls," said Cate. "As they are, they look dingy."

"Terrific!" cried Brooke. "What color are you thinking?"

"A pale peach. Something that complements all colors and softens the room. Cassandra had mentioned the need to replace the carpet. It should go well with most anything you choose."

"Super. Amber and I can choose carpeting tomorrow. She's spending the night," said Brooke. She elbowed Amber with an impish grin. "Tonight, she has a hot date with a certain lawyer."

"Oh?" said Cate, settling her gaze on her.

"It's not going anywhere," said Amber. "He's lonely after losing his wife, and I'm trying to get past my time with Jesse. We both understand that."

Cate gave her a hug. "Oh, hon, we don't mean to make you uncomfortable. We're just teasing."

"I know," said Amber, but they were right. Wynton was hot, and she definitely would be attracted to him if she was ready to even consider dating.

CHAPTER FORTY

AMBER

Amber sat in the guest room in Brooke's house, gathering her thoughts for the evening ahead. She was excited to meet Wynton for dinner. Though she and Jesse hadn't been together for long, and it was several months ago, she wondered if she was moving too fast. With Jesse it was the first time in her life that she'd felt safe enough with a man to trust him. She already felt the same way with Wynton. Was it because both men were older? Successful? Honest? What?

She stared out the window at the winter scene below. She'd been in and out of therapy for several years to deal with her childhood. For the last year or so, she'd finally felt as if she'd properly put the past to rest. She knew now most mothers didn't act the way hers did, most kept their children secure and safe, she was in control of her own life, and good men were not like the one who'd assaulted her. She'd watched and worked with Jesse for a long time before she'd allowed herself even to think of dating him. And he'd proved to her how right her therapist was. Decent men could be kind, loving, and honest.

She sighed, exhaling feelings from deep inside her. After knowing Jesse, thinking of a future with him, and being pregnant with his baby, her heart had opened to all those possibilities. And then her dreams for a future with him had been ripped away from her. Hugging her arms around herself, she admitted, more than anything, she was lonely, aching for a normal, loving life—something she'd been too afraid of finding for way too long.

A soft knock on the door broke through her musing. "Yes?"

The door opened and Brooke slipped inside. "Just wanted to check on you. Are you pleased with everything we saw at the store today? I need to know you're on board with all my plans."

Amber smiled. "I'm definitely okay with the plans for Refresh and I'm glad to help. I'm not sure I even want to start my own agency any longer. Now that I've been away from the business for a while, I don't know if that's what I should do."

"Take your time figuring things out. In the meantime, I'm thrilled you're going to help me in this new venture of mine. After so many years of being mom and wife, I've lost some of my self-confidence about going into business. I need you, Amber."

Amber got to her feet and went to Brooke. "I need you too. You're going to make this the best 'gently used' store ever! And it's for a good cause."

As Amber walked down the stairs in a simple, blue wool dress, she felt like a teenager on her first date—nervous, excited, scared. What was she doing?

"You look lovely," said Brooke standing at the bottom of the sweeping staircase with Wynton and the two girls.

"You're so pretty," gushed Brynn.

"Yeah, P.J. would say you're hot," Bradley said.

"I would too," commented Wynton, bringing giggles to the girls' lips.

At the twinkle in Wynton's eyes, Amber relaxed. It was going to be fine. He was a good man.

Brooke handed him Amber's faux fur coat, and he stood

and helped her put it on. “Another cold winter night, but this looks like it will keep you warm.”

“Yes, it’s cozy and very PC.”

He laughed. “Samantha would agree with your choice.”

“Have a good time,” Brooke said, smiling at them both.

Amber gave her a little wave and exited through the door Wynton held for her.

“Well, we’re off to a good start,” he said. “I enjoyed talking to Brooke and meeting her girls. I’m pleased you have such nice friends.”

“It helps. And after going through the mess with Belinda, I’ve learned to appreciate my true friends.”

“Good,” he responded, “because life certainly has its ups and downs.”

Wynton helped her into his bottle-green Porsche and then got positioned behind the wheel. “I hope you like Italian food. Arturo’s is one of my favorite places.”

“I do like it,” said Amber. “And now that I don’t work for Belinda anymore, I’m going to enjoy doing more than tasting food.”

He gave her a look of surprise. “I’m happy to hear that. That’s one thing I loved about my wife, Barbara. She wasn’t afraid to enjoy life.”

“You still miss her, I’m sure.”

“I do, but this is the year I’ve told myself I’ll open up to new possibilities. Not that I’m in any hurry.”

“This is going to be my year to try and do the same,” said Amber.

“I think you’ll enjoy being out from under Belinda’s rule. She’s a tyrant.”

“Yes, she is. I realize now how unhealthy it was for me to stay. Even my counselor thought so.”

He shot her an approving look. “I like your honesty.”

She shrugged. "I've got that, at least."

He reached over and squeezed her hand. "And so much more. I'm looking forward to knowing you better."

Pleased, she felt her cheeks grow warm.

He pulled up in front of a simple brick building. "Don't be fooled by the exterior. Arturo's has some of the best food I've ever eaten, and it's consistently that way."

He helped her out of the car and with his hand at her waist ushered her inside the main entrance where a number of people were sitting on benches, waiting.

The hostess, a gray-haired woman dressed in a simple black dress noticed him and hurried over. "Wyn, my darling boy, how are you? It's been ages. We're busy tonight, but I've saved your special table." She smiled at Amber. "And who is this?"

Wynton placed a protective arm around her. "Nona, this is Amber Anderson, a friend of a friend. And, Amber, this is Nona Bertelli, Arturo's better half."

"Nice to meet you, Amber," she said, giving Amber a careful inspection. "I hope to see a lot more of you. Now both of you follow me."

Nona led them to a table covered with a red-linen cloth in a back corner. Candlelight shimmered in a cut-crystal votive, setting off the sparkling wine glasses and polished silverware at each place.

"Thanks, Nona," said Wynton as he helped Amber into her chair and accepted menus from her.

"You're welcome, Wyn. Anytime." She left quickly and headed to the front door to greet people.

Amber took a look around the restaurant. As far as she could tell, they were seated in the main dining room. Another room was visible at the far end of the main room. Tables there were covered in red and white-checked cloths with an atmosphere that seemed much more casual.

Wynton saw her staring at it and chuckled. “Families with small children are assigned to that room. Arturo won’t have children spoiling the appreciation of his cooking. Barbara and I were pleased when Sam finally received approval for the main dining area.”

Amber smiled. “Very nice. It does ruin a meal if children are crying and fussing nearby.”

“True, but I haven’t minded having kids around.”

She wondered why Wynton didn’t have more children. He obviously loved Samantha.

The waitress appeared. “Welcome back, Wynton. We’re glad to have you here.”

“Amber, this is Nona’s granddaughter. Annette, Amber Anderson.”

Amber smiled at the young, dark-haired beauty. “It’s so nice that this restaurant is a family affair.”

Annette laughed softly. “Nice? Usually. But Italian tempers can get pretty hot from time to time.”

“What does Arturo have planned for this evening? Anything special or should I stick to my usual?” asked Wynton.

“You might want to try the fettucine with a lemon lobster sauce. It’s delicious, with plenty of tender pieces of lobsters right from Maine waters.”

“Sounds wonderful. How about you, Amber? Do you need time to decide?

“Yes, I’m sorry. I’ve been so busy gazing around, I haven’t looked at the menu yet.”

Wynton smiled at Annette. “I think you might have found another loyal customer. She likes the place, and we haven’t even eaten our food yet.”

Annette grinned and turned to Amber. “How about one of

my favorites—linguine with fresh, grilled vegetables in a light butter and garlic sauce?"

"Perfect," said Amber, grateful she wouldn't have to peruse the menu and keep Wynton waiting.

As Annette left, the wine steward approached.

"Trust me on the wine?" Wynton asked.

Amber nodded. "Of course."

After conferring with the wine steward, Wynton faced Amber with a smile. "I've ordered a nice white wine I think you'll love. I hope so anyway."

"I'm not that knowledgeable about wine, so I'm eager to see what it tastes like."

Wynton leaned forward. "How are things going with that clothing store you mentioned?"

"Good. I'm helping Brooke to get it up and running. I think she's going to be successful and in the meantime, I'm having fun with it."

Wynton chuckled good-naturedly. "I'm glad. Like I said, I'm hoping to get to know you better. I haven't dated in a while. Haven't wanted to. But after meeting you, I decided I'd like to try."

"Yes, me too. Though I have to warn you, I'm a very cautious person about this kind of thing."

"That's okay. Me too."

The wine steward returned with a bottle of wine. He showed it to Wynton, opened it, handed the cork to Wynton, and waited.

Following a routine, Wynton accepted a small amount of wine in his glass, and tasted it before nodding his approval. "Very nice. Thank you."

The steward poured wine into Amber's glass and then refilled Wynton's. "*Buono Appetito!*"

Wynton lifted his glass to her. "Here's to friendship."

"Yes!" Amber quickly agreed, raising her glass to meet his.

They chatted comfortably about the weather, Refresh, Samantha, and other easy topics throughout dinner.

When at last, both of them declared themselves full, Wynton sat back and gazed at her. "I've enjoyed our time together. Would I sound like a lech if I asked you back to my house for coffee? I'm not ready for the evening to end."

Amber laughed. "Not at all. I trust that you're not going to be that way."

He studied her. "I won't be a jerk, I promise you."

As Wynton pulled up to the front of his house, Amber studied it, liking it as much this time as she had before. It was an attractive house, not the least bit ostentatious.

They hurried from the car through the chilly air to the front door and inside.

"I'll light the fireplace in the den. We can sit there," said Wynton, helping her with her coat.

"Sounds good. Want any help in the kitchen?"

"No, but you can keep me company. Living alone, I've learned to make myself handy in the kitchen. In fact, I like to cook."

"You and Cate's fiance, Jackson, would get along nicely. He's a wonderful cook."

"I'd love to meet him sometime."

"Maybe you will," Amber said, knowing already that both Cate and Jackson would like him.

Wynton fixed their coffee, and they each carried a cup of it into the den. "Let's sit in front of the fire." He indicated the love seat. Amber lowered herself into it and moved over so Wynton would have plenty of room, as he was over six feet tall and broad-shouldered.

They stared at the fire for a while and then Wynton said, "I have to ask. How close were you to Jesse? If he hadn't reunited with his wife in Paris, would you have continued to see him?"

Amber set down her coffee cup on the end table beside her. Wynton had said he admired her honesty. She owed him that.

"Yes ... I ... I was pregnant with his baby when he died." Tears stung Amber's eyes. "We'd only dated a couple of months. I never expected anything like that to happen. The truth is, I haven't been close to many men before." Amber covered her mouth and closed her eyes, wondering where to begin, how to end. A wave of embarrassment swept over her.

Wynton's warm fingers wrapped around her cold hand. "Go on. You can tell me."

Amber opened her eyes and let her tears escape. "I lost the baby shortly after I found out I was pregnant, during the time the news about the crash came out. I was heartbroken about it."

Wynton pulled her into his embrace. "Always a crushing time. Barbara and I lost three babies."

He rubbed her back and let her cry.

The humiliation she might have felt with someone else didn't happen. A calm washed over her. The secret she'd promised to keep from anyone else was out, and instead of being ashamed, she was relieved.

As Wynton continued to comfort her, he asked gently, "And those other men?"

Amber straightened and looked him in the face. After years of therapy, she understood it was not her fault that her mother's boyfriends had tried to get her to do things she didn't want to do. "My mother had a lot of boyfriends when I was growing up."

"Did they hurt you?" Wynton said, his brow wrinkled with concern.

"One," said Amber, her lips thinning at the memory, even now. "That's why I haven't dated much. I haven't wanted to until recently when I've learned to trust myself."

"Ah, my sweet Amber. You've had such a difficult time." He lay her head against his broad chest and patted her back. "I want you to know you can trust me."

She leaned into him and let the sobs traveling up from her gut out into the open, finding relief in sharing the truth.

After a while, Wynton said, "Feeling better?"

Amber took the handkerchief he offered and wiped her eyes, then blew her nose. The honking sound of it should have made her embarrassed, but it didn't. She studied Wynton's face full of concern and emitted a long sigh. "I haven't told anybody but Cate and Brooke and my old therapist what happened. But I knew I had to tell you. That's the only way we could become real friends."

"Yes," said Wynton. "The best of friends."

Amber studied him. "You're okay with that?" she asked, praying he would be.

He brushed a lock of hair away from her face and gave her a tender smile. "For now, that's what we'll be. In time, I hope you'll change your mind. I would like more than that."

When she realized how sincere Wynton was, Amber emitted a soft sigh of contentment. He was such a wonderful man.

CHAPTER FORTY-ONE

CATE

On their way to North Carolina for Valentine's Day, Cate sat on the plane beside Jackson trying not to worry about the weekend ahead. She hated conflict and knew she might have to stand firm to keep her wedding the way she wanted. Jackson's mother was sweet but used to being in charge. With six children she'd had to be able to keep everyone in line.

"Excited?" Jackson said, giving her hand a squeeze.

"And worried," she answered honestly. "You know your mother isn't going to like a destination wedding in Florida."

"It's our wedding, not hers," Jackson replied. "Don't worry. She's so happy I'm finally marrying you she might be more pliable than you think."

Feeling better, Cate relaxed.

Later, as they entered the warmer air of North Carolina outside of the Raleigh-Durham International Airport, Cate pushed aside worrying thoughts. Jackson loved his family, and they loved him. This was his time to share his happiness with them.

A white Suburban pulled up to the curb, and Jackson's mother, Laurie, got out to welcome them. Hugging Jackson to her, she bubbled, "I'm so glad you're here. We've got a lot of fun things planned."

She turned to Cate and swept her in her arms. "Welcome,

Cate. I'm so excited about having you here. Just think! Another daughter."

Cate smiled. "Glad to be here, Laurie." But Laurie had already gone around to the back of the vehicle to help her husband load the suitcases.

Jackson's father, Tom, strode over to them. "Good to see you two. Laurie's been planning this day for weeks." He gave Jackson a bro hug and Cate a quick embrace. "Nice to add another member to the family."

"Let's get going, shall we?" Laurie said, hopping inside the back seat. "Jackson, you can sit up front with your Dad. Cate and I are going to chat." She patted the seat next to her and waved Cate inside.

Realizing she had no choice, Cate climbed in beside her while Jackson settled in the passenger seat up front.

Laurie squeezed Cate's hand. "Now, dear girl, I thought we'd spend some time tomorrow looking at a few places I thought you might like for your wedding. Jackson told me you wanted something small and intimate. I think you'll be pleased with what I've found."

"Oh, but ..." Cate began.

"Laurie, honey, slow down. The kids just got here. Give them time to get their breaths," warned Tom.

Laurie fluttered her hands in front of herself. "Oh, right. I will. It's just so thrilling that they're here." She turned to Cate. "We have lots to talk about, but I'll give you a chance to get settled first."

"Mom, I hope you've scheduled time for Cate and me to relax with the family. This is a short trip."

"Of course. We have the engagement party tomorrow night. Then Sunday will be a day of rest and planning. Your flight on Monday isn't until late afternoon."

Cate fought the urge to leap out of the car. She, like most

writers, was shy and content to be by herself. Jackson's family could be overwhelming. Exhausting, in fact.

"Your sisters will be here, along with Jake and Justin," Laurie said with a note of triumph. "Jon is involved in some special project for the government and can't make it. But he promised to be at the wedding."

"Good. Has he found a girlfriend yet?" Jackson responded.

"Not yet. But now that you and Cate are getting married, he knows the pressure is on him to find someone," Laurie said chuckling. "I want all my babies happily settled."

Cate gazed out the window at the scenery, sitting straighter as they entered the gates of the golf community Laurie and Tom loved so much.

"We'd better have time scheduled for a round of golf," Tom announced to his wife. "I need to help Jackson with his game."

"Whoa! Help me? I beat you last time. Remember?" said Jackson, chuckling.

Still laughing, Tom pulled up to one of the larger homes in the community. A successful entrepreneur who'd owned several gas stations and fast food franchises in New Jersey, he'd been able to sell them for a good price and retire early.

Cate got out of the car and followed Jackson inside. She liked the layout of the house, the tile floors, the swimming pool, and the huge lanai outside. Still, the size of his parents' home and the way Laurie, Tom, and the others filled it with their constant chattering and motion were sometimes intimidating.

As soon as they got settled in their bedroom, Jackson said, "C'mon! Let's go meet the girls."

Cate knew by now what the family called the girls were his two older sisters, Janis and Jenn. She'd glimpsed them and their families sitting by the pool when she'd entered the house.

It was interesting to see Jackson with his siblings. Both in their fifties, Janis and Jenn adored him and his younger brothers. Along with exchanging hugs and kisses, good-natured teasing usually occurred. This time was no exception.

"Well," said Janis, a tall, lean women with dark curls, "Cate finally put a noose around your neck."

Jackson held up his hands. "Whoa! I'm the one who had to convince her to marry me."

"Sounds about right," said Jenn, rising from her lounge chair and giving him a hug. She turned to Cate. "Good for you, sister! We've got to keep these guys on their toes."

Her husband, Nick, a big, broad-shouldered man, walked over to her and put his arm around her. "Whatever you say."

Everyone laughed. Nick was an ex-football player and wasn't about to be pushed around by anyone.

Dan, Janis' husband, climbed out of the pool, wrapped a towel around himself, and came over to them. "Hi, Cate." He punched Jackson's shoulder playfully. "So, when's the big day?"

"June 17th," Jackson answered with a grin. "Pack your bags, it's going to be a destination wedding in Florida." He turned to Cate. "Right, babe?"

"Right," said Cate as forcefully as she could when observing the looks of horror on the faces of Janis, Jenn, and their mother.

"Oh, but you can't do that. Florida? June?"

"I'm sorry, Jack, but you'll have to change things around," Janis said. "Bitsy's baby is due in mid-June. I can't miss being there for my first grandchild."

"And it's little Chase's third birthday. Dan and I are taking the whole family to Disney World then."

"Tom and I are cruising with our dearest friends. A trip through the Panama Canal," said Laurie.

Jackson cast a worried glance to Cate. "But we've already booked the Seashell Cottage and a block of rooms at the Salty Key Inn."

"It was the only weekend the cottage had available," said Cate, blinking rapidly to hold back tears. "My friends have already committed to the time."

"Well, now, let's not get too excited," said Tom. "Laurie, you can call our friends and tell them we'll book the next week. This far in advance that shouldn't be a problem. Janis and Jenn, you'll have to work around the date. It's unfair to ask Cate and Jackson to change the date. If Bitsy's baby is anything like the other babies in the family, he'll be here early."

Cate drew a deep breath. Tom didn't speak loudly, but it was clear that he was not going to allow any argument. Her admiration for him grew.

"Thanks, Dad," said Jackson with heartfelt gratitude. "It wasn't easy to get the cottage, and it has a special meaning to Cate and me."

"Well, I guess that's settled then," said Laurie with obvious disappointment. She sighed. "I wish the two of you had warned me earlier. I had so many things planned for here."

"Mom, we told you we wanted something small and simple," Jackson reminded her gently.

"Maybe we can work around the Disney World trip," said Jenn. "Don't worry. We'll be there."

"The Salty Key Inn isn't too far from Orlando," Jackson said. "I've printed off information sheets for you so you have all the details you need. But it's a popular place, so be sure to reserve rooms early. Mom and Dad, we thought you might like to stay in the Honeymoon Suite." His smile was teasing.

"Well, now, that's nice of you," said Tom. "What do you say, Laurie?" He wiggled his eyebrows at her.

Cate laughed with the others when Laurie's cheeks turned bright pink.

"Guess that's a go," said Tom, giving Laurie's behind a love pat.

Observing this, Cate hoped she and Jackson would keep that kind of playful love in their lives.

The next evening, Cate stood with Jackson in their bedroom before the engagement party, wondering if they'd done the right thing.

"Is your mother going to be all right about our wedding?" Cate asked. Though Laurie was being nice about their choice of venue for the wedding, her disappointment was obvious.

Jackson tugged Cate into his arms. "Sweetheart, the wedding is about us. It's important to have the wedding we want. I love my mother, but if we let her plan it, it will become something neither one of us wants. Believe me, the party tonight will be a way to prove that to you."

"Good. I'm not used to having a family to please, and I don't want any hurt feelings."

He lifted her chin and kissed her. "They love you. Don't worry about it."

"Okay." She stepped back and twirled in front of him. "Like the new dress?"

"Like you in it," he said. "It brings out the green in your eyes."

The deep-green, sleeveless linen dress was something Amber had helped her pick out, and it fit her like a glove. Catching a glimpse of herself in the mirror, she was glad she'd joined Brooke's gym class for a good workout three days a week. It was making a difference.

A knock at the door interrupted Jackson's kiss. He pulled

away. "Yeah?"

"Jackson, it's Mom," came his mother's voice through the door.

"Okay, come on in." He went to the door and opened it. "Wow! You look pretty good, Mom!"

She grinned. "Thanks, son. Now, go along. I want to talk to Cate alone before our guests arrive."

Jackson shot a glance at Cate, shrugged, and left.

Cate clutched her hands and smiled at Laurie. "Is there something I can help with?"

"No, my dear, we're all set. I just want to give you this." She handed Cate a turquoise box with a white ribbon. Tiffany & Co. was printed in black on the top.

Cate's pulse raced. She knew about Tiffany's, of course, but hadn't ever shopped there.

"Go ahead. Open it," Laurie said, smiling.

With shaking fingers Cate took off the ribbon and lifted the top of the box. Inside, nestled against velvet, a pearl necklace glistened.

"It's beautiful," gushed Cate. "I've never seen pearls so rich and shiny."

"They're Mikimoto pearls. Janis and Jenn were each given a necklace like it at their engagements. Something special to wear at the wedding. I hope you like them too."

The tears stinging Cate's eyes slipped out and down her cheeks. "Oh, Laurie. I can't think of a sweeter gift. Thank you. They're beautiful and so much more than that. I will treasure them."

Laurie hugged her. "And we treasure you and Jackson together. He's a great guy, and you've made him very happy. You can't know what that means to me."

"I promise to keep him happy." She paused and then blurted, "Unless I can't give him the babies we want. Even though we're not married yet, we're trying."

"Good. He's always wanted a family."

"But what if I ..."

Laurie clasped her hand. "Don't even go there. If it's meant to be, it'll all work out."

Cate couldn't stop herself from saying, "I hope so."

Laurie gave her a hug. "Let me put that necklace on you and then let's go to your party."

The Golf Springs Country Club was an elegant version of several in the area, a step above the norm. Cate had been here once before. The décor included lovely Oriental rugs, original artwork, and a variety of decorative touches that Cate recognized as being special. Fresh flowers in a variety of arrangements throughout the rooms were an added touch.

Tom and Laurie had reserved a private dining room for fifty people. A full bar was set up at one end of the room. Waitresses carried trays of appetizers through the throng of people gathered at the bar and in small groups throughout the room.

Cate dutifully followed Laurie, smiling as she was introduced to so many people there was no way she'd be able to remember the names of any. The writer in her, though, catalogued dresses, bits of conversation, and other tidbits to be tucked away in her mind to be brought out at some point in the future. All things that would add texture to her descriptions in future books.

During a break, Cate headed for the ladies' room, needing a breather. The party was lovely in every detail, the guests pleasant, the family fun. But Cate was glad that she and Jackson had decided on something simpler. After living together for so many years, they wanted to enjoy the moment when they finally made their vows in front of those close to them.

Cate felt a bit of cramping and checked to see if it had anything to do with getting a period. So far, things were all right. But she wouldn't be sure for another week or so. A worrisome thought. Though no mention of it was made to others, the joy behind this engagement was the idea of starting a family.

CHAPTER FORTY-TWO

BROOKE

Now that she'd signed a lease for the store, Brooke dug into the project, establishing a work schedule. Before they left for North Carolina, Jackson and Cate, with her help and Amber's, had painted the interior of the store. Brooke ordered new carpet, and then she and Amber chose a fabric to be made into privacy curtains for the dressing rooms—a peach and green print that was both sophisticated and fun. With the help of both Amber and Cate, she ordered live plants, prints of paintings of women, a loveseat in a dark-green, other pieces of furniture, and decorative items to adhere to the peach and green color theme. Preparing the store was just one part of it. Sorting through clothes, creating ads, and figuring out how best to take care of the business aspects were other issues.

One evening after coming home late, her mother met her at the door. "Where have you been? The girls and I were wondering when you'd get home to start dinner."

Brooke clamped her teeth together. Her mother would be moving into her new house in two days and she didn't want to blow apart the détente they'd created.

Brooke drew a calming breath. "I left a note for the girls and told you I might be late. It's going to take a lot of work to get the store completely ready. Until we get things set up, I can't promise to be here when you expect me."

"What are you going to do when I'm not here with the girls?" her mother said, giving her a challenging look.

"I'll make different arrangements. Don't worry. I'll see that they're properly supervised. Spring sports will be starting soon, and they will be getting out of school later."

"I was always there for you when you came home from school," her mother said, shaking her head.

Brooke couldn't let that go by. "No, you weren't. You had luncheons and bridge games and all sorts of activities. It was Maybelle who gave me afternoon snacks and asked about my day."

"Harumph. Maybe that's why you got so heavy. She spoiled you rotten."

Brooke drew a deep breath. "I'm not going to talk to you about that. It was hurtful then and it's hurtful now."

"Oh, sweetheart. I didn't mean anything by it. It's just that I was so worried about you."

Brooke studied her. "You weren't worried about me. You were worried about having a daughter that didn't look the way you wanted. You constantly put me down, made me feel so ugly, so unworthy. It's time to cut the bullshit. I'm a grown woman now, Mother. So, you don't have to worry about me anymore."

The look of surprise on her mother's face was telling. "Don't be that way, Brooke. I care about you. I do."

"I'm sure you think you do. But you have a poor way of showing it. I'm tired of dealing with your constant belittling. Now, stand aside. I'm going to find the girls. Dinner might be a little late tonight."

Brooke moved past her mother and climbed the stairs feeling better. She'd confront her mother again, if necessary. This move, this year was about new beginnings. She wondered how much work it would take to convince her family she had a life of her own.

The sound of the girls' giggles drew her to Brynn's room.

They were sprawled across the bed, looking at a magazine together.

"Hi! What's up?" she asked.

"A cute boy named Xavier," said Bradley. "He's a singer who's a real hottie."

Brooke blinked in surprise. The girls were ten, not twenty, and growing up too fast. "Where'd you hear about him?"

"Online. Maria at school lent us this magazine," said Brynn. "We promised we'd give it back to her tomorrow."

"May I take a look?"

Bradley handed her the magazine. "She got it from her sister."

Brooke flipped through the pages, finding all sorts of beauty ideas, some articles about dating, and ads for clothing—nothing out of line.

She handed it back. "Okay. Here it is. You're right. Xavier is sort of cute."

"Mom! You're not supposed to say something like that," said Brynn. "You're way too old."

"Yeah, you could be his mother," added Bradley.

"Thank goodness, I'm not," said Brooke. "You two and P.J. are enough for this family."

"What about the dog?" Bradley said. "It's almost spring."

"Let's wait a while. It should be a little warmer in a month or so. Right now, I'm busy trying to set up my business. That has to take precedence."

"No fair," said Brynn.

"It's time for you to understand that I need to get my life here settled in a way that pleases me and helps others. It's going to take cooperation from all of us."

"Okay. But can we have a dog?" said Bradley."

"Not now. Maybe later. In the meantime, you can start to do a search online for puppies or rescue dogs."

"Really?" Brynn scrambled to her feet and gave her a hug.

"I want a big dog," said Bradley. "Maybe a Saint Bernard."

"Too big," said Brooke. "Think more along the lines of small."

"A wiener dog!" cried Brynn.

"Let's see. Shall we?" Brooke left their room and headed downstairs to her own room to get into something more comfortable.

Later, after changing into jeans and a sweatshirt, she headed into the kitchen.

Her mother looked up from the kitchen table. "You're wearing that? Paul will be coming home soon. You want to look your best for him."

"I can't believe you're saying that. It's something out of the 1950s, for heaven's sake. This is the twenty-first century. Remember?"

"I'm just trying to be helpful. Your father expected me to look my best."

Two more days! Brooke couldn't wait until she had her house to herself. Her mother had made a trip to California to supervise the packing of her house, and the three days she'd been gone were blissful.

"Have you heard anything from the moving company?" Brooke asked her while getting out chicken breasts from the refrigerator. She'd do a simple mushroom-stuffed chicken bake with a creamy cheese sauce the girls liked.

"They're on their way. I don't know what I would've done without Rosita to oversee the loading of the truck. And she did all the cleaning before the house officially went on the market."

"I hope you paid her well."

"Oh, I did. Her son is in college and she needs the money."

After Brooke finished preparing the chicken, she set the

table. The girls usually did it, but tonight she didn't want any disagreements about whose turn it was to do what. Tomorrow, she'd post a list of chores for them to do each day.

Her mind was whirling with ideas about finishing touches in the store. She figured she could open the store within two weeks. Amber had brought in a number of articles of clothing and was scheduled to pick up more. Brooke had received a couple of calls from mothers of students at the girls' school who wanted to consign goods. That was another whole procedure to get organized. That, and a simple accounting and sales system. Brooke was meeting with an accountant tomorrow and a salesman to see about leasing a cash register tied into an inventory program.

The sound of the garage door opening caught her attention. She felt her lips curve. Paul was home. With him around, her mother assumed a sweet, caring attitude that calmed Brooke's agitation with her.

The girls rushed downstairs to greet him as he walked into the kitchen.

"Dad! Dad! We're looking for a dog!" cried Brynn.

"I want a wiener dog like Auntie Cate's dog Buddy," said Bradley.

Paul glanced at Brooke. "You okay with this?"

"Yes, but not until later, after I've got my business up and running smoothly. The girls and you need to sit down with me, together as a family because there are going to be some changes around here. I won't be as available to you as I have been."

He raised his eyebrows. "Okay. We'll talk."

Brooke's mother walked into the room. "How was your day, Paul?" she asked, giving her a pointed look.

"Fine, fine. Busy as usual," he answered politely. "I'm going to go and change into something more comfortable."

"Dinner will be ready in thirty minutes or so,"said Brooke. "We have time for a cocktail in the living room. I've got a fire going there."

"Sounds good." Paul disappeared into the master suite.

Brooke resisted an urge to follow him and turned to her mother. "Go ahead. Take a seat in the living room and I'll bring you a glass of wine. After tomorrow night, you'll be on your own."

"Yes. It will be good to have my own space," her mother said. "But I enjoy having you wait on me."

Always, Brooke thought meanly, and then chided herself.

She fixed Paul a glass of Scotch and poured red wine into two glasses. She liked this nightly ritual of a short break before dinner. It was a good time to catch up with one another on the day's activities. Many times, this communication had helped their marriage along. That's why she'd been so upset when Paul had stopped talking to her about what he was going through.

She carried the wine and Scotch into the living room on a tray and set it down on the coffee table in front of the couch facing the fireplace.

"Have you told Paul about all your plans? Does he realize what it's going to do to his schedule?" her mother asked her.

"That's something I intend to talk to the whole family about in time. For the moment, we'll get through this week and your move, and then we can settle down to a more normal routine."

"Be sure to make him seem spoiled," her mother said. "Men want to feel like they're king of the castle, so to speak."

"Mother, stop." Brooke turned as Paul entered the room.

He gave her a questioning look.

She shook her head.

He got her silent message and said, "They say another storm is coming. I hope it won't delay your moving, Diana."

She gave him a flirty smile. “It sounds as if you’re anxious to get rid of me.”

To Paul’s credit, he played along. “You know that’s not true. We love having you here.”

“I was just telling Brooke how important it was to make sure you were happy to come home and be treated like a king.”

Paul glanced at Brooke and faced Diana. “I’m always happy to come home to my beautiful wife.” His tone was gentle but firm in its commitment.

Brooke wanted to hug him for it.

“Well, I hope after I get moved in, you’ll be happy to visit me. I’ve yet to make friends here.”

“I was wondering if you’d like to work at Refresh. It would be a good way for you to meet people and become part of the surrounding area.”

“Me? A shopkeeper? You know how I feel ...”

“Mother, you’d be a part-time employee,” Brooke interjected. “Think of it as volunteer work, though, of course, we’d pay you. And this is no typical thrift store, though its purpose is allowing others a chance to have access to high-end clothing. We plan to use unsold clothing to help young professional women and women who want to enter the job market.”

“I’ll think about it.”

“Please do. Amber, Cate, and I think you’d be perfect for the job because you’re so stylish and you know how to present yourself well. We’re sure you could help others.”

“Oh. Well, let me get moved in and I’ll consider it. Some people have no fashion sense at all.”

“Precisely,” said Brooke, hiding her amusement.

The buzzer sounded from the kitchen. Brooke got to her feet. “I’ll see to dinner. You two relax here.”

As she left the room, Brooke heard her mother say,

"Brooke's right. I'd be good at helping people with their wardrobes. Heaven knows, I've had a lot of practice."

"Yes, you have," said Paul with a note of humor that made Brooke smile.

CHAPTER FORTY-THREE

CATE

Now that she was back home in New York, Cate had time to reflect on her time in North Carolina. She was happy she and Jackson had made the trip. The engagement party was lovely, and more than that, it gave his parents a chance to celebrate with Jackson, and Laurie a chance to plan something special. It also proved to both Jackson and her that a big wedding was something neither wanted. Still, they were glad for the family and friends who'd committed to attend the wedding in Florida.

Laurie and Tom reserved the honeymoon suite at the Salty Key Inn. Jackson's two sisters and one of his brothers, Jerome, also reserved rooms there. His oldest brother, Jake, was waiting to see if he could have the time off, and they were still waiting to hear from Jon, who hadn't been able to make the engagement party.

On Cate's side, Brooke and Amber had reconfirmed they'd stay at the cottage and be part of the wedding. Pleased to be invited, Brooke's mother went ahead and reserved a room at Salty Key Inn for herself and the two girls, and another room for P.J. With the plans underway, Cate grew more excited, and more worried. She'd overheard Jackson talking to his mother about his excitement over starting a family. She knew it might take time to become pregnant, but she felt her sense of failure growing with each disappointment.

She rubbed her abdomen, wishing her menstrual cramps, a sign of yet another miss, would go away. She'd cried when she'd told Jackson it had happened, but he again reminded her that it was still early and they had plenty of time.

Cate gazed out the window of her office. Yet another snow storm was due to arrive. She lifted her phone to call Brooke. They exchanged greetings and then Cate asked, "Any news on your mother's moving van?"

"Yes. They're planning on being here this afternoon and will start unloading then. I was told they'll stay as late as it takes to unload all of it because of the storm headed this way."

"Do you want help?"

"Yes," said Brooke. "My mother is driving me crazy. She insists on going to her house now. If you would come here when the girls get home from school and stay with them until Paul arrives, that would be great. I'll need you to come at four thirty. Can you do that?"

"Sure. I'll set the alarm on my phone."

"Thanks. You sound down. Everything okay?"

"I got my period," Cate replied, feeling the sting of tears.

"Oh, sweetie, I'm sorry. I know how disappointed you must be, but it's still early, so don't give up hope. It'll happen."

"That's what Jackson says. But what if it doesn't?"

"One step at a time, Cate," said Brooke. "Be positive."

"You're right. I need to stop thinking about it. I don't know how you did it, waiting all those years for the girls to come along."

"It wasn't fun," Brooke admitted. "I hope you don't have to go through the same thing. I'm off to take Mother to her new house. Thank goodness, she's shipping her car. Driving her everywhere is getting old. Especially when she insists on giving me directions every step of the way."

Cate laughed. It sounded just like Diana.

"Thanks for your help. See you later."

Cate clicked off the call and went back to her work on

"Girls' Night Out," the contemporary novel she was hoping to sell. Until she got more into the story, she couldn't come up with a compelling synopsis. Though it was easier to write about the three young women living in New York and not on a planet called Galeon, Cate missed Selena and Rondol. She knew everything about them. The three women in this story were still new to her.

She was deep into characterizations when Abby called. "How are you doing on the new book?"

"I'm pulling together the characters, and then I'll write the first three chapters. I should be able to come up with them in two weeks."

"You can't take that long. I promised the editor I'd have it to her by then, and I need time to look it over before I send it to her. Get it to me by the end of next week. Not a day later. Gotta go," she said, and clicked off the call.

Cate let out a long sigh. Didn't Abby understand that beginning a book was no easy task? Cate lay her head down on her desk, drew several deep breaths, and told herself she could do this.

She was in the middle of defining the quirky characteristics of one of the women when her alarm sounded. She glanced at the clock on her phone and gasped. Four fifteen.

"C'mon, Buddy. We've got to run."

Cate loaded the dog in her car and took off for Brooke's house. She loved the twins. Truth was, if she got pregnant, she hoped it would be with a girl.

The girls were just being dropped off by another student's mother when Cate pulled into the driveway behind her.

She and Buddy hurried out of the car and met the girls at the front door.

"Auntie Cate! Buddy!"

Cate waved to the driver and turned to the girls. "Your

mom called and asked me to meet you. She and your grandmother are at your grandmother's new house, waiting for the moving van. Let's go in. I'll stay with you until your father gets here."

"C'mon, Buddy," said Brynn, picking him up.

"We want a dachshund just like him," Bradley announced. "Mom said it was okay, but not now. We had a family meeting. We all need to help her get her business going. Then maybe, after that and warmer weather, we can get one."

"Do you know where you're going to get it?" Cate asked, amused by the way Buddy was licking Brynn's cheeks.

"Will you show us online where you got him?" Bradley said. "We were looking but couldn't find anything close by."

"Sure," Cate said. She followed the girls into the kitchen, read the note Brooke had left, and doled out the snacks Brooke had set aside for them.

"What do you girls think of your mother's new business, Refresh?" Cate asked.

"We have to help her," said Brynn. "Mom said it's time for some changes."

"More work for us," Bradley said. "She's making a list of chores."

"Sounds like she's planning ahead. That's good."

"Yeah, well we already know that if we get a puppy, we'll have to take care of it. Mom even bought us a book by the guy called the dog whisperer. It's a lot to learn." Brynn and Bradley exchanged grins.

"Maybe Mom will let us get two dogs, not one." Bradley held up crossed fingers.

Cate couldn't help the smile spreading across her face. These two girls would keep any mother hopping. The thought of having one baby was scary. The thought of twins, horrifying.

###

For the next week, Cate worked feverishly to write the first three chapters of the book, going back to the beginning and revising several times as new ideas about the characters came to her. It was only as she was writing about them that she was able to add layers to who they were, what their internal goals were, and the external conflicts that might arise to challenge them. By the time Abby called to check on her during the first week of March, Cate was exhausted and totally unsure if what she'd written was worth even looking at.

"Have you got it ready for me?" Abby asked her cheerfully.

"I've done the best I could in the one-week time frame you gave me," Cate replied, trying not to sound snappish. "You know it takes me longer than this to put something together."

"Whoa! I apologize for pushing you, but the particular editor I have in mind was looking for something new. Let's hope she hasn't already filled her slot."

"Sorry for being so grumpy, but I'm not sure you're going to like it."

"Send it to me and then go plan your wedding," said Abby. "I'm thrilled for you that it's finally happening. June 17th, right?"

"Yes. You'd better make room reservations at the Salty Key Inn right away. Our block of rooms is filling up."

"Okay. Thanks. I appreciate the invitation, Cate. You're one of my very special clients. You and I go back a long way."

"I appreciate you too. I'm sending you the synopsis and three chapters now. Let me know what you think."

"Okay, but it won't be for a day or two. In the meantime, don't fret. If I don't like it, we'll fix it together."

"That's what I'm afraid of—a big rewrite."

"Your email came through. Gotta go. Talk to you later."

Cate hung up and clasped her hands together. This was just

one scary part of writing a book—waiting for word on all that was wrong with it.

CHAPTER FORTY-FOUR

AMBER

On this April morning, Amber listened carefully to the salesman demonstrate the inventory program tied to the computer system Brooke was purchasing for the store.

"The old systems used to be complicated, but this one is as simple as possible. There are three categories for each item—price, source, share. The price is obvious. The source determines if this is a consigned item. If not, leave blank. The share is forty percent of the sales price that would go to a consigner. If no consignor, leave blank. It's just that simple."

"What if you change the price?" Brooke asked.

"Simple. Go in and change it. The rest is automatically calculated for you."

"We can start with my donations," said Amber. "For the print function, we print out the price label and stick it on a cardboard tag. Right?"

"Yes. The printout gives you the price and the inventory number so you know where to go to make any changes in the inventory system."

"Good. Because if an item doesn't sell, a consigner can decide to give it to us." Brooke turned to her. "That's when I decide whether to put it on sale or give it away."

Pleased, Amber nodded. A number of charities would love donations like that.

"You can do anything you want with pricing as long as you're tracking it in the inventory program," the salesman said to Brooke. "Your accountant will want a clear trail of how cash receipts and disbursements were managed and how credit card charges and credits were posted. My suggestion is to keep the operation as simple as possible. We can change things for you, but I don't think you want to do that unless it's necessary."

"I agree," said Amber. What had seemed a complicated issue was pretty easy to control. Brooke had already purchased a couple of boxes of different-sized clothing tags and special needles to use to tag the clothes.

"I'll check back in a week to see how you're doing. In the meantime, you can call the office with questions." He smiled at Brooke. "Thank you for your business." He handed her a notebook with instructions and bobbed his head. "Good luck! I like the way you've decorated the store."

He left, and Amber and Brooke grinned at one another.

"It's not bad," said Brooke. "If you're willing, we can take turns inputting the information in the system."

"No problem. You need all the clothes tagged too," said Amber. Brooke had paid a carpenter to come in and build shelves for items like sweaters, and she'd purchased several clothing racks. Large boxes of hangers were ready to use. They'd agreed all hanging items had to be hung using the special store hangers so that it looked consistent and professional. Brooke had also bought a clothes steamer so items could be pressed if necessary. Refresh might feature gently used clothing, but they'd be treated and displayed as if they were brand new.

"Do you think I'm crazy to do this?" Brooke asked, clasping her hands together. "Mother says I'm going to regret putting in this kind of time unless I do it right."

Amber made a face. "That's your mother for you. I thought she was considering helping you."

"She hasn't made up her mind. I'm sure she's waiting to see the reaction I get before deciding. If I do well, she'll join me. If not, she'll say 'I told you so'."

"Sounds like Diana. But I think she'd enjoy working here for a few hours each day. This isn't going to be your average store with average customers." Amber might not like all of her qualities, but Diana might be a wonderful asset to the store. She checked the time. "Sorry. I have to go. I'm meeting Wynton for a late lunch."

"Thanks for meeting me this morning. Have a nice time with Wynton," Brooke said. "You must know how happy I am that you're dating."

Amber paused a moment, uncomfortable. "It's not really dating. It's just spending time together."

Brooke gave her a quick hug. "Whatever you say. He's a nice man, and I'm happy you're ... friends."

Giving her a little wave goodbye, Amber left the store. Wynton was meeting her at Arturo's. It felt so good, so natural to join him for lunch. They'd talked on the phone almost every night and she was more and more comfortable with him. It was as if her time with Jesse had opened her up to a new kind of love. She and Wynton were actually becoming true friends.

She arrived at the restaurant a few minutes early and saw that Wynton's car was already in the parking lot. Knowing how much he enjoyed being with her, she filled with anticipation.

Inside, Annette greeted her. "He's already here, waiting for you."

Amber smiled, and seeing Wynton get to his feet to greet her, she waved, and hurried over to him.

He took hold of her hands and kissed her on the lips.

There was a time when she might not have liked such attention in a public place. But Wynton was an affectionate man and she'd learned to relax with him.

"How did your morning with Brooke go?" he asked after helping her into the chair opposite him.

"Good. She's installing an inventory system that makes a lot of sense. The number of items that need to be entered into the system, tagged, and then hung in the store seems daunting. But I'll help her. She really wants this business to succeed."

"I like the concept as you've explained it," said Wynton. "What are you having for lunch?"

"I'm going to order soup. The *pasta e fagioli* sounds fabulous. I need something hearty after this morning."

He chuckled. "I think I'll have the same thing."

"How was your meeting last night?" Amber asked after Annette had taken their orders. "Everything turn out the way you wanted?"

His expression grew serious. "It's a tough case, but I think I can win for my client."

"I'm sure you can," Amber said with conviction. Wynton was a respected lawyer who worked hard for his clients.

Wynton gave her a grateful smile. "I like that you have confidence in me."

"I do," she said, returning his smile as he reached across the table and caressed her hand.

"I missed talking to you last night," Wynton said. "How about meeting me for dinner tomorrow night?"

"I'd like that." Amber said. "You're spoiling me, you know."

He grinned. "Good."

Their soup came and they ate it in comfortable silence. It was another thing Amber liked about him.

After lunch, Wynton walked her out to her car. "Thanks for meeting me." He cupped her face in his hands and bent down to kiss her.

Heart thrumming happily, Amber met his lips.

When they pulled apart, they smiled at one another.

"See you tomorrow night," said Wynton. He watched as she got into her car and then he walked away.

The next day, Amber and Brooke worked in tandem putting information into the inventory system and tagging clothes, trying to get as much done before an afternoon meeting with Seth Morehead, the accountant Brooke had chosen to work with her. She'd heard he was local, young, and ambitious.

When he arrived for the meeting, Amber hid a smile. With his large round glasses perched on the end of his nose and his serious manner, he looked the part.

He emphasized the need to keep careful records of every expense, along with receipts. He then worked with Brooke to draw up a cash flow plan indicating what she thought she'd need until she began to make enough money to cover expenses.

"I'll have to do a lot of advertising," said Brooke. "In the meantime, I can carry the costs."

"Just be sure to cover all your basic expenses and have enough left over for emergencies. And you'll need to have enough money set aside to pay for any consigned goods sold on a regular basis," Seth warned her.

"I'll use my contacts not only for clothing, but to help spread the word," said Amber. "A few of them might not mind leaving the city to buy some of your things discreetly."

Brooke beamed at her. "If I can get high-end customers, it'll make my life so much easier."

Seth continued working with them, until Amber's mind began to spin. Math had never been her favorite subject.

By the time he left, and Amber packed up to go home, she hoped Wynton would agree to stay in and order food. She was exhausted.

The sound of the doorbell made Amber hurry to answer it. Opening the door, she smiled at Wynton. "Please come in. I'm so happy you agreed to stay in tonight."

"It's perfect. I've had quite a day myself."

Amber took his coat and hung it up. When she turned around, Wynton was standing back, staring at the photograph Jesse had taken of her.

He looked over at her and smiled. "This is so nice. And very revealing."

"Jesse was a special person in my life. It's such a tragedy that he and his family are gone."

"Yes. He was a good guy." He walked over to her and kissed her cheek. "I'm glad you and he met. Otherwise, I might not have met you." He drew her into his arms.

Amber rested her head against his chest and hugged him. It felt good to have this connection with him. As she told people, theirs was a friendship. A friendship that had so much more to offer when she was ready for it.

"Come into the living room. I've opened a bottle of wine and set out a bowl of nuts. I figured we'd want to relax before ordering our food."

"Good." Wynton walked into the room and sat down on the white couch that faced the wide window that looked out to the west. In the dark, lights sparkled from other living quarters like stars resting on window sills before returning to the sky. Soft sounds of smooth jazz filled the room.

Amber sat, poured the wine, and handed him a glass. "Here's to easier days!"

"I'll drink to that. I'm working on a case similar to yours. A twenty-five-year employee is fighting for a bonus that is rightfully his. His employer doesn't see it that way, of course." He shook his head. "Any word from Belinda about getting your 401k transferred to another account?"

"Not yet. I know her well enough to realize she'll find every excuse to delay it. That's how angry she is."

"She should know better," said Wynton. "How's Refresh coming along?"

Amber filled him in on the details. "It's a ton of work to get it set up, but Brooke is trying to keep everything as simple as possible. After it gets up and running, I'll need to either find a real job or decide to go ahead with a business of my own. The more I think of it, I'm not sure I want to stay in the city. It seems so much more livable in West Walles or Ellenton where Cate lives."

"I hear you. I retreat to my house as often as I can. With Samantha away, it doesn't matter much, but I prefer the burbs too."

They exchanged glances. Amber smiled. "However, tonight it's lovely that we have our choice of excellent food brought in. I was thinking Thai. How about you?"

"Blue Ginger is right around the corner. It should be easy." He patted the cushion next to him. "Move a little closer. I like having you next to me."

Happiness flooded through her. She got up from the end of the couch and sat beside him. He always made her feel so good. She'd learned that he didn't care what she wore or whether she had makeup on or not. He liked her, not only her image. Tonight, she was wearing black yoga pants and a long-sleeved tunic that was anything but glamorous.

"I talked to Samantha last night and told her we were dating. In the past, she hasn't liked it, but she seemed okay with it. I think she understands how lonely I've been." He kissed her on the forehead. "I like spending time with you."

"Me, too." She was about to tell him that they weren't really dating, and stopped. She wasn't fooling anyone. Wynton and she spent as much time together as possible. Though he was giving her time to get used to the idea, he'd already made it clear he hoped they'd have a future together. New to the game of lasting love, Amber appreciated each moment with him, becoming more and more comfortable. Though they hadn't yet made love, nestled against him, she thought she might be ready.

With the last of the leftovers stored in the refrigerator and the dishes in the sink, Amber turned to Wynton, standing by.

"Do you want to stay for a cup of coffee or something else?"

"How about something else?" Wynton said, giving her a meaningful look.

She hesitated. "Let's sit for a while."

They returned to the living room and the couch.

Wynton put his arm around her. "I'm falling in love with you, Amber. I hope you know I don't do casual. I couldn't do that after sharing a wonderful marriage to Barbara."

Amber swallowed hard. "I know. That's the way I feel too. It's ironic that I would be dating two different men within six months. That's just not me. In fact, I haven't done much dating at all. It seemed safer that way."

"I won't ever hurt you, Amber," said Wynton, brushing her hair away from her face. He kissed one cheek, then the other before his lips met hers in a kiss so tender that she opened her mouth to it.

As he continued to kiss her, feelings she usually kept under wraps emerged. Longing changed to desire, sending need to her core. She wrapped her arms around his neck, holding onto him as emotion swept through her in wave after wave.

After several moments, he pulled away, "Should we move to your bedroom?"

Wynton's question broke through her pounding senses. "Yes, oh yes. That would be better."

He took her hand and they walked down the hall and into her room.

Trembling now, Amber watched as Wynton started to unbutton his shirt. Before, at this point in a relationship, she'd usually put a halt to it. But, tonight, she wouldn't do that. He was a kind person who'd promised not to hurt her. She needed to prove to herself and to him that she was willing to trust him.

He turned and smiled at her. "Ready?"

She nodded, lifted off her shirt and wiggled out of her pants. She could do this.

Moments later, lying on the king-sized bed beside him, she turned to him. "I think I'm falling for you too."

"Ah, Amber. You don't know what that means to me." He tenderly clasped her face in his broad hands and kissed her, putting feelings into it that she recognized. Satisfied that he needed her as much as she needed him, she responded.

Touch and taste followed.

Later, as Amber lay naked, cuddled against his chest, her eyes filled. Their lovemaking had been more than physical. It had been a meeting of souls, a sharing of what each had to offer.

He lifted her chin and gazed at her with concern. "What's this? Tears? Did I hurt you?"

"No. I'm simply overwhelmed. I haven't ever felt the way you make me feel."

"And how is that?" he asked gently.

"As if we were meant to be together. You're everything I've

ever wanted."

His eyes grew moist. "I love you, Amber."

She let out a sigh of deep contentment as Wynton rubbed her back. With him, she'd found the love and safety she'd been looking for all along.

CHAPTER FORTY-FIVE

CATE

Cate stared out the window at the April day, noticing the tulips pushing through the dirt in the border of plants at the back of the house. They were a promise of the blooms that would follow. Once again, she'd had proof she wasn't pregnant. She hoped with the advent of warmer weather and the appearance of flowers and leaves on the trees that the next month would be a fertile one for her.

She faced her computer. After the big rush on getting a synopsis and three chapters of a new book out to Abby, she'd heard nothing. Now it was time to end the Galeon Wars book. She'd attempted several different endings and hadn't been happy with any of them.

She wasn't ready to give up the characters she loved so much. Why didn't her new editor understand that her readers would feel the same way when they learned the series was ending simply because the editor whom she loved to work with had decided to stay home with her baby?

Sighing, she told herself it was time to let it go, to finish the book.

Taking a deep breath, she began typing, letting words flow through her.

A while later, lost in the moment, she typed The End.

She sat back in her chair, and looked at the pages she'd written. Her heart pounding with warring emotions, she reread the last page:

On a balcony overlooking the crowd below, Serena stood beside Rondol accepting the cheers of the people with an overwhelming sense of gratitude. She'd been born to the role of Queen, but she'd also earned the title, fighting one war after another to secure peace for all the Galeons.

"Well done, my love," whispered Rondol. "They love you, and so do I."

Serena gazed at the man she loved with all her heart, unable to find the words she wanted. Condora settled on her shoulder, her tender dragon skin shivering with excitement. If as Condora had blurted out, there would be many babies in the future, Serena would need her to help protect them.

"Long live Serena!" came the cry from below her.

Tears formed in Serena's eyes. She lifted her hand and waved. She'd survived battles and done her best for her people not out of duty, but out of love for them. Duty meant doing the right thing. Love meant opening your heart to every possibility.

Serena squeezed Rondol's hand, eager to see what life would bring because she loved him most of all.

Cate sat at her desk, staring out at the darkening day, filled with sadness. So often, she wished she could be more like Serena, but the way things were going, life's possibilities were becoming out of reach for her. She felt so frustrated. She hadn't yet conceived a baby or created a new writing life for herself.

Her cell phone rang. *Brooke.*

"Hi, I was wondering if you wanted to join Amber and me for a glass of wine. I'm officially open and we're about to celebrate my first day."

"I'd love to. I'm at loose ends here. I'll meet you at the store as soon as possible."

Grateful for the call, Cate's spirits lifted. She left a note for Jackson, put Buddy in the car, and headed out. Being with her best friends was just what she needed.

As she drove up to the storefront, she studied the building. Brooke had added purple awnings to the two front windows; tall pots filled with decorative grasses sat on either side of the front door; and a wooden bench that Jackson had made at her request was painted a purple to match the front door.

She got out of the car and took a moment to check the windows. Silk flower arrangements, porcelain bunnies, and various spring-like items enhanced the display of clothing focused on a spring theme. It was fun, and tastefully done.

"Everything looks wonderful," Cate said as she and Buddy entered the store. The inside of the store was brightly lit, showcasing the clothing on racks, folded on shelves, or stacked on tables. Soft music played, and the light scent of flowers filled the air.

"Hi," cried Brooke, giving her a hug. "Let me lock the door behind you, and I'll join you and Amber in the dressing area."

Cate walked through the main room to the space where three comfortable chairs were placed opposite four dressing rooms.

Amber smiled up at her and got to her feet to give her a hug. "Hi! Glad you could join us to celebrate the not-so-grand opening."

"Not-so-grand. What happened?"

"Brooke's worried because she had hardly any customers. I told her she'll be all right. This was a soft opening to test equipment and new routines. Her big announcement comes out next week. That'll be the real test."

"Red or white?" Amber asked, indicating the bottles of wine on the table beside her.

"Red," Cate said. "Not too much. I'm still trying to be careful."

"No luck yet?" Amber asked.

"No," Cate said, trying to keep her lip from trembling. "I tell myself not to worry, but I can't help it. I sometimes feel I'll be marrying Jackson under false pretenses if I don't get pregnant before the wedding."

Amber clucked her tongue. "Cate, don't put yourself in that position. You've mentioned before that Jackson isn't worried. It's not like he's going to drop you if it doesn't happen."

"Not a chance," said Brooke joining them.

Cate plopped down in one of the chairs. "I know. I just feel like nothing is working out for me right now. Abby hasn't called about the book proposal I wrote for her, and I just finished the last book for my new editor and don't know if she'll like it."

"If she doesn't like it, what will you do?" Brooke asked, giving her a look of concern.

"I'll rewrite it if I have to. She and I don't see eye to eye about things. We probably never will."

"Just relax," said Amber. "I feel as unsettled as you do. I think I'm going to put my condo on the market and move out here. But then, I'm not sure if that's what I should do."

"How are things going with Wynton?" Cate asked. '

A pretty pink colored Amber's cheeks. "Even though it might seem too early to others, we're in love."

"It has happened fast," said Cate, "but you're not one to be foolish. Especially about men."

"That's it. I think Jesse opened my heart to possibilities, and Wynton is making me believe in them."

Cate thought about what she'd written. *Duty meant doing*

the right thing. Love meant opening your heart to every possibility. "Sounds to me as if it's the real deal."

Amber's smile brightened her features. "I think so too."

"You shouldn't make any decisions about your condo now. What if Wynton asks you to marry him?" said Brooke.

"I think we're all in a holding pattern," said Amber.

"Yeah, I'm waiting to hear from my mother whether she'd be willing to help us out," Brooke explained. "Amber's been great to help me, but neither of us want to spend every day at the store. After a while, I'll hire a manager, but in the meantime, I need to have some time away from it."

"But you're only open Thursday through Saturday," said Cate.

"Yes, but I have to have all the stock ready to go for those three days," Brooke responded. "And that's a lot of work because I want things done right."

"And she needs to thin out the articles that aren't selling. There's a lot more to it than most people would guess," added Amber.

"I can see that," Cate replied amicably. "It's the same with the book business. People think if you write a book that's all there is to it. You sit back and collect your money. It's not that way at all. Writing the book is only the first step in rewriting many, many times. And don't get me started on all the PR stuff, social media and everything else."

"Aside from getting my mother on board with the store, I have to make sure my family can do much more for themselves, that I'm not going to be the house mom I used to be. On top of everything else, the girls want to get a dog like Buddy."

Hearing his name, Buddy sat up and barked.

Brooke rubbed his ears. "I know what an imp Buddy was as a puppy. The girls are going to have to assume the care of any dog we might get. And P.J. is another story. I love that boy, but he's a whirling dervish wherever he goes, leaving a trail of clothes and a mess behind him."

"What are you planning to do with all this free time you fight for?" asked Cate.

Brooke grinned at her. "I know it can't happen right away, but someday I'm going to take some painting classes and start painting again."

"Great! But, wait! Opening this store isn't what you really want to do?" Cate asked, dismayed by the thought of all the work going to waste.

"Though I couldn't say much about it when I was setting up the business, my plan has always been about getting it started and then turning it over to women who might not find work otherwise. Women whose second language is English, or who haven't been able to afford to go beyond high school."

"Oh, I like that," said Cate.

"It would be a partnership. I wouldn't simply hand over the business to them," said Brooke. "And it might take a lot of time to find the right people and train them. But if I can make this work for all concerned, it is a great way to do something for the community and keep me busy for a while."

Cate lifted her glass. "Here's to you and all the good work you can do."

"Hear! Hear!" cried Amber, laughing as they all clinked glasses.

CHAPTER FORTY-SIX

BROOKE

Brooke arrived home to an empty house and a note from Paul that they'd gone out to eat since dinner hadn't been prepared. She was both relieved and annoyed. Couldn't they have waited for her? It wasn't that late. Six-thirty.

She opened the refrigerator and pulled out a piece of chicken left over from last night's meal. She was eating it when she heard the garage door opening and Paul's car entering.

Moments later, the girls rushed into the kitchen.

"Mom! Where were you?" cried Brynn.

"Dad said you should be home any minute, but you didn't come," Bradley said giving her a worried look. "We ate without you."

"I told you this morning that I might be late, that the store was opening for the first time today," Brooke said. "Remember?"

"Yeah, but I didn't think it would be this late," grumped Brynn. "Are you going to be home on time tomorrow? You said we could have a pajama party."

"Hold on!" Brooke said to her. "I didn't say that could happen this weekend. You've known all about the store opening. I can't be there and here at the same time."

"Hi, Brooke! You're home, I see!" said Paul with a little edge to his voice.

"Yes, of course. I'm a little late, that's all. I wanted to celebrate the first day of Refresh being open with Amber and

Cate. It's a big deal for me."

"I get it. I'm happy for you, I really am," said Paul. "But I didn't think you'd be so late. That's all."

Brooke faced the three of them. "You're going to have to get used to some changes around here. We've talked about it before. Now that I'm running the store, there will be times I won't be available."

"The store is only open three days a week, right?" Paul said.

"Yes, but on some of the other days, I'll be working at the store getting everything ready for the time we're open. I am in business, after all." She held up her hand to stop the girls' chattering. "Listen, girls. In the past, I've always been available for all of you. Now, we'll have to do some further planning to work around my schedule."

"But ..." Paul began.

Brooke cut him off. "Don't make this more difficult than it needs to be. It's time for me to do something for myself."

She realized how tied to her family's needs she'd been, how, in many ways, she'd lost her freedom to their demands. She drew a deep breath and told herself to stay calm.

"You girls can learn to help more in the kitchen, and on days when the girls need to be picked up from school, you can do it, Paul, or we can make other arrangements. But my new schedule is firm."

"Okay," said Paul. "Not a problem. Right, girls?"

"It's okay, Mom," said Brynn.

"We know you're busy," Bradley added.

"Now, it's time for you to do your homework and then take baths." Guilt, like a sneaky snake, stood coiled, ready to strike. She forced it away. Freedom to do her own thing wouldn't come easily, but she'd fight for it.

The girls grabbed their books from the kitchen counter and headed upstairs, unusually quiet.

After they left, Brooke turned to Paul. “I’ve already talked to a temp agency about hiring someone to stay with the girls after school on Thursdays and Fridays, and all day every Saturday. But until we find someone, you, or, heaven forbid, my mother will have to cover for me.”

“Let’s hope we can find someone soon,” said Paul. “I’m not sure what would’ve happened if I had had to stay late.”

“You agreed to pick up the girls,” Brooke reminded him.

“Yes, but I might not be able to get away as easily as I did today,” he countered.

“That’s why we’re going to hire someone to help. Because I need to do this store project for me.”

He gave her an encouraging smile. “You deserve it, hon.”

Some of the tension left Brooke’s shoulders, and when he kissed her, she kissed him back. One step at a time, she told herself, because she was finding her wings.

CHAPTER FORTY-SEVEN

AMBER

On a clear May morning, Amber stood in the middle of the cabin on Cate's property and gazed around. "This will be perfect. Are you sure you don't mind my staying?" Four weeks of commuting back and forth from the city to the burbs to help manage the store was enough.

Cate grinned. "Are you kidding? It's going to be great to have you here. You're welcome to stay as long as you like."

"Only as long as you'll let me pay rent for it, as we'd agreed," Amber said. She had no intention of free-loading off anyone. She'd worked hard to earn her money and was proud of it.

"It's not necessary, but all right. And don't worry about your coming and going. The cabin is private. One reason we decided to fix it up for me. I wanted to feel as if I'd escaped to my own special place."

"But my staying here means you have to keep your office in your house for a while longer. Will that affect your writing?"

Cate sighed and shook her head. "Nothing is going to help my writing. I'm still waiting to hear from both my agent and my editor. If it was good news, I'm sure I would've heard by now. It's mid-May for heaven's sake!"

"I can only imagine how hard it is to wait for any word, but, Cate, you've been successful. That can't be ignored."

"We'll see," Cate said, grimacing.

"How's the other issue?" Amber asked, and hoped she wasn't prying.

"I won't know for a while. I don't want to take any pregnancy tests until the time for my period has come and gone."

"I'm keeping my fingers crossed for you."

"On the brighter side of things," Cate said, "plans for the wedding are moving along. Jackson is thrilled that all but one of his siblings will be there. I think you'll enjoy them. They're a fun bunch."

"It's going to be fabulous. I've waited a long time for you two finally to marry. Thank you for including Wynton and inviting him to share the house with us."

"Not at all. Jackson and I both liked him when we met him at dinner."

"I'm so glad," Amber said, remembering how gracious Wynton had been hosting an impromptu dinner at Arturo's for all of them one Saturday after the store closed for the day.

Cate elbowed her. "Are you sure you don't want to take him up on his offer to have you stay at his house?"

Amber paused before answering. "Not yet. I love him, but so much has happened to me in the last year that I don't want to rush into anything. He understands what I've been through and is not pushing me at all."

"That's sweet, because anyone can see how he adores you."

"Yes. For the first time in my life, I feel secure in a relationship. His wife must have been a wonderful woman because even though he's ready to be with me after her death, she'll always be a part of his life. I like that about him."

"Me too," said Cate. "I'll leave you here to settle in. If you need anything, I'm not far away."

Amber hugged her and walked her to the door.

Alone, she walked through the small but well laid-out space. In time, if things continued to go well with Wynton, she might move in with him. In the meantime, this was perfect.

Her cell rang. *Wynton.*

Smiling, she clicked on the call. "Hello."

"How are the new digs?" he asked.

"Great for now," she answered. "I can't wait for you to see it. How's your day going?"

"Busy as usual, but I thought you might like to meet me for dinner. Is it too much to ask of you to come into the city? That way, with an evening meeting of mine, it won't be such a late night."

"Actually, that works out nicely because I want to pick up a few more of my things for this place."

"Great! Why don't I meet you at *Chez Simone* at eight o'clock, and then we can drive out to Ellenton together."

"That'll be perfect." Amber clicked off the call basking in the warmth that talking to Wynton made her feel.

As soon as Amber walked into the restaurant, she felt as if she was in Paris at a tiny neighborhood restaurant that only the natives knew. Fresh flowers were everywhere, softly played music filled the background, and the aroma of fine food wafted about her nose.

An attractive woman dressed in a simple black sheath approached her. "May I help you?"

"Yes, I'm meeting Wynton Barr."

"Ah, *oui,*" she said. "Follow me."

Amber was led to a table in a back corner. Seeing her, Wynton got to his feet and beamed at her. "So glad you could make it, darling."

"Me, too," she responded, accepting his kiss.

She turned at the noise of a commotion behind her. Horrified, she watched Belinda approach her with loud, belligerent steps.

"Well, it didn't take you long to find a replacement for Jesse. What is this one famous for?"

"I won't dignify that with an answer, Belinda." Amber's voice wavered but she faced Belinda with determination. "I used to admire how you built your business on your own, but now I understand what a vicious person you are."

"Yeah? Well, you can tell that lawyer of yours to stop harassing me about your 401-K savings. It will be transferred in due time."

"You might want to tell him yourself," Amber said, motioning to Wynton who'd moved to stand beside her.

Belinda's eyes widened. She stepped back. "You? Her lawyer? Well, you heard me. It will be taken care of. So, stop having your people call me about it."

"The issue is real. We're contemplating a lawsuit for your withholding funds that are due to my client, in addition to your attempt to assault her in a very hostile work environment. It's a simple matter, Ms. Galvin. If you don't do what you should, I'll move forward with it."

Observing his broad shoulders, hearing the command in his voice, Amber realized how intimidating he could sometimes be. She hid a smile.

Belinda shook a finger at her. "I've found a replacement for you, and she does a better job than you ever did."

"Good for you, Belinda. We'll see how long she stays. I heard she's the second one you've hired since I left."

"Anything else we need to discuss?" Wynton asked in a voice that dared Belinda to say anything.

She swore under breath, moved away, grabbed her coat from a chair toward the front, and left the restaurant in a huff.

"I'm sorry for her disturbance," said Amber, as Wynton helped her into her chair. "She's such a difficult, unhappy person."

Wynton shook his head. "It's amazing you even worked for someone like that. It couldn't have been easy."

"No, it wasn't, but I at least knew where I stood with her."

He studied her a moment. "I guess brutal honesty is better than being jerked around all the time. Is that it?"

"Yes," Amber answered, remembering how, growing up, she didn't know if it was going to be one of her mother's good days or bad.

Wynton ordered a bottle of red wine, and as their dinner progressed, Amber's childhood memories left her.

And later when she showed Wynton around the cabin, new, loving thoughts filled her mind. Still later, as they lay together, all she could think of was how much she loved him.

CHAPTER FORTY-EIGHT

CATE

Cate waited for two weeks beyond her normal period before using the pregnancy test kit she'd bought last November. Sitting in the bathroom, waiting for results, she whispered, "Please, please, please!" over and over again.

When she checked and saw the two lines indicating she was pregnant, she buried her face in her hands and cried. She knew she was lucky, that it had been only six months of trying, but the worry that had consumed her could now be a thing of the past and she could enjoy her wedding.

She stood and washed her hands, trying to think of a special way to tell Jackson. They'd agreed they wouldn't talk about it until she knew for sure.

Buddy scratched at the door.

She opened it and patted his head. "Well, little guy, it looks like you're going to have some competition around here."

Buddy looked up at her with those adoring brown eyes and barked.

"Yeah, I thought you'd like it," she said. She picked him up and twirled in a circle. "Wait until Daddy hears about it!"

Bubbling with happiness, Cate went into her office. She'd been doing some online research about weather in Florida in June and was trying to decide what to pack for the wedding and the honeymoon that would follow in Naples, down the coast. Brooke and Amber had helped her pick out her wedding dress—a simple, sleeveless maxi dress in ivory crepe with a nipped-in waist that was flattering. But she needed sundresses and outfits for the heat of summer.

When her phone rang, she checked the number and drew in a deep breath, hoping for more good news. "Hi, Abby! What's up? I've been worried about not hearing from you. Did you like the synopsis and three chapters I sent you? Were you able to do anything with them?"

"I'm sorry, Cate. I tried everything I could think of, but I couldn't get a sale out of it. I have a feeling your heart wasn't in the writing. That's why I'm calling. I think you should start a whole new sci-fi series, this time focusing on YA. That's your true voice."

Cate felt her shoulders collapse as a sigh of disappointment left her body. Could she start again? Create another whole world with all kinds of unique complexities? She'd loved Serena and Rondol from the beginning. Could she create other characters she'd love as much?

"What do you think?" Abby asked.

"Who would buy it? The editor I'm working with on the Galeon Wars series hasn't even had the courtesy to call me back."

"That's another reason I'm calling. Your old editor has decided she doesn't want to be a stay-at-home mother. She and I have already talked. She'd like to work with you again. She'll work on the last book in the Galeon series, but you also need to come up with another proposal. This time you don't even need to give her three chapters. Just come up with a brief synopsis to present to her."

"Ah, Abby, you make it sound so easy. You know I'm going to have to develop all the details of a whole new world before I can tell the story."

"Not necessarily. It's your characters who carry the story. The world can be worked out around them."

Cate remained quiet while her mind spun with ideas.

"Okay. So, maybe this girl meets a guy she thinks is a little weird but it turns out he's a prince in a different world, that he's just on earth to meet the challenge of beating out his cousin for the crown, or something like that."

Abby's soft chuckle caught her attention.

"What?" Cate asked, afraid Abby thought it was a dumb idea.

"See? You've already started the next series. Don't worry, Cate, you've got many more stories inside you. You're going to be fine. I was wrong to encourage you to do something different. You need to write what is natural to you, not what I or some editor tries to make you do."

Relief swept through Cate. "Thanks. You don't know how much I've needed to hear that."

"Are we all set? I'd like you to get something off to me before the wedding. Is that possible?"

"Probably. I've been going crazy without something to write."

"That's my girl," Abby said, a satisfied lilt to her voice.

Cate smiled and hung up the phone. Her life was back in order. She picked up Buddy, and holding him tight once again, danced for the pure joy of it.

Cate heard the sound of Jackson coming in the back door and hurried to greet him. Quickly, before he could recognize it, from behind her back she handed him a package of diapers.

"What's this?" he asked, then let out a whoop. "We're pregnant?"

"Yes. Now, when Buddy and I call you Daddy, it will be for real."

Jackson swung her up in his arms and held her tight.

Cate clung to him. "Now, we can have a real wedding."

He set her down on her feet and looked at her with confusion. "What are you talking about?"

"You wanted to get married and have children. If I couldn't get pregnant, it wouldn't be fair to you."

Jackson cupped her face in his hands. "Cate, don't you understand? I'm marrying you because I love *you*, not because of any kids we might or might not have. It's great that we're going to have a baby, but you have to know what you mean to me. We've been together for almost seven years. How else could I have proved it to you?"

She saw the pain in his eyes and lifted a hand to touch his cheek. "You prove to me every day how much you love me. I'm sorry. I didn't mean to hurt your feelings. I just want to make you happy in every way."

"You do make me happy." His expression brightened. "And now you're making me a father."

She hugged him back, so thankful they'd been given this wonderful gift.

The next morning, after seeing Jackson off to work, Cate walked out the door. On her way to Refresh, she stopped at Margie's Pastry Shoppe for croissants and fresh brewed coffee. She couldn't wait to tell Brooke and Amber her good news. Carrying the treats, Cate walked into the store with a spring to her step. Brooke looked up at her from behind the counter where she was ringing up a sale and waved. "Go on in the back room. I'll meet you there."

In the dressing area, Amber was talking to two women about the dress one of them was wearing. She smiled at Cate and continued talking.

Cate walked into the back room, set down the goodies, and checked the clothes hanging on a rack waiting to be tagged.

She was admiring a pale, pink sundress when Brooke entered the room.

"Hey! Good to see you! What brings you here on this sunny May morning?"

Cate felt a huge grin spread across her face. "I'm pregnant!"

Brooke rushed forward and embraced her. "Wonderful news! I'm so happy for you!"

"What's going on?" Amber said, hurrying toward them.

"Cate's pregnant!" Brooke cried, turning and waving a fist in the air.

"Oh, hon! That's fantastic news!" Amber threw her arms around her and squeezed tight. "I'm pleased for you and Jackson. You're going to make great parents for this lucky baby."

At Amber's words, Cate looked down at her belly, wondering what the next few months would do to it. Then, without warning, a wave of nausea washed over her. She gripped the table beside her.

"Are you okay?" Brooke asked.

She nodded. "Just pregnant. I brought you two some treats, but I'm not going to stay. I just wanted to share my good news."

One moment she was standing talking to them; the next, she was throwing up in the store's bathroom.

"I'm so sorry," she said, when she returned to them. "How long does this go on?"

Amber and Brooke looked at each other and turned to her.

"It depends," said Brooke. "With the twins, it was the first six months."

"Six months! Does that mean I'll be sick for the wedding?" The thought of throwing up in her wedding dress was horrible. "I don't want anything to spoil it. We've waited a long time for it."

"I want your wedding to be perfect too," said Amber.

Cate couldn't stop the tears that filled her eyes. She hugged her. "If you and Brooke are there, it will be."

Brooke wrapped her arms around the two of them.

CHAPTER FORTY-NINE

CATE

On an early May morning, Cate left the doctor's office in awe of what was happening to her body. Her pregnancy's progress was confirmed, and by all estimates the baby would arrive at the end of the year. Jackson's mother had already warned his siblings that she'd be on standby for the baby's arrival, no matter what else was going on. Cate had been amused, and now she was grateful. The job ahead of her seemed overwhelming. The doctor had spoken of various tests she and the baby would undergo to ensure that the baby was healthy and growing well. It was frightening to think of it.

She decided to stop by the store.

It was quiet when she entered it. "How's business?" she asked Brooke, doing her best to hide her concern at the lack of customers.

Brooke surprised her with a smile. "Very good. The website I had set up is doing better than the store. I don't mind being here, though. I'm taking in more and more clothing from good sources. A lot of women like to get rid of old things as they buy new stuff. It works for me."

"Oh, good," said Cate. "Where's Amber?"

"She called and asked if she could be excused for the weekend to spend time with Wynton."

"I'm so happy that things are going well between them."

"Me, too. How are you doing, Cate?"

Cate told her about her visit to the doctor. "It's such an

exciting time, but I worry about all those tests."

"The best thing is not to think about it. You're healthy, and I'm sure the baby will be too. It's annoying that doctors today have to reveal everything that could go wrong. My mother said it wasn't like that when she had me."

"How is Diana?" Cate asked.

"She decided that instead of my hiring someone to come in to take care of the girls while I'm working, she would do it. I thought she'd complain about all the things I was doing wrong. Instead, she's been praising me for doing as much as I can. The greatest thing though is the relationship she has with the girls. It's precious, the way they've gotten along."

"That's fantastic," said Cate. "Better than her having to work here."

"Exactly. She'd rather be a doting grandmother in everyone's eyes than a shopkeeper."

Cate and Brooke shared a hearty laugh.

A week before the wedding, on a sunny morning, Cate packed her suitcase and carefully placed her wedding gown in a plastic bag, along with a couple of dressy outfits she'd chosen to take with her. Jackson and she had decided to drive to Florida so they could take Buddy. Cate liked the idea of being able to stop whenever she needed and had purchased a few audio books to listen to along the way. As a writer, she needed to read and listen to other books on a regular basis.

"All set?" Jackson asked.

"I think so," she said. "Several months ago, I had no idea I'd be packing for my wedding."

"Wait until we have to load all kinds of baby gear. That will be something else," said Jackson.

They smiled at each other. They'd started a list of all the

things they'd need, and each of them had been shocked by the number of suggested items.

As Jackson pulled into the driveway of the Seashell Cottage, Cate felt a sense of homecoming. There was something about the house that spoke to her. Maybe because it was here that she'd decided to let go of her worries and marry Jackson with the understanding they'd start a family. She'd been so afraid then but was deeply content with the idea now.

"Here we are, Buddy!" Jackson announced, getting out and opening the back door for the dog. With a yip of excitement, he allowed Jackson to set him down on the ground before taking off and running in circles as fast as his short legs could carry him.

"Guess he's happy we finally made it," said Cate laughing. She lifted her arms to the sky and took in several deep breaths of the salty air. "I love it!" She turned to Jackson. "I'm so happy we decided to get married here."

"Me too. This is where you promised you'd marry me. It'll always be a special place for me."

Cate wrapped her arms around him. "I love you, Jackson Hubbard!"

As he kissed her, Buddy danced around them, barking.

Jackson stepped away from her and frowned at the dog. "C'mon boy. Give me a break. I haven't kissed her since this morning."

Laughing, Cate said, "Let's unload the car."

Later, after they'd brought their things inside and unpacked, Cate headed for the beach. The sound of the gulf water rolling into shore and out again was a steady beat in her ears as she faced it. She dipped her bare toes into the foamy edges of the water finding it surprisingly warm against her skin.

Jackson joined her. "Beautiful, huh?"

"Yes. There's something so timeless about watching the waves. I feel as if I was meant to be here at this moment. With you."

Jackson squeezed her hand. "I love when you say things like this. No wonder your readers love your books."

"Even on Galeon, life and love exist." She felt a frown mar her smile. "I'm not sure how they're going to like a moon called Ouris."

"Don't worry. You'll come up with a good story. You've already started by naming the place where your new characters live."

Cate nodded. She had to learn to trust herself, to listen to the words coming from deep inside her.

She watched Buddy chase the frothy edges of the waves as they pulled away from kissing the sand. She laughed when a returning wave startled him by wetting his face. Above her, seagulls flew, their white wings making moving patterns against the background of blue sky.

Contentment filled her, chasing her doubts away. It was time simply to enjoy the day.

The day before the wedding, guests arrived throughout the day. First came Brooke and Paul, and their family, then Jackson's parents, then several of his siblings, Abby, and finally, Amber and Wynton.

"Sorry we're a little late," said Amber, giving Cate a hug.

"I had some important business to take care of," said Wynton, beaming at Cate as he wrapped an arm around Amber.

Amber held out her left hand.

"Oh, my God!"

Amber smiled at Wynton and turned to Cate. "We got engaged last night."

Cate wrapped her arms around Amber. "I'm so happy for you two!" She gave Wynton a quick hug. "Wait until Brooke hears the news! She's at the beach now."

"No, I'm not, I'm here," said Brooke. "What's happening?"

"Amber and Wynton are engaged!" Cate couldn't rein in the happy trill in her voice. Amber looked starstruck and Wynton couldn't stop smiling at her.

"Engaged? How wonderful!" Brooke cried, hugging Amber.

The others crowded around to extend their congratulations.

"I wanted my wedding to be perfect. Now, it is, because of the two of you," said Cate. It doubled her happiness to know Amber and Brooke were moving forward, just like her.

People traveled easily from the Seashell Cottage to the Salty Key Inn and back again, enjoying one another as they walked the beach, or swam in the pool at either place or just sat and talked. Buddy tried to keep track of everyone until fatigue set in. By late afternoon, Cate found him curled up in his bed in the bedroom she shared with Jackson.

After the constant commotion at the house, Cate was relieved that she and Jackson had reserved a private room at the Purple Pig for dinner for the wedding guests.

Later, sitting at one of the tables at the restaurant, Cate studied the members of Jackson's family. They were a congenial group who shared a lot of the same facial features.

Sitting next to her, Jackson's mother smiled. "You look wonderful, Cate. I can't tell you how pleased I am that Jackson is marrying you. He's simply gleaming with happiness."

Cate glanced at Jackson talking with his sister, Jenn, and smiled. He sensed her looking at him and winked at her. "I'm happy too. He's such a good man."

"Like his father," Laurie said. "Here's to a beautiful day tomorrow." She lifted her glass of wine and clinked it against Cate's water goblet.

Later that night, while their men slept, Cate sat with Amber and Brooke in the living room of the cottage.

"Remember when we met here at Seashell Cottage last year? I said then that this year, with all of us turning forty, would be one to remember. Who could've guessed all that has happened to us?" said Brooke. "And we haven't even officially turned forty. That's right ahead of us."

"It's turned out to be a good year, though I certainly had my doubts," said Cate. "But then life is bittersweet at best."

"Wow! Your books make me believe that isn't true," said Amber. "I love that about them."

Cate held up a warning finger. "You can't write about love if you don't know about pain."

"That's true of people everywhere. If I hadn't met Jesse, I might never have known I was capable of love. And my love for Wynton is much, much deeper."

"Oh, my! I've just realized something," Brooke said. "We've each opened ourselves up to life and experienced more meaningful love this year."

"I feel like we're thirteen again, facing whole new lives ahead of us," said Cate. "Here's to us!"

"The Beach Babes!" cried Amber and Brooke together, making them all laugh like the friends they were and always would be.

CHAPTER FIFTY

AMBER, BROOKE, AND CATE

The day of the wedding was as beautiful as Cate and her friends had hoped. Blue skies held puffy clouds, like dollops of whipped cream floating above them, keeping the hot sun at bay from time to time.

Amber and Brooke helped Cate dress for the ceremony. They would walk Cate to the beach in place of the father she'd never known. The minister, whom the wedding coordinator at the Salty Key Inn had helped to find, was waiting with Jackson and Buddy to greet them. Guests had formed a circle around them.

"You truly look beautiful, Cate," said Brooke. "Pregnancy looks good on you."

Amber smiled at her. "Love too. You're glowing."

Cate stole a glance of herself in the mirror and fingered the pearl necklace she'd been given. She could hardly believe the confident woman staring back was her. The past few months shared with her friends had helped her discover a more nurturing part of her. She was ready to begin a new phase of her life with the man who'd made her understand that she was worthy of attention and love.

She could hardly wait to begin. "Let's go!"

They headed to the beach—Amber leading, Brooke following, and then Cate.

After they were situated on the sand, Amber stood beside

Wynton in the circle of people gathered on the beach for Cate's wedding. The musical notes from the guitar player lifted into the air and danced around her. She sighed at the beauty of the scene, the magical moment for her friend.

Wynton reached over, wrapped his fingers around her hand and gave it a gentle squeeze as if he knew what she was thinking. She turned to him and smiled. The past year was one she couldn't ever have imagined. She felt as if she'd grown from a child to a woman. A late bloomer for sure. The future lay ahead of her full of promise. She hadn't yet decided if she would open her own business, but the thought remained.

She'd learned so many things about herself. She had the right to protect her body. Nobody should ever try to take that away from her. And in loving someone, she'd learned what a gift it was to share the joy of that love, both physically and spiritually.

Observing Cate and Jackson taking their positions in front of the minister, Amber squeezed Wynton's hand. He was the love of her life, the man she trusted with her heart for now and the future.

He turned to her with a smile, his gaze full of tenderness. He was steady, strong, and safe.

She lifted his hand to her lips and kissed it.

Brooke left Cate with Jackson and joined her family in the circle of family and friends who'd come to celebrate the wedding.

Her thoughts flew back to the first time she'd seen Seashell Cottage and the reunion with the two best friends that would always be part of her. The year of turning forty was proving to be a milestone for them all. She'd found a new inner strength, a new independence that she'd desperately needed. Her marriage had been tested in ways she'd never thought possible and had become even stronger. Paul was a good man, a decent man, a wonderful father. Without him, she wouldn't have the confidence to expand her horizons while remaining true to her role of mother. She'd learned that it wasn't a case of choosing between her own desires and her family's, that one balanced the other. Her family was what kept her feet on the ground while their love gave her wings.

Paul leaned over and whispered in her ear, "Love you."

Her eyes misted with gratitude. "Love you too," she said, meaning it with her whole heart.

Cate stood before the minister on the beach opposite Jackson, filled with such love she wondered how she could get the words out. Jackson had just vowed to be there for her always, to love and cherish her, and to protect her, sounding a lot like Rondol might to Serena if he'd had the chance to do so.

Cate tightened her fingers around Jackson's hand. Her vision blurred with tears as she began to speak.

"I love you, Jackson, more than you'll ever know. I've treasured my made-up world and the hero and heroine in love, meeting challenges, and surviving. But I know now that I've been writing about you all along. You're my hero. You've given me the love and confidence I needed to grow. But more than that, you've made it possible for me to learn how honesty and trust and kindness can work their magic on a young woman afraid to open her heart to the idea of a loving family. I promise to try to be all that you are to me, to take care of you and be by your side for the rest of our lives. I promise you this with all I am."

Jackson drew her into his arms and kissed her, deepening

his kiss as she responded.

After a few seconds, the minister said, “I guess I don’t need to pronounce you husband and wife.”

Chuckling, Cate and Jackson broke apart.

The small gathering of people standing around them began to clap.

Glancing at them, Cate filled with gratitude. Her gaze rested on Brooke and Amber, The Beach Babes, her dearest friends. At that moment, with them cheering her on, Jackson at her side, and Buddy at her feet, she felt every bit like Serena. But this wasn’t fantasy; it was real.

Overwhelmed by all she’d been given, she gazed at those around her and said softly, “Thank you!” to the bright blue sky above and anyone who might hear.

# # #

Thank you for reading *The Beach Babes*. If you enjoyed this book, please help other readers discover it by leaving a review on Amazon, Goodreads, BookBub, or your favorite site. It's such a nice thing to do.

To stay in touch and to keep up with the latest news, here's a link to sign up for my periodic newsletter!

http://bit.ly/2OQsb7s

Enjoy an excerpt from my book, *Waves of Hope,* Book 1 in The Sanderling Cove Inn Series:

PROLOGUE

Eleanor "Ellie" Weatherby sat on the front porch of the home she and her deceased husband, William, had built in the 1970s at Sanderling Cove on the Gulf Coast of Florida. Since its original construction, the house had been renovated several times, buildings had been added to the oversized property, and Ellie was now co-owner of an upscale operation called The Sanderling Cove Inn.

She'd invited her three granddaughters to visit her. At the thought, waves of hope swept through her. She loved her granddaughters with all her heart and hoped to settle a family issue with them. Born within eighteen months of one another, they were a remarkable trio. But which one of them would be willing to do as she asked? They were each unique. But then her three daughters were very different and, to her disappointment, not close.

At fifty-nine, Vanessa, her oldest, was overly involved in

New York society, a woman focused on appearance. Vanessa herself was a stunning, auburn-haired, gray-eyed woman who was used to being noticed. She'd had a tragic first marriage that fell apart after her three-year-old son drowned in the surf not far from Sanderling Cove. Charlotte, Vanessa's twenty-nine-year-old daughter, was still trying to find her place in the world. It was no wonder. Neither of her parents was the warm, cuddly type. Ellie sighed.

Ellie thought of JoAnne, her middle daughter. Two years younger than Vanessa, Jo was a single mother. Of all her daughters, Jo was the sweetest and the one who'd suffered most in life. She'd struggled with depression for years and now fought every day with numerous symptoms of fibromyalgia and the problems associated with it. Jo's daughter, Brooke, just turned twenty-eight and was a strong supporter of her mother, but, in Ellie's opinion, her granddaughter should be out on her own. Both Brooke and Jo needed to add sparkle to their lives, brighten their appearance, buy some new clothes, enjoy what fun they could. Jo made a good living working from home doing IT work for an understanding company, and Brooke worked in an accounting office. They lived in upstate New York, where Jo had been her happiest before her fiancé was killed in Iraq.

Last but certainly not least, Leigh, her youngest and her father's favorite, entered her thoughts. She was a beauty with caramel-colored hair and green eyes that sparkled. At 49, Leigh still attracted attention and favors from others, but it hadn't always been easy. She'd had her daughter out-of-wedlock at 20, and after going back to work when Olivia was less than a year old, she'd ended up marrying her boss a few years later. Her husband, Jack, pampered her, which seemed appropriate after she gave him two sons, whom they both adored. But it was Olivia, with strawberry-blond hair, blue eyes, and a short figure, who was Ellie's favorite.

Ellie kept in touch with her daughters frequently, but she didn't often see them. Vanessa hated Florida after losing her son there, Jo didn't like to travel, and Leigh was a social butterfly, a southern belle who was usually too busy. However, all three daughters encouraged their girls to visit her in Sanderling Cove. Ellie loved their times together, loved them in a way that was easier than being a parent to them. Grandmothers could get away with saying quite a lot, and Ellie was known for not holding back. She tried to be a supportive, loving figure in the family and did her best to hold them all together.

Ellie stared out at the waves that filled her with hope. They rushed into shore to embrace the sand and quickly pulled away again, like a shy teenager after her first kiss. Seagulls and terns floated in the sky, riding the wind, their white wings like the sails of a boat against the blue background. The air on this May day caressed her skin. She lifted her face to the breeze, enjoying the tangy taste of salt.

She glanced around. Sanderling Cove held only five houses and the Inn and hadn't changed that much from all those years ago when she and William first bought land there. She loved it and never wanted to leave her home.

If only things would work out the way she wanted.

CHAPTER ONE

CHARLOTTE

Charlotte Bradford told herself not to stomp back to her office at the North Public Relations company in New York City, but it took every bit of will power to keep from doing it. Rand Michaels, her co-worker, had once again attempted to take credit for work she had done for a client. Rather than be called out for it, their boss had praised Rand for adding to Charlotte's campaign, though neither couldn't deny that the idea had been Charlotte's to begin with.

She went into her office and closed the door before taking a seat at her desk and staring out at the scenery below. Charlotte knew she was excellent at her job. Clients loved her and her work. but she was tired of constantly fighting for the recognition she deserved. She knew damn well that Rand Michaels would be made partner before her. That wasn't fair.

The six o'clock traffic below had created a scene that reminded her of the movement in an ant farm she'd owned as a child. Cars moved as best they could in the streets and the sidewalks filled with people moving faster than they. Was she like an ant working hard but going nowhere?

She sighed. It was time for a change but she didn't know how, when, or where.

"I'll be there as soon as I can, Gran. Thanks."

Charlotte Bradford ended the call with her grandmother and impulsively danced around her room. An extended visit with Gran was just what she needed. She hated her job, knew she didn't want to stay in New York, and needed to do something that resonated with her. Not something that pleased her mother.

Charlotte felt she'd been a disappointment to her mother from a young age, that she could never measure up to her brother, David, who'd died in a drowning accident when he was just three years old. Two years younger, she'd never really known him though her mother talked about him frequently. By the time Charlotte came to understand what had happened to him and why she'd never have another sibling, he was already on a pedestal she could never climb.

Her parents divorced a year or so after David died. Her father kept his commitment to Charlotte with financial support and the occasional visit, but he'd moved to California and had a busy, happy life with his new family, one she wasn't a part of. Shortly after her divorce, her mother married Walter Van Pelt and he provided her with an upscale lifestyle that was more suited to her.

Charlotte had plenty of friends, but in her restlessness, she was ready to move on and away from their expectations of what life should be like in their high-society circle. She especially wanted to get away from Jeremy Probst, the man her mother wanted her to marry. Her mother and Jeremy's mother had planned this romance for years, but it was never going to work. There was no physical attraction, and though she'd never discussed it in depth with anyone else, she was pretty sure Jeremy was gay. She knew he'd be much happier after he had the courage to come out. And if she ever were to meet a man whom she'd consider marrying, Charlotte had to feel she couldn't live without him. He had to be someone she could trust to love her for herself.

The next day, Charlotte went into work and gleefully gave

her resignation letter to her boss. In the competitive marketing company where she constantly had to fight for recognition, Charlotte had no real regret about leaving.

Later, at home, Charlotte was busy sorting through her things at the apartment she shared with a roommate when her mother called. “I understand you’re moving to Florida for the summer. When did this happen, and why wasn’t I told? I had to hear it from Marjorie Probst, of all people. She said Jeremy is devastated that you broke it off with him.”

Taking a deep breath and letting it out slowly, Charlotte sank onto her bed. “I was going to tell you when we met for lunch this weekend. And, I don’t believe Jeremy is the least bit upset. We both know it wasn’t going to work. My stay with Gran is for an unspecified amount of time. I’m just trying to figure things out. You know I didn’t like my job.”

“You shouldn’t have to be worried about a job. There are opportunities for you to get involved in various volunteer positions and plenty of other suitable young men for you to consider. You’re a beautiful woman, Charlotte. And being Walter’s step-daughter is a big plus.”

“Mother! Do you realize how archaic you sound?”

“The reality is that you could have a nice life going forward, Charlotte. Don’t waste the opportunity to meet new people.”

“You mean here in New York,” Charlotte said. “I need to get away, and being with Gran for a while is the perfect solution. She’s always been honest with me.”

“She’s never appreciated all I’ve done for you, my charity work, or the life I’ve made,” said her mother with an edge to her voice.

“I’m not sure that’s true,” said Charlotte. “But she knows I want something different.”

“Well, try not to burn too many bridges. Life has a lot of surprising twists and turns/ Some of them are heartbreaking.”

Charlotte knew her mother was talking about David and said softly, "I know."

"Well, I hope you know what you're doing. I suppose there's no way I can get you to change your mind."

"No, Mother," said Charlotte. Thinking of the future she'd have if she'd decided to turn Gran down. Her spirits lifted at the thought of leaving that life behind.

Several days later, Charlotte drove her BMW convertible down Interstate 95, intent on getting to Sanderling Cove as quickly as she could. She had stuffed the trunk of her car and the backseat with suitcases and bags full of shoes and things she wanted in her new life. She'd left most of her dressy clothes behind at her mother's house. She knew from earlier visits she wouldn't need them. A pleasant thought.

When at last, after a couple of days of hard driving, she saw the sign for The Sanderling Cove Inn off to the side of Gulf Drive, she filled with excitement. She'd always felt Gran's love and acceptance. Her unwavering devotion meant the world to her.

She turned into the driveway and pulled up to the main building. The white clapboard siding of the building was trimmed in turquoise, a nod to some of the colorful homes and buildings in this area of the Gulf Coast of Florida.

A man wearing a New York Yankees baseball cap came out to the front entrance to greet her.

"Hey, Charlie, I'm glad you made it," he said, giving her a wide smile. "I've already called your grandmother to let her know you've arrived."

Charlotte smiled with pleasure. Here in Florida, Charlie seemed a much more suitable name than Charlotte. Far less formal, especially when spoken by John Rizzo, Gran's long-time business partner and special friend. Charlotte hadn't been very old when she realized Gran and John were more than two people who owned a business together. But no formal announcements were made about their relationship. It was simply a fact. And now, they lived together in Gran's house.

Tall, in great shape for his age, and with a shock of gray hair that couldn't be totally covered by the cap, John was a handsome, jovial man whom all the guests loved.

John gave her a peck on the cheek. "Better go see Ellie now. She's been waiting to see you."

Charlotte gave him a little wave and headed over to Gran's house sitting in a corner of the property. Gran and her husband had purchased the two oversized lots that provided enough space for the main building and its wing, along with the owner's house, all with beach access and Gulf water views. In today's market, the land itself was worth a small fortune.

She parked in the back of Gran's house, got out of the car, and let out a soft groan as she stretched. The trip took longer than she thought it would.

"You're here!" cried Gran, rushing out of the house to greet her.

Charlotte flew into her grandmother's open arms. "Thought I'd never make it." She stepped back and studied her grandmother. "How are you?"

Gran's blue eyes sparkled as she returned Charlotte's smile. "I'm fine. A little older and not much wiser. And definitely not thinner."

Charlotte laughed. At barely five-foot-three, her grandmother had gray curly hair that she kept short, forming a halo of sorts around her head, and didn't seem to realize how adorable she was. At the moment, Gran was wearing a T-Shirt that said, "*Love Happens*," a pair of khaki shorts, and pink flip-flops with sparkly pink bows.

"It's starting to feel like home already." Charlotte hugged her. All the constraints of living a lifestyle she didn't like fell away from her. Gran was all about being yourself without judgment from her. The T-shirt she wore would have made Charlotte's mother shudder.

Charlotte turned as a young man approached. He saluted Gran with a bob of his head. "John sent me over to help with the luggage."

"I'm glad you came," said Gran. "It looks like we're going to need your help. Jake McDonnell, meet my granddaughter, Charlotte Bradford."

Charlotte gazed into his chocolate brown eyes that seemed to reach inside her. Jake had straight dark hair and a buff body.

"Jake is a financial consultant and our accountant. He's looking over the numbers for the business," explained Gran.

Charlotte stared at his horned-rimmed glasses, wondering how such a nerdy guy could be that sexy.

"It's an interesting operation that your grandmother runs," Jake said.

"I told him he could take as long as he wants to complete the work," Gran said, smiling at both of them in a way that Charlotte thought was a blatant attempt at matchmaking. But Jake didn't seem to mind.

"Well, guess I'd better help you unload," said Jake, winking at her as if he knew what she was thinking.

Charlotte opened the trunk of her car and began lifting boxes from the back seat, hoping he hadn't noticed how she'd reacted to him.

"Okay, Charlie, I've got your old room ready," said Gran.

Jake turned to her with a grin. "Charlie, huh? I like it."

Charlotte followed Jake up the stairs to the second story,

where four bedrooms and three bathrooms were situated. The master suite was on the first floor. Gran told her she planned it so when her granddaughters got together, they'd each have a room of her own upstairs. The last room was reserved as a formal guest room with an ensuite bathroom.

Charlotte stood at the threshold to her room and took a moment to survey it. She'd chosen sunny yellow paint for the walls, white trim, white plantation shutters at the windows, and white wicker furniture. The king-size bed was covered with a blue and yellow patchwork quilted spread that she loved.

Jake set down the suitcases. "Guess I'd better get back to work." He smiled at Charlotte. "Hope to see you around."

"Oh, you will," said Gran. "Charlie's here to help me."

Charlotte hid her surprise. She'd come for a visit and to get a better idea of her future. And if that included a way to help Gran, it was even better.

# # #

About the Author

A ***USA Today* Best-Selling Author,** Judith Keim is a hybrid author who both has a publisher and self-publishes. Ms. Keim writes heart-warming novels about women who face unexpected challenges, meet them with strength, and find love and happiness along the way—stories with heart. Her best-selling books are based, in part, on many of the places she's lived or visited, and on the interesting people she's met, creating believable characters and realistic settings her many loyal readers love.

She enjoyed her childhood and young adult years in Elmira, New York, and now makes her home in Boise, Idaho, with her husband, Peter, and their lovable miniature Dachshund, Wally, and other members of her family.

While growing up, she was drawn to the idea of writing stories from a young age. Books were always present, being read, ready to go back to the library, or about to be discovered. All in her family shared information from the books in general conversation, giving them a wealth of knowledge and vivid imaginations.

Ms. Keim loves to hear from her readers and appreciates their enthusiasm for her stories.

"I hope you've enjoyed this book. If you have, please help other readers discover it by leaving a review on Amazon, Goodreads, Bookbub, or the site of your choice. And please check out my other books and series:

The Hartwell Women Series
The Beach House Hotel Series
The Fat Fridays Group
The Salty Key Inn Series
The Chandler Hill Inn Series
Seashell Cottage Books
The Desert Sage Inn Series
Soul Sisters at Cedar Mountain Lodge Series
The Sanderling Cove Inn Series
The Lilac Lake Inn Series

ALL THE BOOKS ARE NOW AVAILABLE IN AUDIO on Audible, iTunes, Findaway, Kobo, Google, and others! So fun to have these characters come alive!"

Ms. Keim can be reached at **www.judithkeim.com**

And to like her author page on Facebook and keep up with the news, go to: **http://bit.ly/2pZWDgA**

To receive notices about new books, follow her on Book Bub:

https://www.bookbub.com/authors/judith-keim

And here's a link to where you can sign up for her periodic newsletter! **http://bit.ly/2OQsb7s**

She is also on Twitter @judithkeim, LinkedIn, and Goodreads. Come say hello!

Acknowledgments

As always, I am eternally grateful to my team of editors, Peter Keim and Lynn Mapp, my book cover designer, Lou Harper, and my narrator for Audible and iTunes, Angela Dawe. They are the people who take what I've written and help turn it into the book I proudly present to you, my readers!

I also wish to thank my coffee group of writers who listen to and encourage me to keep on going. Thank you, Peggy, Lynn, Cate, Nikki Jean, and Megan.

A special 'thank you' to you, sweet reader, for your continued support and encouragement.

www.ingramcontent.com/pod-product-compliance
Lightning Source LLC
Chambersburg PA
CBHW051218190726
48288CB00006B/2019

* 9 7 8 1 9 6 2 4 5 2 1 8 2 *